ECONOMICS
OF THE LAW

ECONOMICS
OF THE LAW

TORTS, CONTRACTS,

PROPERTY, LITIGATION

Thomas J. Miceli

New York   Oxford
Oxford University Press
1997

Oxford University Press

Oxford   New York
Athens   Auckland   Bangkok   Bogota   Bombay   Buenos Aires
Calcutta   Cape Town   Dar es Salaam   Delhi   Florence   Hong Kong
Istanbul   Karachi   Kuala Lumpur   Madras   Madrid   Melbourne
Mexico City   Nairobi   Paris   Singapore   Taipei   Tokyo   Toronto

and associated companies in
Berlin   Ibadan

Library of Congress Cataloging-in-Publication Data
Miceli, Thomas J.
Economics of the law : torts, contracts, property, litigation / by
Thomas J. Miceli.
p. cm.
Includes bibliographical references and index.
ISBN 0-19-510390-4
1. Law and economics.   I. Title.
K487.E3M53   1996   340—dc20
96-25958

9 8 7 6 5 4 3 2 1

Printed in the United States of America
on acid-free paper

For my mother and the memory of my father

PREFACE

This book arose from a one-semester graduate course in law and economics that I taught at the University of Connecticut. My purpose in the course was to acquaint students with the "state of the art" of law and economics scholarship in a way that would prepare them to write either a masters or a Ph.D. thesis in the area. To that end, I chose to go into detail in a few core areas of the law with an emphasis on methodology, rather than to attempt a comprehensive overview of the field. That decision is reflected in this book, which undertakes a detailed analysis of the traditional common law topics of torts, contracts, and property, along with issues associated with the litigation-settlement decision (e.g., the selection of disputes for trial, evolution of the law toward efficiency, and frivolous litigation), while omitting consideration of other topics that fall under the heading of law and economics (most notably, corporate law and the economics of crime).

The stated objective of the book necessitated the use of a fair amount of technical analysis (primarily algebra and basic calculus), though no more than is commonly employed in the standard law and economics journals. Thus, the book will be useful as a text in graduate courses on law and economics and as a reference for those doing research in the field. At the same time, I have attempted as much as possible to provide intuitive explanations of the results and to illustrate the basic concepts with examples from actual cases. Thus, the book could also be accessible to advanced undergraduate economics and business students, and quantitatively oriented law students with an interest in economics.

I would like to acknowledge the input of my students in helping to shape both the content and the organization of the material. There is no better way to organize one's ideas on a topic than to have to prepare a course on it and subject it to questioning students. I would also like to acknowledge the comments of several reviewers of the manuscript. The current version incorporates many of their suggestions. I also greatly appreciate the enthusiasm and support that Ken MacLeod and Herb Addision at Oxford showed for the project, especially at its early stages. Finally, I wish to acknowledge the support and encouragement of my wife Ana throughout the preparation of the manuscript.

Storrs, Connecticut   T.J.M.

January 1996

CONTENTS

ECONOMICS
OF THE LAW

ONE

INTRODUCTION

The application of economic analysis to the law is based on the proposition that economic efficiency is useful for examining legal rules and institutions. Although this is not an uncontroversial proposition, the continuing vitality of the field of law and economics suggests that it has at least some validity, as I hope this book exemplifies.

When we say that economic efficiency is "useful" for examining the law, we can mean one of two things. First, we can mean that efficiency is useful in explaining the actual structure of the law. This type of argument, which is a form of *positive analysis*, suggests that the law tends to evolve in the direction of greater efficiency, not necessarily as a result of the conscious choices of judges or other participants in the legal process, but by the accumulation of the decisions of rational agents acting in their own self-interest. Thus, positive claims about the tendency of the law toward efficiency closely resemble Invisible Hand–type arguments regarding the efficiency of markets.[1]

The second sense in which efficiency is useful for examining the law is in suggesting how legal rules and institutions can be improved, or, more specifically, how they can be made more efficient. This type of *normative analysis* therefore views efficiency not as a theory for explaining how the law has evolved (or how it will evolve in the future), but rather as an ethical foundation for prescribing how it ought to be structured.

Although the positive and normative approaches to the economic analysis of the law can be quite distinct, much of the law and economics literature has elements of both. For example, the standard economic analysis of tort (or accident) law typically begins by describing the socially efficient outcome in a risky situation by deriving, as the solution to a maximization problem, the optimal allocation of liability (see chapter 2). This is purely normative analysis (given the social objective of minimizing expected costs). However, the analysis then goes on to suggest that several actual liability rules can duplicate this result—a positive assertion. In examining the various areas of the common law in this book, I will attempt whenever possible to engage in this sort of combined positive-normative analysis, for it is my view that such an approach demonstrates the greatest strength of the economic analysis of law.

In the remaining sections of this chapter, I will briefly discuss two preliminary issues. The first is the use of expected wealth maximization as the predominant efficiency concept in law and economics, and the second is the Coase theorem.[2] I will then use the discussion of the Coase theorem to suggest several themes that recur throughout the book. Finally, I will provide an overview of the topics to be covered in subsequent chapters.

1. Efficiency Concepts

Most of the law and economics literature employs wealth maximization, or the Kaldor-Hicks criterion, as the concept of efficiency (Posner, 1992, chap. 1). I will therefore do the same in this book. Nevertheless, it will be useful at this point to relate the Kaldor-Hicks criterion to other concepts of efficiency commonly used in economics—namely, Pareto efficiency (or Pareto optimality), the Pareto criterion, and social welfare maximization—and to provide some justification for the choice of the Kaldor-Hicks concept.[3]

The easiest way to relate the various efficiency concepts is to apply them to a particular situation. Consider two individuals, A and B, who have utility functions $U_A(w_A)$ and $U_B(w_B)$ that are increasing in their wealth levels, w_A and w_B. Suppose further that w_A and w_B are functions of a variable Y, which may be thought of as a particular allocation of resources or assignment of legal entitlements (rights). Thus, $w_A = w_A(Y)$ and $w_B = w_B(Y)$. The social problem is to choose Y in an efficient manner.

Under the concept of Pareto efficiency, Y should be chosen to maximize the utility of one individual, say person A, subject to the constraint that the other individual, person B, achieves a minimum level of utility. Formally, we can write this problem as

$$\text{maximize } U_A(w_A(Y)) \quad \text{subject to } U_B(w_B(Y)) \geq U_B^0. \tag{1.1}$$

The solution to this problem defines a *utility possibility frontier* (UPF) that gives the maximum level of U_A for all possible choices of U_B^0. The UPF arising from (1.1) is shown by the curve labeled AB in figure 1.1. Its negative slope implies that the utility of person A can be increased only by reducing the utility of person B (and vice versa).

The Pareto criterion is related to Pareto efficiency in that it also solves the problem in (1.1), but it does so for a *particular* starting point, say point C in figure 1.1. For example, if the utility of person B is constrained to be the level at C, then the set of points Pareto-superior to C are those on segment CD. Alternatively, if the utility of person A is fixed by point C, then the Pareto-superior points are those on segment CE. In general, therefore, all points above CE and to the right of CD constitute the set of points that are Pareto-superior to C. In this region, both parties are at least as well off as at C.

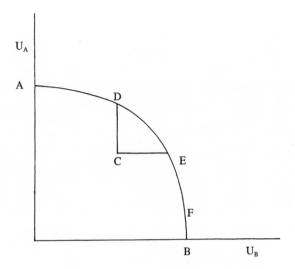

FIGURE 1.1 The utility possibility frontier.

It is interesting to note that a point like F, which is *not* among the set of points that are Pareto-superior to C, *is*, however, among the set of Pareto-efficient points. This is a consequence of the fact that the Pareto criterion (or Pareto superiority) relies on the particular starting point. This observation points out a general weakness in employing the Pareto concepts for determining efficiency: although point C is not Pareto-efficient (in the sense that there are points Pareto-superior to it) and point F *is* Pareto-efficient, we cannot rank points C and F. Indeed, we cannot use either of the Pareto concepts to rank any two points where one party prefers one of the points and the other party prefers the other point. It therefore follows that all points on the UPF are *non-comparable* under Pareto. Unfortunately, most interesting policy questions involve a movement between noncomparable points (i.e., there are both winners and losers).

One way to resolve this noncomparability is to specify a social welfare function, or a *utility function* for society.[4] Such a function has as its arguments the utility levels of all members of society. Thus, in our two-person example, the social-welfare function would be written $W = W(U_A, U_B)$. The purpose of the social-welfare function is to attach implicit weights to individuals in order to allow a ranking of all possible allocations, including those that are Pareto-noncomparable. If the form of W were known, then the optimal (social-welfare maximizing) point on the UPF could be located by finding the highest "indifference curve" of W that just touches the UPF. Of course, in reality it is impossible to know the particular form of W, or even if one exists. Consequently, this approach has little practical applicability.

Given the incompleteness of Pareto and the impracticality of social-welfare maximization, consider finally the concept of Kaldor-Hicks efficiency. This concept offers an alternative to the social-welfare function for choosing among points that are noncomparable according to Pareto. To see how it does this, consider points D and E in figure 1.1. Both points are Pareto-efficient, but they are noncomparable because person A is better off at point D, and person B is better off at point E. Kaldor-Hicks ranks these points by asking whether one is "potentially" Pareto-superior to the other. That is, if we contemplate a move from point E to D, for example, we would ask whether person A gains enough from the move to compensate person B for his loss so that both parties are left better off (or at least no worse off). If so, we say that point D is more efficient than point E in a Kaldor-Hicks sense, *even though we do not actually require A to compensate B*. (If compensation were required, then the move would be a Pareto improvement.)

As suggested above, the Kaldor-Hicks concept is equivalent to maximization of aggregate wealth. This equivalence can be seen by rewriting (1.1) as

$$\text{maximize } U_A(w_A(\Upsilon) - T) \quad \text{subject to } U_B(w_B(\Upsilon) + T) \geq U_B^0 \qquad (1.2)$$

where Υ is a reallocation, T is a potential transfer payment from A to B (or, if T is negative, from B to A), and U_B^0 is B's initial utility. If we form the Lagrangian for (1.2) and choose Υ and T optimally, we get the following first-order conditions:

$$U_A'(\partial w_A/\partial \Upsilon) + \lambda U_B'(\partial w_B/\partial \Upsilon) = 0 \qquad (1.3)$$

$$-U_A' + \lambda U_B' = 0 \qquad (1.4)$$

where λ is the multiplier. Substituting (1.4) into (1.3) yields:

$$\partial w_A/\partial \Upsilon + \partial w_B/\partial \Upsilon = 0, \qquad (1.5)$$

which is the first-order condition for the choice of Υ that maximizes $w_A(\Upsilon) + w_B(\Upsilon)$.

The fact that wealth maximization (Kaldor-Hicks), in contrast to the Pareto concepts, allows a complete ranking of points, however, does not by itself justify its use as an efficiency concept. For example, an important consequence of abandoning Pareto in favor of Kaldor-Hicks as the criterion of efficiency is that one sacrifices the notion of *consent* as the ethical foundation for efficiency. In particular, since Kaldor-Hicks does not require actual compensation to be paid to losers, one cannot claim that they have consented to the change.

In response to this problem, Richard Posner has argued for the replacement of *actual consent* with the concept of *implied consent* as the underlying basis for wealth maximization.[5] In short, the argument is that, by implicitly consenting ex ante to a social institution (e.g., a particular common law doctrine) which promotes wealth maximization, members of the society also consent to any uncompensated losses that they may sustain ex post as a result of the operation of that institution. The method by which we look for implied consent, according to Posner, is "to answer the hypothetical question whether, if transaction costs were zero, the affected parties would have agreed to the institution" (Posner, 1980, p. 494).[6] As we shall see, this type of counterfactual inquiry is a common strategy for evaluating the desirability of legal doctrines or judicial decisions in the economic analysis of the law. For example, the doctrines of contract law are commonly viewed by the economic approach as attempts to fashion contract terms ex post that the parties would have written ex ante if they could have bargained with perfect foresight and low transaction costs. Likewise, tort rules are often evaluated by asking how well they reflect the manner in which the parties would have assigned liability if they could have bargained before the accident occurred.

Note that this approach is similar to that employed by Rawls (1971) in his derivation of a theory of justice. Rawls likewise viewed consent as being implicit, having been given by individuals from behind a "veil of ignorance" about what their particular place in society would be. Posner's argument differs from that of Rawls, however, in the claim about the objective function that the individuals would maximize—Rawls argued that it would be the utility of the worst-off individual, whereas Posner argues that it would be aggregate wealth.

Posner concedes, however, that wealth maximization as the standard of efficiency may not be justifiable on consent grounds in all cases. For example, one circumstance where it would not be justified is when the distribution of wealth resulting from a particular institution or rule is expected to be systematically biased against some members of society, for in that case, individuals behind a veil of ignorance would not likely consent to it. Fortunately, this is not apt to be the case with regard to the common law (in contrast to legislation), which Posner (and others) have contended is not an effective means for redistributing wealth.[7] And, when parties have no systematic belief ex ante that they will be on the winning or losing side of disputes, they might as well choose to maximize the aggregate wealth produced by the adjudication of those disputes. In contrast, if systematic redistribution is a concern, as when rent-seeking by interest groups is effective, wealth maximization is less defensible on the ground of implied consent because any increases in wealth may be funneled to a small segment of the population. However, since most modern economic analysis of the law concentrates on the common law rather than the behavior of legislatures,[8] the problem of redistribution and rent seeking is typically ignored.

2. The Coase Theorem

The manner in which economic analysis can be applied to legal rules was perhaps first demonstrated in the influential article by Ronald Coase, "The Problem of Social Cost" (1960). In this article, Coase reconsidered the traditional economic analysis of external costs. In doing so, he demonstrated a result that has since come to be called the Coase theorem.

To illustrate his argument, Coase used the example of a rancher whose cattle strayed and damaged crops planted by a neighboring farmer. To formalize Coase's example, let $\Pi(x)$ be the profit of the rancher as a function of his herd

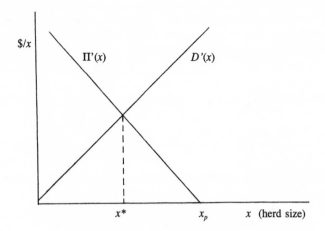

FIGURE 1.2 The socially efficient herd size.

size, x, where $\Pi' > 0$ for $x < x_p$, $\Pi' < 0$ for $x > x_p$, and $\Pi'' < 0$. Thus, a herd size of x_p is privately optimal for the rancher. Suppose, however, that straying cattle cause damage to the farmer in an amount $D(x)$, where $D' > 0$ and $D'' > 0$. The socially efficient herd size, x^*, therefore maximizes $\Pi(x) - D(x)$.[9] The resulting first-order condition is[10]

$$\Pi'(x) = D'(x). \tag{1.6}$$

Figure 1.2 depicts this condition graphically. Note that the socially optimal herd size is smaller than the privately optimal size as a result of the external cost D.

According to the traditional (Pigouvian) view of externalities, the rancher imposes an external cost on the farmer that results in a market failure requiring correction by the government, generally in the form of a tax imposed on the producer of the external cost (the rancher).[11] Note that underlying this view of the externality problem are two implicit assumptions: first, that because externalities are sources of market failure, the rancher must be induced via a government-imposed tax to reduce the "offending" activity to the efficient level; and second, that the rancher is *the* cause of the externality.

Coase challenged both of these assumptions. He challenged the first by showing that government-imposed remedies are not necessary if the parties can bargain with each other at low cost, since in that case they will always be able to achieve the Pareto-optimal allocation of rights through voluntary exchange. To see this, suppose initially that the rancher has a herd of size x_p in figure 1.2. Starting from this point, note that the farmer would be willing to pay any amount up to $D'(x_p)$ (the farmer's marginal damage at x_p) to induce the rancher to reduce his herd size to $x_p - 1$, and the rancher would be willing to accept any amount greater than zero (which is $\Pi'(x_p)$, the rancher's marginal profit at x_p) to make this adjustment. Since $D'(x_p) > \Pi'(x_p)$, a mutually acceptable price can be set to complete this transaction. Based on this reasoning, the parties will agree to reduce the rancher's herd size as long as $D'(x) \geq \Pi'(x)$, or until the socially efficient herd size, x^*, is achieved. At this point, bargaining will cease because no more mutually beneficial exchanges exist. It should be easy to see that similar bargaining will achieve the efficient herd size if we start at $x = 0$, where in this case the rancher will pay the farmer to be allowed to increase his herd size as long as $\Pi'(x) \geq D'(x)$. This type of argument shows that bargaining between the parties can achieve the efficient outcome without government intervention.

Coase's response to the second assumption underlying the Pigouvian view is that both parties are simultaneously the cause of the externality in the sense that, if the farmer were not present, the rancher's straying cattle would not harm anyone. In other words, both parties satisfy the "but for" test used to determine causation in tort law: the externality would not have occurred but for the presence of both the farmer and rancher.[12] This recognition of the "reciprocal nature" of externalities indicates that the particular assignment of legal rights in externality situations is irrelevant with regard to efficiency. To see why, note that the designation of the rancher as the cause of the externality represents an implicit assignment to the farmer of the right to be free from the offending activity. The rancher therefore has to "purchase" the right to impose the cost on the farmer, as was the case above when we started at $x = 0$ in describing bargaining between the farmer and rancher. On the other hand, suppose we treat the farmer as the cause of the externality by allowing the rancher to expand his herd to x_p without first having to purchase the right. Perhaps the rancher predated the farmer at this location, so straying cattle became an externality only when the farmer arrived. This approach thus awards the legal right to engage in the offensive activity to the rancher. As shown previously, the efficient herd size is achieved in this case as well (assuming low transaction costs) because the farmer will bribe the rancher to reduce his herd from x_p to x^*.

The preceding arguments establish the Coase theorem, which says that if transaction costs are low enough to permit bargaining between the parties to an externality, and if property rights are well defined, then the initial assignment of rights will not affect the ultimate allocation of resources, which will be efficient.[13] Although this result seems surprising at first, it becomes intuitively clear once we recognize that the externality simply concerns the assignment of a property right over which the parties can bargain, like any other good. And as the Invisible Hand theorem tells us, when transactions are costless, the parties will bargain until they exhaust all mutual gains, and rights are assigned in an efficient manner.[14]

Although the assignment of legal rights does not matter for efficiency in a world of zero transaction costs, the two bargaining scenarios above show that it does matter for the distribution of wealth. This also makes sense because, by reallocating legal rights, we are taking something of value away from one party and giving it to the other party.[15] Although subsequent bargaining will ensure that the ultimate allocation is efficient, the initial assignment dictates the direction of any monetary payments.

Coleman (1982) has argued, however, that the assignment of rights will not matter for the distribution of wealth either, to the extent that the expected liabilities associated with a given assignment will be reflected in the price that the parties pay when they make their initial location decisions. For example, when a farmer moves near a rancher, the price of the land will be lower if the rancher has the right to expand his herd without liability than if the farmer has the right to be free from crop damage.[16] As a result, the farmer's wealth is independent of the assignment of rights. Although this argument is correct with regard to the farmer, it ignores the fact that, at the point that a change in legal rights occurs, the *existing* landowner (the owner who sold to the farmer) either suffers a capital loss or realizes a capital gain.[17] Thus, a change in legal rights will always affect someone's wealth, even if it does not affect efficiency.

Of course, the Coase theorem is of limited practical interest because most actual externality settings are not characterized by low transaction costs.[18] In that case, the initial assignment of rights *does* affect efficiency because the parties cannot be counted on to reallocate rights through mutually beneficial exchange. Thus, it is in these contexts that the choice of the rule of law matters. Consequently, perhaps the most important implication of Coase's article for the economic analysis of law is the importance of transaction costs, for a world without transaction costs is one in which the law does not matter for efficiency.[19]

The importance of the choice of legal rules in the presence of transaction costs brings us back to the earlier question of what notion of efficiency should be used to make that choice. As noted earlier, most current economic analysis of the law follows Posner's lead in applying expected wealth maximization, which is equivalent to saying that the assignment of rights should be chosen to reflect who would have paid the most for them if bargaining were possible (i.e., to "mimic" the market). Alternatively stated, legal rules in externality situations should be designed to impose the cost on the "cheapest cost avoider."[20] Since the aim of this book is to reflect the current approach to law and economics rather than to critique it, I will for the most part employ this approach without further comment.[21]

3. Themes

The preceding discussion of the Coase theorem highlighted several themes that have been very important in the modern economic analysis of law and will therefore recur throughout this book. The first is the notion of optimal precaution against risk or harm. In general, law and economics is concerned with internalization of external costs that arise because of risky or harmful activities. The economic problem is to reduce these risks or harms in an optimal manner by balancing the costs of precaution against the benefits of reduced damage. (In Coase's example, precaution takes the form of reductions in the herd size by the rancher.) The model that economists have developed to examine this problem has been described as the *model of precaution* (Cooter, 1985a).

A recurrent theme in the economic analysis of law, therefore, is how legal rules are, or should be, designed, given the objective of inducing optimal precaution against "harm," broadly defined. The usefulness of this approach is obvious in the context of tort law, where the goal is prevention of accidents, and in nuisance law, where the goal is control of external costs. However, it also has proved useful in examining optimal precaution against the cost of excessive breach in contract law and in the analysis of takings law where a developer's investment in his land affects the opportunity cost of acquiring or regulating it for public benefit.

A second theme raised by Coase is the importance of transaction costs. As the above discussion of the Coase theorem indicated, the cost of transacting between the parties to an externality situation has an important impact on whether they can be expected to resolve the dispute on their own or if legal intervention is necessary. The higher the transaction costs, the more important legal rules will be in determining the allocation of resources.

More generally, the relevant question is the *relative* cost of voluntary resolution of the dispute by the parties themselves compared to the cost of resolving it through the legal system. In a sense, this comparison determines the optimal division of labor for dispute resolution (all else equal) as between the parties themselves and the court. This theme emerges frequently in the economic analysis of the law. More broadly, it is a version of the fundamental problem in the philosophy of law of the choice between "rules" and "discretion."[22] In this book, I will try to show the manner in which economic theory can inform this choice. In general, the argument will take the following form. As transaction costs rise relative to litigation costs, courts should take a larger role in resolving disputes by implementing rules that allow greater judicial discretion. Conversely, as transaction costs fall relatively, courts should take a lesser role by implementing mechanical rules that facilitate bargaining between the parties.[23] In the following chapters, this argument will manifest itself in several ways: for example, in tort law, in the choice between strict liability and negligence; in contract law, in the choice between court-imposed damages and specific performance; in property law, in the choice between property rules and liability rules; and in legal rule making, in the choice between precedent and judicial discretion.

4. Plan of the Book

This book examines the basic common law areas of torts, contracts, and property as well as the economics of litigation and settlement. The order of topics is based on the fact that the model of precaution is most literally relevant in the context of accidents. Thus, torts are treated first. Once the basic model is laid out in this context, the principles are then easily transferred to the areas of contracts and property.[24]

Each topic is covered in two chapters. Generally, the first chapter describes the basic economic model and the second examines extensions and additional topics. The following is a brief overview of the content of each chapter.

Chapters 2 and 3 examine the economics of tort law. Chapter 2 begins by describing the basic accident model that has been used to examine the structure of tort law. This model is based on the notion that parties engaged in risky activities can take precautions to reduce the expected costs of accidents. An important conclusion of the model is that one can draw a close correspondence between optimal (cost-minimizing) precaution and the due standard of care under negligence law, a correspondence that is exemplified by the Hand test for negligence proposed by Judge Learned Hand in the case *U.S.* v. *Carroll Towing Co.*[25] In addition to examining optimal precaution and the Hand rule, chapter 2 considers the role of causation in tort law. Although causation plays an important part in the actual assignment of liability, economists have had some difficulty in developing economic models to explain its importance. Chapter 2 also considers whether the due standard of care under negligence should be individualized or based on the average injurer. An information-cost argument explains why negligence law generally opts for the latter in the form of the reasonable-person standard. Chapter 2 next considers the impact of activity levels, as distinct from precaution, on accident risk. This impact is illustrated in the context of products liability law, given that an important example of an injurer's activity level is the output (as opposed to the safety) of a dangerous product. Finally, chapter 2 examines several issues that affect the determination of damages, including punitive damages, defendant insolvency, and apportionment of damages among multiple defendants.

Chapter 3 extends the analysis of tort law to consider three further topics. The first is the impact of litigation costs. In particular, the analysis shows how litigation costs (the plaintiff's costs of bringing suit and the defendant's cost of defending himself) affect the functioning of the tort system. The second topic is uncertainty. Four types of uncertainty are considered: uncertainty by injurers about the due standard of care, uncertainty by the court about whether an injurer (or victim) satisfied the due standard, uncertainty by the court about the cause of an accident, and uncertainty by injurers about the riskiness of their activity or product. The final topic in chapter 3 concerns sequential-care accidents, or accidents in which the injurer and victim choose their precaution in sequence rather than simultaneously. These accidents are of interest because they are pervasive and because they present an important problem for courts in assigning liability—namely, the threat of strategic behavior. The discussion focuses on ways in which the law addresses this threat.

Chapters 4 and 5 turn to the economics of contract law. Chapter 4 begins by examining legal remedies for breach of contract. It first asks whether the various court-imposed remedies provide efficient incentives for breaching the contract, for investing in contract-specific capital (reliance), and for risk sharing. Chapter 4 next examines the efficiency of the rule from *Hadley* v. *Baxendale*[26] that limits a promisor's liability from breach to those damages that the promisee could have reasonably foreseen. Chapter 4 then turns to the question of when courts should enforce breach remedies that the parties specify themselves (liquidated damage clauses), and concludes by examining the conditions under which specific performance is preferred to money damages as the remedy for breach.

While chapter 4 focused on remedies for breach of enforceable contracts, chapter 5 considers the question of what contracts should be enforced in the first place. It begins with a brief discussion of the traditional elements of an enforceable contract: offer, acceptance, and consideration. It then turns to an examination of formation defenses (focusing on mistake) and performance excuses (focusing on impossibility). The chapter concludes by examining the enforceability of contract modifications. The theme of chapter 5 is that courts attempt to supply ex post solutions to contract problems that the parties failed to account for as part of the original contract.

Chapters 6 and 7 examine the economics of property law. The first part of chapter 6 examines the distinction between property rules and liability rules for protecting legal entitlements (rights), and suggests that the structure of trespass and nuisance law is broadly consistent with this distinction. It then develops a formal economic framework for comparing the efficiency of property rules, liability rules, Pigouvian tax subsidies, zoning, and land-use covenants for controlling externalities. The second part of chapter 6 examines legal rules governing land transfer between private individuals. It first considers the systems that have developed to organize voluntary (consensual) transfers of land and then examines involuntary (nonconsensual) transfers, focusing on the doctrine of adverse possession.

Chapter 7 concerns the acquisition and regulation of private property by the government. Government acquisitions of private property are covered by the government's power of eminent domain, which allows it to take property without the owner's consent provided it pays just compensation. The discussion of eminent domain offers an economic justification of this power based on transaction costs, considers the proper definition of *just compensation*, and examines the impact of eminent domain on the investment decisions of owners of private property. When the government does not physically acquire private property, but merely regulates it, courts have generally found that no compensation is due under the government's police power. However, some cases have established limits to the government's regulatory power, beyond which a regulation becomes a compensable taking (a *regulatory taking*). The second part of chapter 7 uses an economic model of land use and regulatory decisions to determine where that limit should be, and argues that the result is consistent with the limits that the court have actually established. It then extends the analysis to several related issues, including the investment-backed expectation requirement and capitalization of the threat of regulation into the price of land.

Chapters 8 and 9 examine the resolution of legal disputes, focusing primarily on the choice between settlement and trial. Chapter 8 considers several models that have been used to distinguish between cases that settle and cases that go to trial. The results of these models are used to examine several issues, including the selection of disputes for trial, the question of whether the law evolves in the direction of efficiency, the impact of various legal rules for allocating litigation costs (e.g., the American rule versus the English rule and Rule 68 of the Federal Rules of Civil Procedure), and whether pretrial discovery is an effective means of promoting settlement of disputes and reducing overall litigation costs.

Finally, chapter 9 turns to the problem of frivolous litigation, or lawsuits that succeed in obtaining settlements despite the fact that they have little or no legal merit. The discussion first reviews several models used to explain the success of these suits, and then uses the results to examine various policies for reducing their success, including different cost-allocation rules and the imposition of monetary sanctions (e.g., under Rule 11 of the Federal Rules of Civil Procedure). The chapter concludes by addressing two questions: (1) Do contingent fees tend to promote frivolous suits, as is often claimed? and (2) Can repeat defendants (like insurance companies and manufacturers of dangerous products) successfully deter frivolous suits by developing reputations for taking cases to trial rather than settling?

Throughout the book, I have made an effort to provide references to the literature from which the material was drawn, as well as related literature, so that the interested reader can pursue a particular topic in greater depth. In some cases I have presented previously unpublished material (examples include portions of the discussion of causation in section 2 of chapter 2; the discussion of the optimal standard of proof for determining negligence in section 2.2.4 of chapter 3; some portions of the discussion of sequential care torts in section 3 of chapter 3; some portions of the discussion of discovery in section 4 of chapter 8; and some portions of the discussion of sanctions against frivolous suits in section 4.3 of chapter 9). It is my hope that this material will provide a stimulus for further work in these areas.

TWO

THE ECONOMICS OF TORT LAW

The Basic Model

From an economic perspective, tort law is concerned with internalizing the costs associated with accidental harm. This chapter develops the basic accident model that economists have employed to examine the structure of tort law.

The economic analysis of tort law is primarily concerned with the incentives that various assignments of liability create for injurers and victims to take precautions against accidents.[1] In most accident settings, if injurers do not face the threat of liability for the victims' injuries, they have no incentive to take precautions because the victims' costs represent an externality.[2] Alternatively, if victims always expect to be fully compensated for their injuries, they too will have little or no incentive to take precaution. This two-sided "moral hazard" presents a difficult problem for tort law, and the economic model of accidents (the model of precaution) shows how negligence rules elegantly solve it. More broadly, the basic principles that arise from this analysis turn out to be applicable to problems in both contracts and property, thereby demonstrating the ability of the model to provide a unifying framework for the economic analysis of law.[3]

The first section of the chapter develops the basic accident model and examines the effect of various liability rules on the incentives of injurers and victims. It is therefore largely normative. The second section takes a more positive approach by examining the well-known Hand test for negligence and the role of causation requirements in the economic model. The third section considers the question of whether standards of care for negligence (or any legal standard) should be individualized or based on a representative person (the so-called reasonable person). The fourth section examines the role of activity levels as distinct from precaution as determinants of accident risk. Since an important example of an injurer's activity level is the number of units of a dangerous product produced by a manufacturer, the economics of product liability is examined in this section. Finally, the fifth section considers several issues relevant to the determination of damages: specifically, whether damage awards should be individualized or based on the losses of the average victim, the impact

15

of errors in measuring damages, the economic function of punitive damages, the problem of injurer insolvency, and the apportionment of damages among multiple injurers.

1. The Basic Accident Model

The basic accident model consists of a single risk-neutral injurer and a single risk-neutral victim.[4] Consider, for example, the driver of an automobile and a pedestrian. In the unilateral-care version of the model, only the injurer can take care to reduce the expected damages from an accident—for example, by deciding how fast to drive. In the bilateral-care version, the victim can also take care—for example, by crossing the street only at well-marked crosswalks.

1.1. Unilateral-Care Accident Model

Let x represent the dollar cost of care undertaken by the injurer, and let $D(x)$ be the victim's expected damages, where $D' < 0$ and $D'' > 0$.[5] Thus, care reduces expected accident costs, but at a diminishing rate.[6] The socially optimal level of care by the injurer should minimize total expected accident costs, including the cost of care. That is, x should be chosen to

$$\underset{x}{\text{minimize}} \quad x + D(x). \tag{2.1}$$

The first-order condition for (2.1) is given by

$$1 + D'(x) = 0 \tag{2.2}$$

and the resulting optimal care level is denoted x^*.[7]

The problem for the legal system is to induce the injurer to choose x^* by appropriately choosing the liability rule. A *liability rule* is simply a rule that specifies how the damages from an accident will be allocated. In the context of the unilateral-care model, I will consider three rules: (1) no liability, (2) strict liability, and (3) negligence. A rule of no liability simply says that the injurer is not liable for the victim's injuries. Thus, the injurer's problem is to minimize x, which obviously results in no care. More generally, no liability results in too little care by the injurer. In contrast, strict liability holds the injurer fully liable for the victim's injuries.[8] The injurer's problem is thus identical to (2.1) and he therefore chooses optimal care, x^*.

Finally, a negligence rule says that the injurer is liable for the victim's injuries only if he failed to take a minimum level of care, referred to as the *due standard of care*, and he avoids liability altogether if he met (or exceeded) the due standard. If z is the due standard, then the injurer's problem under negligence is to

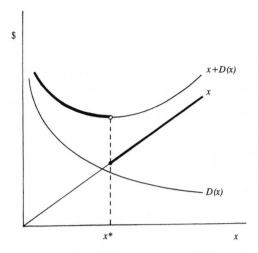

FIGURE 2.1 Efficient care under a negligence rule.

$$\text{minimize} \atop x \quad \begin{cases} x, & x \geq z \\ x + D(x), & x < z \end{cases} \qquad (2.3)$$

Suppose that the court sets the due standard equal to the optimal care level—that is, $z = x^*$. In that case, the solution to (2.3) is x^*. This follows from the fact that

$$x^* < x^* + D(x^*) \leq \min_{x < z} x + D(x). \qquad (2.4)$$

The solution to (2.3) is shown in figure 2.1. The graph shows that the negligence rule induces efficient care because it creates a discontinuity in the injurer's expected costs, shown by the darkened segments. In particular, the injurer avoids liability by choosing at least x^*, and he minimizes his costs of care by choosing *no more than* x^*.[9] This "threshold" feature of negligence plays an important role in the economic analysis of tort law and in other areas of the law as well.

This section has shown that strict liability and negligence are equally good at inducing optimal care in the unilateral-care model. If we include the administrative costs of the rules, however, strict liability seems preferable because it places a lower fact-finding burden on the court, since the plaintiff needs to prove only causation rather than causation *and* fault.[10]

1.2. Bilateral-Care Accident Model

Now suppose that the victim as well as the injurer can take care to reduce the expected costs of an accident. Let y be the expenditure on care by the victim, and let $D(x,y)$ be accident costs, where

$$D_x < 0, \quad D_y < 0, \quad D_{xx} > 0, \quad D_{yy} > 0, \quad \text{and} \quad D_{xy} > 0. \qquad (2.5)$$

The final inequality implies that inputs of care by the two parties are substitutes in a sense that will be noted below. The socially optimal care levels by the two parties now solve the problem

$$\text{minimize } x + y + D(x,y), \qquad (2.6)$$
$$x,y$$

which yields the first-order conditions

$$1 + D_x(x,y) = 0, \quad \text{and} \qquad (2.7)$$

$$1 + D_y(x,y) = 0. \qquad (2.8)$$

Equation (2.7) defines a locus of points, $x^*(y)$, which represents the injurer's optimal care level for any choice of victim care y. Equation (2.8) similarly defines a locus of points $y^*(x)$ for the victim. The social optimum occurs at the intersection of these loci such that $x^* \equiv x^*(y^*)$ and $y^* \equiv y^*(x^*)$.

It will be useful to derive the characteristics of the functions $x^*(y)$ and $y^*(x)$. It follows from (2.5) that

$$\partial x^*/\partial y = -D_{xy}/D_{xx} < 0, \quad \text{and} \quad \partial y^*/\partial x = -D_{xy}/D_{yy} < 0. \qquad (2.9)$$

These derivatives show the sense in which care is substitutable. Specifically, as the care of one party falls, it is efficient for the other to increase his or her care. Though this need not always be true, it seems to be the most sensible specification of the accident technology. For example, pedestrians can compensate for careless drivers by being more careful themselves.

I now ask whether any of the above liability rules can induce optimal care by both parties in equilibrium. I assume that the parties choose their care simultaneously and derive the Nash equilibrium.[11] First consider a rule of no liability (which is, in effect, strict liability for the victim). As in the unilateral-care case, the injurer's problem is to minimize x, which yields $x = 0$ for all y. The victim's problem is thus to minimize $y + D(0,y)$, which yields $y^*(0)$. By (2.9), $y^*(0) > y^*$. Thus, under no liability, the injurer takes too little care and the victim takes too much care, though the victim's care is optimal *given* the injurer's care choice. The outcome is exactly reversed under strict liability. Specifically, the victim is never liable and chooses $y = 0$, while the injurer is fully liable and chooses $x^*(0) > x^*$. Thus, neither rule induces optimal care by both parties in equilibrium.

Now consider negligence and assume, as earlier, that the due standard is set equal to the injurer's optimal care level (i.e., $z = x^*$). I will show that (x^*, y^*) is a Nash equilibrium in this case. To demonstrate this, let us suppose $y = y^*$. The injurer's problem is therefore to

$$\text{minimize} \quad \begin{array}{ll} x, & x \geq x^* \\ x + D(x,y^*), & x < x^* \end{array} \qquad (2.10)$$

As in the unilateral-care case, the solution to this problem is $x^*(y^*) = x^*$. Now consider the victim's problem and let $x = x^*$. In this case, the victim is "strictly liable," so she chooses y to minimize $y + D(x^*,y)$, which yields $y^*(x^*) = y^*$. Thus, the outcome is efficient. Note that, in contrast to strict and no liability, the negligence rule works because it combines two methods for inducing optimal care: it imposes the full damages on one party (the victim), and it allows the other party to *avoid* liability by taking optimal care (the injurer). This dual method for achieving efficiency in bilateral-care settings will arise in various contexts later.

Let us now consider three variations on the negligence rule. The first two are obtained by adding a defense of contributory negligence to the strict liability and "simple" negligence rules, and the third is comparative negligence. A defense of contributory negligence essentially allows the injurer to avoid liability, even if he was negligent, if the victim was also negligent (i.e., if she chose $y < y^*$). Contributory negligence therefore bars victim recovery regardless of the injurer's care. In contrast, comparative negligence shares liability between the parties when both are negligent. I will show that, in principle, all of these rules can achieve the optimal solution in equilibrium.

Consider first strict liability with a defense of contributory negligence, and assume initially that $x = x^*$. In this case, the victim's problem is identical to the injurer's problem under simple negligence. That is, she can avoid all liability by choosing y^*; otherwise she is fully liable (the victim's problem is simply (2.10) with y replacing x). The victim thus chooses y^*. Since the injurer is therefore strictly liable, he minimizes costs by choosing x^*.

Under negligence with contributory negligence, the injurer avoids all liability if *either* $x \geq x^*$ or $y < y^*$ (i.e., if he is nonnegligent or the victim is contributorily negligent). Suppose initially $y = y^*$. The injurer's problem is thus identical to that under simple negligence (problem (2.10)), and he chooses x^*. As for the victim, when $x = x^*$, she is fully liable regardless of her care choice, so she chooses y^* to minimize her expected accident costs. The outcome under this rule thus appears to be identical to that under simple negligence, given optimal care by both parties in equilibrium. This equivalence disappears, however, if the injurer knows the victim has chosen $y < y^*$, for in that case he can freely choose $x = 0$ because of the contributory negligence defense. This difference is important if some parties are inadvertently negligent.[12]

Finally, consider a comparative negligence rule. In reality, at least three different forms of comparative negligence have been adopted by various states.[13] I consider the form employed by Shavell (1987) and Landes and Posner (1987). Specifically, let $\beta(x,y)$ represent the fraction of damages borne by the injurer, where

$$\beta_x < 0, \quad \beta_y > 0,$$
$$\beta = 1 \text{ if } x < x^*, \text{ and } y \geq y^*$$
$$\beta = 0 \text{ if } x \geq x^* \tag{2.11}$$
$$0 < \beta < 1, \text{ if } x < x^* \text{ and } y < y^*.$$

Thus, the rule works like simple negligence except when both parties are negligent, in which case they share liability instead of the injurer's bearing all liability. This form of comparative negligence therefore retains the threshold feature from the injurer's perspective.

To show that this formulation of comparative negligence induces the efficient outcome, suppose $y = y^*$. In this case, the injurer's problem is to

$$\text{minimize}_x \quad \begin{cases} x, & x \geq x^* \\ x + \beta(x,y^*)D(x,y^*), & x < x^*. \end{cases} \tag{2.12}$$

Since $\beta(x,y^*) = 1$ for $x < x^*$ and $y = y^*$, this problem is identical to the injurer's problem under simple negligence. He therefore chooses x^*. And, when $x = x^*$, $\beta = 0$ for any y. Thus, the victim is fully liable and therefore also chooses optimal care.[14]

2. The Hand Rule and Causation

The preceding analysis represents the way economists have formalized accident law. An important question for the positive economic theory of law is how closely this model resembles the way courts actually assign liability. To answer this question, I consider two topics in this section. The first is the Hand rule for determining negligence, and the second is the role of causation in assigning liability.

2.1. The Hand Rule

The Hand rule for determining negligence was formulated by Judge Learned Hand in the case of *U.S. v. Carroll Towing Co.*[15] According to the Hand rule, a party is negligent if an accident occurred as a result of a party's failure to take a particular precaution, and if the following inequality holds: $B < PL$, where B is the burden (or cost) of the untaken precaution, P is the probability of the accident given that the precaution was not taken, and L is the injury from the accident. Thus, a defendant is judged to be negligent if the burden of the untaken precaution is less than the expected harm.[16]

Economists have understandably been attracted to this rule given its apparent resemblance to the economic model developed earlier.[17] To examine this resemblance, let x be the actual care of an injurer and let $x' > x$ be some higher level of care. Thus, $x' - x$ is the untaken precaution, and, assuming that the marginal cost of care is constant at \$1, $B = x' - x$. Further, note that $PL = D(x) - D(x')$, where $D(x') \geq 0$, depending on whether or not x' would have prevented the accident with certainty. Thus, according to the Hand rule, an injurer is negligent if he failed to take care of $x' - x$, and if

$$x' - x < D(x) - D(x'). \tag{2.13}$$

Dividing both sides by $x' - x$ yields

$$1 < [D(x) - D(x')]/(x' - x). \tag{2.14}$$

That is, a defendant is negligent if the marginal cost of the untaken precaution is less than the marginal benefit in terms of reduced costs. Note that (2.14) is simply a discrete version of condition (2.2) (Landes and Posner, 1987, p. 87).

An important implication of the Hand rule as defined in (2.13) and (2.14) is that, whether or not it is satisfied depends on the particular untaken precaution that the court is considering. To see this, let x^* denote the optimal care level as shown in figure 2.1. Observe that the left-hand side of (2.14) is the slope of the cost of care curve, x, and the right-hand side is the negative of the slope of the damage curve $D(x)$ between any two points x and x'. Thus, the slope of $D(x)$ is greater than one to the left of x^*, equal to one at x^*, and less than one to the right of x^*. As a result, if the injurer's actual precaution is larger than x^*, *no* choice of an untaken precaution $x' - x$ will satisfy (2.14). In contrast, if $x < x' \leq x^*$, then *any* untaken precaution will satisfy (2.14). Finally, if $x < x^* < x'$, then $x' - x$ *may or may not* satisfy (2.14), with the likelihood decreasing as x' becomes larger (given x).

In general, notice that the left-hand side of (2.13) is increasing in $x' - x$ at a *constant* rate, whereas the right-hand side is increasing in $x' - x$ at a *decreasing* rate (given a diminishing marginal benefit of care). Thus, for $x < x^*$, (2.13) is more likely to hold the *smaller* $x' - x$ is, and it will not hold for a large enough x'. In other words, the plaintiff is more likely to succeed in proving that the defendant is negligent under the Hand rule the smaller the untaken precaution is. This argument has led Grady (1989) to suggest that, because it is up to the plaintiff to present the court with the defendant's untaken precaution, she will increase her chances of prevailing by making it small. This makes sense, since the smaller the alleged untaken precaution is, the more likely it is the court will find that it was cost-effective and therefore that it should have been taken.[18] I will return to this point in the discussion of proximate cause later.

Any analysis of how courts actually assign liability for accidents is incomplete unless it considers the role of causation. In order for a negligent injurer to be held liable for damages, his negligent act must also be both cause in fact and proximate cause of the victim's harm. I will discuss both concepts in turn.

2.2. Cause in Fact

The usual test for cause in fact is the "but for" test: if the victim's injuries would not have occurred but for the injurer's negligent act, then the act is a cause in fact of the harm. Determination of cause in fact is therefore a backward-looking, counterfactual inquiry that compares the actual circumstances of the case to the circumstances that would have existed if the injurer had taken due care. For example, in the case of *Perkins* v. *Texas and New Orleans Ry. Co*,[19] the railroad was absolved of liability for damages caused by one of its trains, despite the fact that the train was traveling beyond the safe speed limit, because the court found that the engineer could not have avoided the accident even if he had been traveling at a safe speed.

One reason economists have had difficulty incorporating cause in fact into their models is that efficiency is determined by a forward-looking analysis—that is, it is concerned with the defendant's optimal choice of care *before* the accident occurs. It is this notion of causation that is implicit in the damage function $D(x)$ and that relates care to expected (as opposed to actual) damages.[20]

It is difficult to provide an economic theory of cause in fact based purely on efficiency. Indeed, the fact that causation limits the liability of injurers seems at first glance contrary to efficiency by insulating injurers from some of the damages that result from their actions. It turns out that this need not be the case. To see why, suppose that injurers are held liable only for the damages that result from their failure to take due care, x^*. In other words, they are *not* liable for damages that would have occurred even if they had taken due care. Formally, an injurer faces expected damages of $D(x) - D(x^*)$ if he chooses $x < x^*$, where $D(x^*)$ is expected damages when the injurer takes due care.

The injurer's problem under this modified negligence rule is to

$$\underset{x}{\text{minimize}} \quad \begin{cases} x, & x \geq x^* \\ x + D(x) - D(x^*), & x < x^*, \end{cases} \tag{2.15}$$

which differs from (2.3) by the subtraction of $D(x^*)$ in the second line. Nonetheless, it is easy to see that the solution to this problem continues to be x^*, given that $D(x^*)$ is a constant. The reason can be seen graphically in figure 2.2, which is identical to figure 2.1 except for the dashed curve, which shows the effect of subtracting $D(x^*)$. Notice that the minimum point of the injurer's expected costs in (2.15)—(the darkened curve)—continues to be at x^*. However, the discontinuity in the injurer's costs depicted in figure 2.1 has been eliminated by the cause-in-fact limitation.[21]

Cooter (1989) has argued in response to the preceding analysis that uncertainties associated with ex post causal attribution will cause the discontinuity in costs at the due-care level to remain in many cases.[22] For example, if a plaintiff has insufficient information to distinguish those injuries that would have been avoided by due care, courts may respond by shifting the burden of proof to the

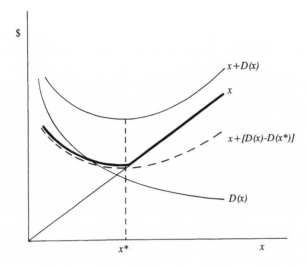

FIGURE 2.2 The negligence rule with a cause-in-fact limitation.

defendant to show that his or her negligence would have caused damages only of $D(x) - D(x^*)$, rather than some larger amount.[23] The costs associated with this shift of the burden will continue to create a discontinuity in the defendant's costs at x^*. Of course, this only reinforces the incentives for due care under negligence.

The preceding argument has shown that, although economists have had difficulty in formulating a positive role for the cause-in-fact limitation in tort law, at least it need not distort the incentives of injurers under a well-functioning negligence rule. The next question is whether there exists an economic basis for the proximate-cause limitation.

2.3. Proximate Cause

Even when an injurer's negligent act is judged to be the cause in fact of a harm, the injurer can still escape liability if the relationship between his act and the resulting harm is in some sense "too remote." For example, one test of proximate cause is whether the injurer could have reasonably foreseen the harm to the victim.[24] Note that this reasonable-foresight doctrine is therefore based on a forward-looking view of the accident, in contrast to the backward-looking orientation of cause in fact. Consequently, it can be formulated in terms of the expected damage function.

For this purpose, let us define $D(x) = p(x)L$, where $p(x)$ is the probability of an accident and L is constant damages. As in the discussion of the Hand rule earlier, let x be the actual care of an injurer $(x < x^*)$, and let x' be some higher level of care (i.e., $x' - x$ is the untaken precaution). One way to measure foreseeability is to ask, after the fact, if $p(x) - p(x') > T$, where T is some threshold.

That is, did the defendant's failure to take care of $x' - x$ increase the likelihood of an accident enough that a reasonable person could have foreseen it?

Recall from the discussion of the Hand rule that $D(x) - D(x') = PL$, or, in the case of constant damages, $[p(x) - p(x')] = P$. Notice, therefore, that if we rewrite the Hand rule as $P > B/L$ and let $T = B/L$, then the condition for proximate cause, $P = p(x) - p(x') > T$, is identical to the condition for determining negligence. This suggests that the two inquiries—breach of duty and proximate cause—are essentially redundant, a result that reinforces the view of those scholars who believe that causation is an unnecessary component of accident law for efficiency purposes, or that it serves purposes other than efficiency.[25]

Although the preceding discussion suggests that proximate cause and the Hand rule are redundant, in that they can be formulated as identical ex ante tests for negligence, there is an important difference between them that relates to the idea that it is the plaintiff's role in a tort case to propose the untaken precaution by the defendant to which these tests will be applied. Recall that it is in the plaintiff's interest to propose a small untaken precaution in order to maximize her chances of satisfying the Hand rule, a result that arose from the diminishing marginal benefit of care in reducing expected accident costs.

In contrast, the plaintiff is *more* likely to satisfy the test of proximate cause the *larger* the proposed untaken precaution. To see this, notice that $p(x) - p(x')$ is increasing in x' (given x). thus, for any T, $p(x) - p(x') > T$ is more likely the larger is x'. Intuitively, the more broadly the plaintiff states the untaken precaution, the easier it will be to argue that the defendant could have foreseen the resulting accident.[26]

This suggests that, in order for the plaintiff to prevail on both counts—that is, breach of duty and proximate cause—she must carefully select the untaken precaution (Grady, 1989, p. 150). Further, by its choice of the threshold T, the court in principle can induce the plaintiff to choose the "right" untaken precaution. In particular, suppose that the Hand rule alone were used to determine negligence. As shown earlier, this will create a downward bias in the plaintiff's choice of an untaken precaution, and as a result, tort cases might establish standards of care that are on average too low. To counteract this bias, the court needs to set a lower bound on those untaken precautions that will result in defendant liability. As the analysis suggested, the requirement of proximate cause with an appropriate choice of T can serve this role.

2.4. Res Ipsa Loquitur

The tort doctrine of *res ipsa loquitur* (which means "the thing speaks for itself") can be invoked by a plaintiff who is unable to prove that the defendant's negligent failure to take a particular precaution was the cause of the plaintiff's injuries. The doctrine allows the plaintiff to prevail if the circumstances of the accident are themselves sufficient evidence that the defendant was negligent.[27] In other words, the plaintiff does not have to prove either proximate cause or that the defendant's untaken precaution was cost-effective according to the

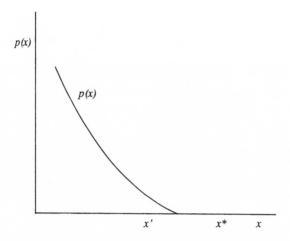

FIGURE 2.3 Accident technology for which *res ipsa loquitur* is relevant.

Hand rule (Grady, 1989, pp. 155–156). The inability of plaintiffs to specify an untaken precaution, however, does not by itself justify use of this doctrine to allow plaintiffs to recover, at least as far as efficiency is concerned. In addition, it must be the case that the efficient level of precaution x^* is such that $p(x^*) = 0$. That is, efficient precaution must prevent the accident altogether.

To see the significance of this requirement, consider figure 2.3, in which x' is the injurer's actual precaution and x^* is the efficient precaution. Note that when the accident technology has the form shown, occurrence of the accident *is* sufficient evidence that $x < x^*$ since $p(x) = 0$ for any $x \geq x^*$. It therefore implies that the defendant's untaken precaution is proximate cause (as defined above with $T = B/L$) and that it satisfies the Hand rule. In addition, the fact that care of x^* prevents the accident with certainty implies that, whenever an accident occurs, the defendant's failure to take care of x^* is cause in fact in the sense that it satisfies the "but for" test (i.e., the accident would not have occurred but for the defendant's failure to take care of x^*). In practice, however, the use of *res ipsa loquitur* will be limited because, in most cases, efficient precaution does not guarantee avoidance of accidents.

3. Individualized versus Average Standards: The Reasonable Person

Up to now, I have implicitly assumed that all injurers and victims are identical. In reality, of course, injurers and victims differ in many relevant respects. In this section, I examine how tort law handles differences in injurer costs of care and how this affects the determination of standards for care under negligence.[28] For simplicity, I focus on the unilateral-care accident model.

Assume that injurers differ in their unit costs of care, denoted c_i.[29] (Note that up to now, we have assumed $c_i = 1$ for all i.) Thus, the total expected costs from an accident involving an injurer of type i are given by

$$c_i x + p(x)L, \tag{2.16}$$

where L is damages conditional on an accident occurring. The level of care that minimizes expected costs therefore solves

$$c_i + p'(x)L = 0. \tag{2.17}$$

It is easy to see that the solution to this condition, denoted x_i^*, is decreasing in c_i.[30] That is, it is efficient for injurers with higher costs of care to invest less effort in accident avoidance.

This result implies that an efficient negligence rule should set a different due standard of care for all injurers, depending on their individual cost of taking care. In reality, the law does not generally do this. Rather, it holds all injurers to the same standard of care—namely, the reasonable-person standard.[31] According to this standard, "negligence is a failure to do what the reasonable person would do 'under the same or similar circumstances'."[32] Let x_R be the reasonable-person standard in the above model.

Landes and Posner (1987, pp. 123–131) argue that the use of a single standard for all injurers reflects the law's sensitivity to the high costs of information that would result if courts had to inquire into the value of c_i in every negligence case, given that c_i will generally be difficult to observe. This benefit must be balanced, however, against the costs of using a single standard. To see these costs, note that a single standard applied to a continuum of injurers will lead to three groupings of injurer behavior. The first group consists of injurers with a unit cost of care less than that of the reasonable person, so that $x_i^* > x_R$. Although it is socially desirable for these injurers to take more than due care, they will find it individually optimal to choose due care and no more since $c_i x_R < c_i x_i^*$ (given that they would not be negligent in either case). These injurers therefore take too little care from a social point of view.

The second group of injurers consists of those with a unit cost of care equal to or just below that of the reasonable person. In particular, this group consists of injurers for whom $x_i^* \leq x_R$ and

$$c_i x_i^* + p(x_i^*)L \geq c_i x_R. \tag{2.18}$$

It follows from (2.18) that, although these injurers have higher costs than the reasonable person, it is cheaper for them to increase their care up to the due standard to avoid liability than to choose their individually optimal level of care. These injurers therefore take too much care.

The final group includes injurers with very high costs of care such that $x_i^* < x_R$ and

$$c_i x_i^* + p(x_i^*)L < c_i x_R. \tag{2.19}$$

For these injurers, the reasonable person standard is so much higher than their individually optimal level of care that they actually find it cheaper to violate the due standard and choose x_i^*. Thus, the behavior of this group alone is consistent with social efficiency (yet they alone are found negligent).

In aggregate, these groupings of injurers in equilibrium may result in too many or too few accidents, given that the behaviors of the first two groups work in opposite directions. Also, note that, in contrast to negligence, a strict liability rule would result in *all* injurers choosing their individually optimal care levels. That is, there is no inefficiency. This benefit of strict liability over negligence must be weighed, however, against the superiority of negligence in inducing efficient victim care in bilateral accidents, as shown earlier, and the possibility that strict liability will lead to a larger number of accident suits, a point that will be discussed in the next chapter (section 1.4).

4. Activity Levels and Accident Risk

In addition to a choice of care, injurers and victims can affect the risk of an accident by their choice of how frequently or intensively to engage in a risky activity. This factor is referred to as the party's activity level. For example, the driver of an automobile decides how carefully to drive, but also how often and how many miles. Or, in the context of products liability (which I discuss in section 4.3), the producer of a dangerous product chooses how safe to make the product (care), but also how much of it to produce (activity).

4.1. Unilateral-Care Model

The simplest way to capture the activity level in the unilateral-care accident model is to define a variable z to represent the injurer's activity level and then redefine $D(x)$ as expected damages *per unit of activity* (Shavell, 1980b).[33] Thus, total expected damages are given by $zD(x)$, which is increasing in z and decreasing in x. Also, define $w(z, x)$ as the injurer's expected income from engaging in the activity at level z and with care x. Assume that $w_x < 0$, $w_{xx} \le 0$, for all z, and that w_z is initially positive but ultimately negative, with w reaching a maximum at $z_p(x)$. Finally assume $w_{zz} < 0$.

Given this model, the socially optimal levels of care and activity for the injurer solve

$$\underset{z, x}{\text{maximize}} \ w(z, x) - zD(x). \tag{2.20}$$

The first-order conditions for z and x, respectively, are given by[34]

$$w_z - D = 0. \qquad (2.21)$$

$$w_x - zD' = 0 \qquad (2.22)$$

Denote the solutions z^* and x^*. Note that (2.21) implies that $z^*(x) < z_p(x)$ for any x, given that $z_p(x)$ solves $w_z = 0$..

Now consider the outcome under the various liability rules. First, under a rule of no liability, the individual will choose an activity level equal to $z_p(x)$, which is too high. Similarly, for any z, the individual will choose $x = 0$, or too little care in the absence of liability. These results are consistent with the model in which only care was chosen. Under a rule of strict liability, the injurer faces the full cost of any accidents, making his problem identical to the social problem in (2.20). He therefore chooses z^* and x^*. Again, this is similar to the earlier model. Finally, under negligence, the injurer's problem is to

$$\text{maximize} \quad \begin{aligned} w(z, x), & \qquad x \geq x^* \\ w(z, x) - zD(x), & \qquad x < x^*. \end{aligned} \qquad (2.23)$$

Based on the reasoning from above, he will choose x^* to avoid liability. His choice of z therefore maximizes $w(z, x^*)$, which yields $z_p(x^*) > z^* \equiv z^*(x^*)$. Thus, he chooses an excessive activity level. Intuitively, since the due standard under negligence is defined solely in terms of care, the injurer does not bear the marginal damage costs associated with greater activity. The usual reason given for making negligence conditional only on care is that the task of calculating optimal activity levels is prohibitively costly for courts to undertake.[35] Thus, whereas strict liability and negligence were equally efficient in unilateral care models in the absence of activity levels (administrative costs aside), strict liability is preferred when the injurer's activity is an important source of accident risk.

4.2. Bilateral-Care Accidents

As was the case with care, the activity level of victims may also contribute to accident risks. For example, how many miles a pedestrian walks, in addition to whether she walks on the proper side of the road, contributes to her risk of being injured. The victim's activity level is introduced into the model in the same way as the injurer's activity (Shavell, 1980b). Specifically, define u as the victim's activity level and $b(u, y)$ as her benefit from engaging in the activity at level u and with care y. Thus, expected damages are now $zuD(x, y)$ and the social problem becomes

$$\text{maximize} \quad w(z, x) + b(u, y) - zuD(x, y). \qquad (2.24)$$
$$z, u, x, y$$

Without going into detail, it is easy to prove a general result in this case—namely, if the due standard for injurers and victims cannot be conditioned on their activity levels, then none of the liability rules we have considered can induce optimal care and activity by both parties. The intuition is easily seen from the unilateral-care case. In order for a party to choose the optimal activity level, he must bear the full accident costs in equilibrium, given that a threshold for activity is assumed not to be feasible. And, since both parties cannot simultaneously bear the damages in equilibrium (given the assumption that any damages imposed on one party are paid to the other), they cannot both be induced to choose their optimal activity. Thus, the party that actually bears the damages in equilibrium will choose the optimal activity level, and the other party will choose too much activity.[36] However, both will choose optimal care under the three negligence rules and under strict liability with contributory negligence.

4.3. Products Liability

As noted above, accidents caused by dangerous products (products liability cases) represent a example in which activity levels are important. In this case, the output of firms (injurers) and the amount consumers (victims) purchase can be interpreted as their activity levels. Product-related accidents differ from those we have been considering, however, in that injurers and victims are not strangers.[37] That is, they have previously engaged in a market exchange, presumably in the knowledge that the product might later cause injuries to the consumer. This is important because, with complete information about risks, we will see that the price of the product will adjust in equilibrium to reflect both the residual risk and the relevant liability rule.[38] In this section, I examine how the market relationship between the injurer and victim affects the equilibrium care and output levels under the various liability rules.[39]

I will employ the bilateral-care accident model from section 1.2, where x is expenditure on care by the producer, y is expenditure on care by the consumer, and $D(x,y)$ is expected damages, all defined to be *per unit of output*. In addition, let q be the number of units produced per firm. Thus, from a social perspective, total expected accident costs per firm (including the consumer's cost of care) are $q[x + y + D(x,y)]$. Let $v(q)$ be the consumer's marginal consumption benefit of the good, where $v' < 0$ (indicating diminishing marginal benefit), and let $c(q)$ total production costs of the producer.[40] Finally, let n be the number of identical firms. Thus, total output is given by nq.

Given these definitions, the social problem is to choose q, n, x, and y to maximize total welfare:

$$W = \int_0^{nq} v(z)dz - nc(q) - nq[x + y + D(x,y)]. \tag{2.25}$$

Note that, because expected accident costs are assumed to be linear in output, the optimal choices of x and y are independent of q and n. In particular, the first-order conditions for x and y are given by (2.7) and (2.8). The first-order conditions for q and n, respectively, are given by:

$$v(nq) = c'(q) + x + y + D(x,y) \tag{2.26}$$

and

$$v(nq) = c(q)/q + x + y + D(x,y). \tag{2.27}$$

According to (2.26), q^* equates marginal consumption benefits to marginal production plus accident costs, and according to (2.27), n^* equates marginal consumption benefits to average production plus accident costs.[41]

The questions we wish to answer are: Do any of our liability rules achieve the social optimum? and What is the role of the market in internalizing accident costs? The second question represents the unique feature of accidents between producers and consumers as opposed to accidents between strangers. In examining the role of the market, I assume firms are competitive in order to exclude market power issues.[42] I will, however, allow the possibility of certain Coasian bargains between buyers and sellers in a sense to be described below.

A convenient way to examine the impact of liability rules in a general manner is to specify a parameter, $s \in [0,1]$, which represents the share of damages borne by the consumer ($1 - s$ is the producer's share). Thus, for example, $s = 1$ corresponds to no liability for producers ('caveat emptor'), $s = 0$ corresponds to strict liability, and conditioning s on x and or y corresponds to the various negligence rules (Landes and Posner, 1985). Given this approach, the problem for consumers is to choose the number of units of the good to consume, Q (where, in equilibrium, $Q = nq$), and the level of care to take, y, to maximize

$$\int_0^Q v(z)dz - RQ - Q[sD(x,y) + y] \tag{2.28}$$

where R is the price of the good. In solving this problem, the consumer takes as given the legal rule, s, the producer's level of care, x, and views the price as being independent of output (i.e., $\partial R / \partial Q = 0$). I will, however, allow the possibility that the consumer and producer can bargain over the price with regard to the consumer's choice of care (i.e., $\partial R / \partial y$ may not be zero). Given these assumptions, the first-order conditions for y and Q, respectively, are

$$\partial R / \partial y + sD_y + 1 = 0 \tag{2.29}$$

and

$$v(Q) = R + sD + y. \tag{2.30}$$

An individual producer's problem is to choose q (output per firm) and x to maximize

$$Rq - c(q) - q(1-s)D(x,y) - qx. \tag{2.31}$$

In solving this problem, the producer takes as given the legal rule, the consumer's care, y, and also views the price as independent of output. As in the consumer's problem, however, I allow possible bargains over the price with regard to producer care (i.e., $\partial R/\partial x$ may not be zero). The first-order conditions for the producer's problem are therefore

$$\partial R/\partial x - (1-s)D_x - 1 = 0 \tag{2.32}$$

and

$$R = c'(q) + (1-s)D + x. \tag{2.33}$$

Finally, free entry of firms results in zero profits per firm, or

$$Rq = c(q) + q(1-s)D(x,y) + qx. \tag{2.34}$$

Equations (2.29), (2.30), and (2.32) to (2.34) characterize the equilibrium (along with $Q = nq$). The efficiency properties of the equilibrium are found by comparing these conditions to (2.7),(2.8), (2.26), and (2.27). First, combine (2.30) and (2.33) to get

$$v(nq) = c'(q) + D(x,y) + x + y \tag{2.35}$$

and combine (2.30) and (2.34) to get

$$v(nq) = c(q)/q + D(x,y) + x + y. \tag{2.36}$$

Comparing these to (2.26) and (2.27) shows that, given any levels of producer and consumer care, both output per firm and the number of firms are efficient, *regardless of the liability rule* (i.e., s drops out of (2.35) and (2.36)). The reason for this "irrelevance" result is that, given full information about risk, the price of the good internalizes the damages.[43] Specifically, if $s = 0$ (strict liability), the equilibrium price of the good (as given by (2.33) or (2.34)) reflects the full damages, and consumers reduce their purchases accordingly. In contrast, if $s = 1$ (no liability), the price will reflect only production costs, but the consumer will purchase an amount dictated by the full cost, $R + D + y$ (as in (2.30)). For negligence rules, the price will reflect the equilibrium allocation of damages.[44] In any case, (2.35) and (2.36) imply that q and n are efficient, given the values of x and y.

The equilibrium care levels are determined by (2.29) and (2.32). Assume initially that $\partial R/\partial x = \partial R/\partial y = 0$; that is, the price is independent of the parties' choices of x and y. In this case, it is clear that efficient care by both parties cannot be achieved by either strict liability ($s = 1$) or no liability ($s = 1$). Under strict liability, the victim will take no care and the injurer will take efficient care given the victim's choice (i.e., he will choose $x^*(0)$). Under no liability ($s = 1$), the reverse will be true. In contrast, it is easy to show that the various negligence rules that condition s on x and/or y can induce both injurers and victims to take efficient care. Thus, when one of these rules is in place, the equilibrium is efficient in terms of output, number of firms, and care.

Landes and Posner (1985, 1987) argue, however, that even strict and no liability can lead to an efficient equilibrium if producers and consumers can bargain at a low cost. Specifically, suppose that the parties can write and enforce contracts that condition price on care. For example, in the case of no liability, we saw that producers take no care because they are not liable for damages. Suppose, however, that the parties strike a bargain whereby producers take care (i.e., produce a safer product) and charge a higher price for the good. Notice that, in this case, consumers would pay up to $R = v(Q) - D(x,y) - y$ for the good (from (2.30) with $s = 1$), from which it follows that $\partial R/\partial x = -D_x > 0$. Substituting this into (2.32) (with $s = 1$) yields the condition for efficient producer care. Intuitively, the producer now chooses care up to the point where the cost of one more unit ($\$1$) equals the marginal increase in the price it can charge ($-D_x$), which yields the efficient level.

The same story holds for a strict liability rule. In this case, the producer is willing to lower the price in exchange for a promise of greater consumer care in order to reduce the producer's expected liability. Specifically, the price the producer charges is now given by $R = c'(q) + D(x,y) + x$ (from (2.33) with $s = 0$), which implies that $\partial R/\partial y = D_y < 0$. Thus, the consumer will commit to taking more care until the cost of the last unit of care equals the marginal price reduction. Again, this leads to efficient care by the consumer (substitute $\partial R/\partial y$ into (2.29) with $s = 0$).[45]

The preceding argument suggests that the legal rule is irrelevant for care (as it was for output). However, there are serious questions regarding the feasibility of the proposed bargaining, in that both contracts require the parties to make correct assessments of the risks of the product and the efficacy of the safety measures adopted by the other party. In particular, under no liability, consumers must accurately observe the increased safety of the product such that they make the correct consumption choice given the higher price. Under strict liability, the problem is more serious because the producer must somehow be able to monitor the consumer's care *after she has purchased the product and paid the lower price.* Both of these solutions pose significant informational demands on the parties, the cost of which may exceed the benefits of less court involvement (as compared to negligence rules, which have higher administrative costs but provide good incentive for care without the need for bargaining).

Nevertheless, Landes and Posner (1985, 1987) have argued that economic theory does a good job of explaining the major historical developments of products liability law.[46] The two major changes in the law have been: (1) the abandonment of privity of contract, which barred suits against anyone except the direct seller (rarely the producer); and (2) the gradual move from negligence to strict liability. Landes and Posner argue that these changes are largely consistent with efficiency based on information costs. In particular, as products have become more complex, consumers have less ability both to judge the riskiness of products and to prevent accidents relative to producers. Both of these factors favor greater producer liability. First, under strict liability we saw that the price of the product rises to reflect expected damages, thereby inducing the consumer to purchase the correct amount without the need to evaluate risk. In contrast, under negligence, consumers bear the damages in equilibrium (given due care by producers), which will result in overconsumption if consumers underestimate risk and underconsumption if they overestimate risk. Second, under a negligence rule, the consumer will generally find it difficult to prove negligence by the producer, given the complexity of the production process for most products. As for the privity doctrine, it often represented a bar of liability for producers, which is also inconsistent with producers' superior knowledge about risk in a modern economy.

As the preceding argument suggests, consumer misperceptions about risk tend to favor strict liability (unless consumer care is very important) because it induces efficient producer care and causes the product price to signal accurately the risk of the product so that consumers purchase the correct amount.[47] Polinsky and Rogerson (1983) have shown, however, that if producers have market power, this conclusion may not be true. The reason is that, in the absence of risk, firms with market power (monopolists or oligopolists) produce too little output from a social point of view. Thus, if consumers underestimate risk, a negligence rule might dominate strict liability because the tendency for consumers to consume too much in this case will act to offset the firm's incentive to produce too little.

5. Issues in the Determination of Damages

To this point I have treated the level of damages awarded in accident cases as if it were set equal to the victim's losses. In this section, I consider some factors that complicate the determination of actual damages. These include variations in the level of damages across victims, errors by the court in measuring the victim's damages, the awarding of punitive damages, the possibility of insolvency of a defendant (the judgment-proof problem), and the problem of assigning liability among multiple defendants.

5.1. Individualized versus Average Damages:
The Eggshell Skull Rule

Potential accident victims differ according to their susceptibility to injury. In terms of the simple accident model we have been using, this implies that the value of L varies over the population of victims. Although the optimal level of care by injurers should ideally adjust to variations in L (specifically, x^* should increase with L), this is not possible since L is generally unobservable to injurers ex ante. Although the court could individualize the standard ex post, this will not result in individualized care; rather, injurers will simply act as if the standard were a random variable (see section 2.1 in chapter 3).

The discussion of the reasonableness standard, however, raises the question of whether damage awards should be individualized or whether all victims should receive the average level of damages. Economic analysis suggests that, on balance, it is preferable to individualize damages when injurers are held liable. This is true for two reasons. First, if injurers were only assessed the *average* damages in cases involving high L victims, then the distribution of damages would be truncated (assuming that injurers could not be charged average damages in cases where victims sustained less than average damages), thereby reducing incentives for injurer care. Second, the information costs of determining L ex post are much lower than was the case with variations in injurer costs of care, since L is revealed by the accident. Landes and Posner (1987, pp. 249–250) argue that the law is consistent with the conclusion that damages should be individualized in that defendants generally cannot use unknown preexisting conditions of the victim (e.g., an "eggshell skull")[48] as a defense against higher than average damage awards.

5.2. Errors in Measuring Damages

Courts may make errors in assessing the actual losses of victims. The impact of these errors on the behavior of injurers and victims depends, first of all, on whether they are *biased* or *unbiased*. If they are unbiased in the sense that the expected value of the court's assessment of damages equals the victim's actual losses, then injurers and victims will choose optimal care regardless of the errors (assuming risk neutrality).

In the case where the court's errors are biased in the sense that damage awards are systematically set higher or lower than the victim's losses, the impact of the errors depends on the liability rule. Under strict liability, injurers will take more than optimal care if damages systematically exceed losses, and they will take less than optimal care if damages systematically understate losses. Although we saw earlier that victims have no incentive to take care under strict liability with damages equal to losses, when damages systematically understate actual losses, victims *will* have an incentive to take care, and their care level will be increasing in the expected amount of undercompensation.

The impact of systematic errors by the court is quite different under a negligence rule. Because of the discontinuity in costs facing the injurer under negligence (see figure 2.1), he will choose the due care level x^* for a wide range of damage levels. Clearly, he will choose x^* for overassessments of the victim's losses, and he will also choose x^* for underassessments as long as the error is not too large.[49] To demonstrate the latter claim, let αL be the court's assessment of the victim's actual losses (which are given by L), where $\alpha < 1$. Also let x_α be the level of injurer care that minimizes $x + p(x)\alpha L$, where x_α is increasing in α and $x_\alpha < x^*$ for $\alpha < 1$. In this case, the injurer will choose care of x^* provided that

$$x^* \leq x_\alpha + p(x_\alpha)\alpha L \tag{2.37}$$

and x_α otherwise. Note that this will always hold for $\alpha = 1$, for in that case $x_\alpha = x^*$, and it will never hold for $\alpha = 0$. Moreover, since the right-hand side is increasing in α,[50] there exists a critical level of α (which is between zero and one) such that the injurer chooses x^* for α greater than this value and x_α for α less than this value. Thus, in contrast to strict liability, the injurer will choose efficient care under negligence as long as the underassessment is not too large (i.e., as long as α is not too small).[51]

If injurers satisfy the due-care level, victims bear their own losses, so they will choose efficient care. In this case, the court's errors do not affect them. If, however, injurers fail to satisfy the due-care level as a result of a large under-assessment of the victim's losses, victims receive partial compensation. Thus, they too will take less than efficient care.

The foregoing analysis of the negligence rule changes when the causation requirement is added, for then the discontinuity in the injurer's costs disappears (see figure 2.2). In this case, *any* underassessment of damages by the court will lead to less than efficient care by injurers (Kahan, 1989).[52]

5.3. Punitive Damages

Punitive damages are damages awarded to the victim in excess of his or her actual losses in an effort to "punish" the injurer. Punitive damages are therefore generally reserved for cases in which it is judged that the defendant acted in a willful, wanton, or malicious manner. From an economic perspective, the question is how damages in excess of the victim's injuries promote the goal of minimizing accident costs, and whether the actual use of punitive damages corresponds to their economic function.

The principal economic explanation for punitive damages has to do with the possibility that injurers will occasionally escape liability for accidents they cause owing to imperfect detection or enforcement error.[53] Specifically, consider the manufacturer of a dangerous product that expects to face liability only a fraction α of the times that its product actually causes an injury. In that case, it will choose a level of care (product safety) to minimize

$$x + p(x)\alpha L. \tag{2.38}$$

As noted above, this will result in less than the efficient level of care whenever $\alpha < 1$.

To correct this problem, suppose that in the event it is found liable for an accident, the injurer faces not only compensatory damages of L but also punitive damages of R. The injurer's problem is in that case is to minimize

$$x + p(x)\alpha(L + R). \tag{2.39}$$

In order to induce an efficient level of care, we need to choose R such that $\alpha(L + R) = L$, or

$$R(\alpha) = L[(1 - \alpha)/\alpha] \qquad (2.40)$$

where it is easy to see that R is decreasing in α and $R(1) = 0$. Intentional torts is an area where punitive damages are often awarded. This is consistent with the preceding argument, in that those who intentionally cause injuries are likely to take conscious steps to avoid detection, resulting in $\alpha < 1$ (Landes and Posner, 1987, pp. 160–163; Cooter 1982b).

There is a popular perception that large punitive damage awards are routine and that limits on punitive damages are therefore necessary.[54] Such an argument is not supported by the above theory or by the available data. Theoretically, a preset limit could prevent R from being chosen to satisfy (2.40) in a given case. Empirically, punitive damage awards appear to be neither frequent nor excessive, especially when reversal of awards on appeal is taken into account (Landes and Posner, 1987, pp. 304–307; Shanley, 1991).

5.4. Defendant Insolvency: The Judgment-Proof Problem

In some cases, defendants who are found liable for a plaintiff's injuries may have insufficient assets to pay compensatory damages. In the extreme case, a defendant may have no assets (e.g., a bankrupt manufacturer), in which case he is referred to as *judgment-proof*. From an economic perspective, the question is how the possibility that he will have insufficient assets to pay damages affects the incentives of potential injurers. The answer differs depending on whether the rule is strict liability or negligence.[55]

Under strict liability, the impact of insufficient assets is analytically identical to both the case of systematic underassessment of damages by the court and imperfect detection. In particular, suppose the injurer expects to have assets of αL at the time that he causes an accident inflicting losses of L, where $\alpha < 1$. He will therefore choose the level of care, x_α, that minimizes (2.38), where we have seen that x_α is less than efficient care, x^*. Under negligence with due care set at efficient care, the injurer will choose due care if (2.37) holds, which will be the case as long as α is not too small—that is, as long as the injurer's expected wealth is close enough to (though still less than) his expected liability. Otherwise, he will choose less than due care.

5.5. Multiple Injurers

So far we have considered only the case of a single injurer. In many accident settings, however, the actions of several individuals contribute to the risk of an injury. An example is when several firms dispose of hazardous waste in a single dumpsite, which subsequently causes contamination of groundwater. The problem is how to apportion the resulting damages among the multiple defendants.

To examine this problem, consider a model in which n injurers can take care to reduce the risk of a loss.[56] Let x_j be the expenditure on care by injurer j, $j = 1, \ldots, n$, and let $D(x_1, \ldots, x_n)$ be the expected damages, where

$\partial D/\partial x_j \equiv D_j < 0$ for all j.[57] The socially optimal levels of care, x_j^*, therefore minimize total expected costs:

$$\Sigma_j x_j + D(x_1, \ldots, x_n). \tag{2.41}$$

The resulting first-order condition for each injurer is

$$1 + D_j = 0, \quad j = 1, \ldots, n. \tag{2.42}$$

Now consider the actual choice of care by the injurers under different liability rules. First, consider a rule of strict liability under which each injurer will be held liable for a share, s_j, of the damages regardless of his or her care, where $\Sigma_j s_j = 1$. In that case, each injurer j will choose care to minimize

$$x_j + s_j D(x_j, x_{-j}^0) \tag{2.43}$$

where x_{-j}^0 is the vector of care levels taken by all injurers, except j in a Nash equilibrium. Clearly, injurers will take less than efficient care given $s_j < 1$. Under the doctrine of joint and several liability, the plaintiff has the right to collect the full damages from any subset of the n injurers, including any single injurer. Typically, under strict liability the plaintiff will pursue the injurer with the deepest pocket to avoid the judgment-proof problem. This will tend to increase the s_j for wealthier injurers and reduce it for less wealthy injurers, with corresponding effects on their care choices.[58]

Now consider a negligence rule. Specifically, suppose that each injurer can avoid liability by choosing its efficient level of care, x_j^*, whereas each injurer choosing less than efficient care will incur a share r_j of the liability, where the r_j's sum to one. (Note, however, that the sum is only over the *negligent* injurers.) In this case, it can be shown that each injurer will choose efficient care in a Nash equilibrium.[59] Under joint and several liability, any single negligent injurer (or any subset of the negligent injurers) could be held liable for the full damages. This should not affect the incentives for care unless an injurer is fairly certain that he would *not* be among those pursued (i.e., his $r_j = 0$), since in that case, he could behave as if he were judgment-proof.

6. Summary

In this chapter I have laid out the basic economic model of accidents and used it to examine several aspects of tort law. I first showed that negligence rules are generally superior to strict liability in providing incentives for efficient care by injurers and victims in bilateral accident cases. The reason is that negligence rules combine two methods for inducing efficient care: they simultaneously impose liability on one party and establish a threshold, or due standard, for the other. We shall see that this basic approach to resolving bilateral-care problems will arise in several contexts throughout this book.

Economic analysis not only prescribes optimal tort rules but also explains several aspects of the law. For example, we saw that the Hand rule for determining negligence corresponds closely to the economic theory of negligence. And, although causation requirements limit defendants' liability under negligence, they are consistent with (though not necessarily required by) efficiency. These and other examples demonstrate the ability of the economic theory of accidents to help us understand the actual structure of tort law. In the next chapter, I extend the model to allow consideration of several more realistic aspects of accident cases, including the costs of resolving disputes, uncertainty, and the possibility of strategic behavior.

THREE

THE ECONOMICS OF TORT LAW

Extensions

This chapter extends in several directions the basic accident model from the previous chapter. The first concerns the impact of litigation costs, or the costs that victims and injurers incur in resolving an accident claim through the legal system. Consideration of these costs is important, not only because they represent a substantial expenditure of resources, but also because they potentially affect the incentives for care created by the liability system. As we shall see, litigation costs tend to reduce the incentives for injurers to take care, though the effects differ under strict liability and negligence. Thus, litigation costs introduce an extra dimension along which to compare liability rules in terms of their ability to reduce the social costs of accidents.

The second extension of the basic model concerns the impact of uncertainty on the operation of the liability system. I first consider the impact of uncertainty by injurers about what the due standard of care is under a negligence rule. I then consider the impact of uncertainty by the court both about whether a given injurer violated the due standard care, and whether he was the cause of an accident. Finally, I consider the impact of uncertainty by injurers about whether the products they are producing or the activities they are engaged in pose a risk of injury in the first place.

The final topic I examine in this chapter is sequential-care torts, or torts in which the injurer and victim choose their care levels sequentially. Although accidents of this sort have not received extensive treatment in the law and economics literature, they are of interest because they are fairly common, and also because they create the potential for strategic behavior by the parties. As a result, we shall see that they present unique problems for the design of efficient liability rules.

1. Litigation Costs

The economic analysis of accidents to this point has ignored the costs of litigation (except for general references to administrative costs). In this section I briefly describe how the costs of litigation affect the ability of the legal system to internalize accident risk.[1] In chapters 8 and 9 I consider in more detail the role of litigation costs on settlement and litigation decisions after a dispute has arisen.

To keep the model simple, I consider only the unilateral-care case, though I will modify the basic model in two ways. First, I will write expected damages as $p(x)D$, where $p(x)$ is the probability of an accident $(p' < 0, p'' > 0)$ and D is constant damages. Further, I will assume that D differs across victims according to a known distribution function $F(D)$, $F' > 0$. The second modification is that there is a cost of bringing suit for victims, c_v, and a cost of defending themselves for injurers, c_i. In what follows I will consider how litigation costs affect optimal deterrence, first under strict liability and then under negligence.[2]

1.1. Strict Liability

Under strict liability, a victim will file suit for damages if the benefit of filing exceeds the cost, or if $D > c_v$. Thus, if an accident occurs, the injurer faces a probability of a lawsuit equal to $1 - F(c_v)$. It follows immediately that the likelihood of a lawsuit conditional on an accident is decreasing in the victim's litigation costs. Given this probability, the injurer's care choice solves

$$\text{minimize}_{x} \ x + p(x) \int_{c_v}^{\infty} (D + c_i) dF(D) \tag{3.1}$$

where the integral represents the injurer's expected liability plus litigation costs in the event of an accident. The first-order condition from (3.1) is

$$1 + p'(x) \int_{c_v}^{\infty} (D + c_i) + 0. \tag{3.2}$$

Denote the resulting care level x_i.

Condition (3.2) determines actual care under strict liability. I will now compare this to socially optimal care in the presence of litigation costs. In the absence of litigation costs, optimal care by the injurer minimizes $x + p(x)E(D)$. The resulting level of care, x^*, is what a planner would like to impose. I will refer to this as the "optimal zero-litigation cost outcome." In reality, injurers will only have an incentive to take care if faced with a lawsuit. Optimal care in this case must take account of the cost of litigation.[3] The optimal level of care in the presence of litigation costs takes the victim's decision to file suit as a given and therefore solves

$$\text{minimize}_{x} \ x + p(x)[E(D) + (1 - F(c_v))(c_i + c_v)] \tag{3.3}$$

where $1 - F(c_v)$ is the probability of a lawsuit given that an accident has occurred, and

$$E(D) = \int_0^\infty D dF(D).$$

Let x^s be the solution to (3.3). Note that $x^s > x^*$ since the expected cost of an accident is higher when lawsuits are unavoidable.

Let us now compare the injurer's equilibrium level of care under strict liability, x_i, which solves (3.1), to the optimal level of care in the presence of litigation costs. To do this, note that (3.3) can be rewritten as

$$\underset{x}{\text{minimize }} x + p(x)\left\{\int_{c_v}^\infty (D + c_i)dF(D) + \int_0^{c_v} D dF(D) + [1 - F(c_v)]c_v\right\}. \quad (3.4)$$

Comparing (3.4) and (3.1) shows that social costs in the event of an accident exceed private costs by the final two terms inside the brackets. Thus, $x^s > x_i$; that is, injurers take too little care under strict liability. The extra terms in (3.4) show the two sources of inefficiency. The first is because injurers do not face the full damages they impose, but rather an amount discounted by the probability of a suit, $[1 - F(c_v)]$. The second inefficiency is because the injurer does not consider the victim's litigation costs in the event of a suit.

The presence of litigation costs raises the question of whether lawsuits are socially desirable.[4] Under a strict liability rule, the social function of a suit is to induce injurers to take care. Thus, suits are socially desirable if the reduced accident costs owing to increased care offset the costs of litigation. Specifically, if no suits are allowed, and therefore injurers do not take care, expected accident costs are $p(0)E(D)$. Alternatively, if suits are allowed, victims file suit when $D > c_v$ and injurers take care of x_i (the solution to (3.1)), yielding total costs of

$$x_i + p(x_i)[E(D) + [1 - F(c_v)](c_i + c_v)]. \quad (3.5)$$

Thus, suits are socially desirable if

$$p(0)E(D) > x_i + p(x_i)[E(D) + (1 - F(c_v))(c_i + c_v)]. \quad (3.6)$$

In general, this inequality may or may not hold. Thus, it is not possible to conclude that a strict liability rule results in too many or too few lawsuits.

1.2. Decoupled Liability

Damage awards in torts are generally structured so that the amount the plaintiff receives is equal to the amount that the defendant pays (both of which are equal to the plaintiff's damages in the absence of punitive damages). Economists have recognized, however, that social costs can be lowered if, under a strict liability rule, the amount the plaintiff receives is "'decoupled" from the amount that the defendant pays.[5] This strategy can lower social costs because the defendant's incentive to take care and the plaintiff's incentive to sue can be manipulated by two policy variables rather than one. Moreover, additional discretion is obtained if neither amount is necessarily equal to the plaintiff's damages.

To illustrate the benefits of decoupling in the context of the earlier model, let $a \cdot D$ be the award to the plaintiff, where D is her actual damages and a is an adjustment factor; and let $b(D) \leq m$ be the defendant's liability, which may be a function of D, where m is the maximum amount that can be assessed (e.g., m may be the defendant's wealth). The condition for a victim to sue is now $aD > c_v$, which makes the probability of a suit conditional on an accident $1 - F(c_v/a)$. Thus, the following problem replaces (3.1) for determining the injurer's choice of care:

$$\underset{x}{\text{minimize}} \; x + p(x) \int_{\frac{c_v}{a}}^{\infty} [b(D) + c_i] dF(D). \tag{3.7}$$

Note that this expression is increasing in both $b(D)$ and a. The social problem is to choose a and $b(D)$ to minimize social costs, which are now given by

$$x + p(x)[E(D) + (1 - F(c_v/a))(c_i + c_v)], \tag{3.8}$$

where $b(D)$ enters implicitly through x.

First consider the choice of $b(D)$. It is easy to show that $b(D) = m$ is optimal; that is, it is optimal to set $b(D)$ as high as possible. To see why, suppose $b(D) < m$ and $a > 0$. Now increase $b(D)$ to m and lower a in (3.7) in such a way that the injurer's expected costs in the event of an accident (liability plus expected litigation costs) are unchanged. This results in the same choice of x by the injurer. Thus, the terms involving x in (3.8) are unaffected. However, the decrease in a lowers expected litigation costs in (3.8) (i.e., the term $(1 - F(c_v/a))(c_i + c_v)$ becomes smaller), thereby lowering overall social costs. Thus, $b(D) < m$ could not have been optimal.

With $b(D) = m$ (which, note, is independent of D), the injurer's choice of care now solves

$$\underset{x}{\text{minimize}} \; x + p(x)[1 - F(c_v/a)](m + c_i), \tag{3.9}$$

which yields $x^*(a)$. It is easy to see that $x^*(a)$ is increasing in a, since higher a increases the probability of a suit when an accident occurs. The optimal choice of a can now be found by substituting $x^*(a)$ into (3.8) and minimizing with respect to a. The resulting first-order condition is

$$\partial x^*/\partial a + pF'(c_v/a^2)(c_i + c_v) = -p'(\partial x^*/\partial a)[E(D) + (1 - F(c_v/a))(c_i + c_v)]. \tag{3.10}$$

The left-hand side is the marginal cost of increasing a—the first term is the increased cost of care and the second is the higher expected litigation costs as a is increased. The right-hand side is the marginal benefit of increasing a, which is due to the lower probability of an accident as care increases. Note that decoupling necessarily improves on (or at least is no worse than) the standard strict liability rule with $a = 1$ and $b = D$ in that the latter is a special case of the more general decoupled rule. Thus, decoupling will generally result in lower combined accident and litigation costs.

1.3. Negligence

Under a perfectly functioning negligence rule,[6] a victim will file suit if $D > c_v$ and if the injurer was negligent. Thus, if an accident occurs, negligent injurers face a lawsuit with probability $1 - F(c_v)$, and non-negligent injurers face no suits.[7] If z is the due standard of care, the injurer's problem is to

$$\underset{x}{\text{minimize}} \quad x + p(x) \int_{c_v}^{\infty} (D + c_i)dF(D), \quad \begin{matrix} x, & x \geq z \\ & x < z \end{matrix} \tag{3.11}$$

The solution to this problem depends on the due standard. Suppose as above that z is set equal to the zero litigation cost optimum, x^*. Note that the second line of (3.11) differs from social costs in the case of zero litigation costs by the truncation of damages at c_v and the presence of c_i. Since these have offsetting effects (the first term lowers costs and the second raises them), the value of x that minimizes the second line of (3.11)—which is simply x_i, the solution to (3.1)— may be larger or smaller than $z = x^*$. If it is *larger*, then the injurer will clearly comply with the due standard. In this case, no victims will file suit and the optimal zero-litigation cost outcome is achieved (i.e., the injurer chooses care of x^* and no suits are filed).

If, however, x_i is *less* than x^*, then the injurer may or may not choose to comply with the due standard. He will comply if the minimized value of the second line is larger than x^*, in which case the result is identical to the previous case. He will not comply, however, if the minimized value of the second line is less than x^*. In this case, the outcome is identical to that under strict liability. That is, the injurer chooses care of x_i, which is less than both the zero and positive litigation costs optimal-care levels (x^* and x^s, respectively), and all victims for whom $D > c_v$ file suit.

It is important to note that, even when a negligence rule achieves the optimal zero-litigation cost outcome and no suits are filed, victims must be *willing* to file suits in the event of negligent behavior, otherwise injurers have no incentive to comply with the due standard.[8] The fact that no suits are *actually* filed in this case therefore implies that victims will not have a socially excessive incentive to file suit under negligence. However, when injurers do not comply with the due standard, it is because there is an insufficient incentive to sue. Specifically, recall that the term $1 - F(c_v)$ tends to reduce the injurer's incentive to satisfy the due standard. Indeed, if this term were close enough to 1, the injurer would always comply with the due standard, and the optimal zero-litigation cost outcome would be achieved.[9]

1.4. Strict Liability and Negligence Compared

The preceding analysis of litigation costs provides a way to compare the efficiency of negligence and strict liability in a unilateral-care model. (Recall that in the absence of litigation costs, they yielded identical results.) Specifically, we saw that negligence can induce optimal care while deterring lawsuits, whereas strict liability requires lawsuits for injurers to take care (Landes and Posner, 1987, p. 65). Thus, negligence reduces the *number* of claims compared to strict liability. Offsetting this, however, is the fact that a *given claim* is costlier under negligence because the court has the extra task of calculating the due standard and then determining whether the injurer complied with it.[10] Indeed, it is this extra activity by the court that allows a negligence rule to deter suits. Consequently, the overall comparison between the two rules based on litigation costs is ambiguous.

More generally, the choice between strict liability and negligence can be viewed in the context of the general problem of choosing between rules and discretion. Strict liability has more of the character of a rule since, as noted, it involves relatively little factual inquiry by the court,[11] whereas negligence has more of the character of discretion because it involves greater fact finding.[12] The economic approach to choosing between rules and discretion is based on transaction costs between the parties involved in the dispute. When transaction costs are low, rules are preferable because the parties can be expected to resolve the dispute on their own according to the Coase theorem. However, when transaction costs are high, the parties cannot be expected to resolve the dispute, so discretion in the form of greater court involvement is preferred. When applied to the typical accident case involving strangers, this argument suggests that discretion will generally be the better alternative given the inability of parties to bargain over the allocation of liability beforehand. This conclusion is consistent with the fact that most accident law is in fact governed by negligence law.

The trend toward strict liability in products liability law is also consistent with this argument because, unlike accidents between strangers, consumers and producers have a contractual relationship that theoretically allows them to "bargain" ex ante over the assignment of liability. (Note that the same argument applies to strict liability in workers' compensation law.) The fact that liability waivers are not generally enforceable therefore works against this argument. However, Landes and Posner (1987, p. 281–282) argue that this is a consequence of lack of consumer information about risk. In other words, it is a rational response to the high costs of information for consumers.

2. The Impact of Uncertainty About Legal Standards, Causation, and Risk

The model of accidents in the previous chapter made the following assumptions: (1) the parties to an accident are perfectly informed about the prevailing legal standards; (2) courts administer legal rules without error; and (3) the parties have accurate information about the risk of a particular activity. All of these concern the availability of information to various decision makers. In this section I relax these assumptions. In sections 2.1 and 2.2, I focus on the functioning of the negligence rule under uncertainty by injurers and by courts, respectively. In section 2.3, I consider uncertainty by the court over the cause of an accident. Finally, in section 2.4, I examine the case where the riskiness of an activity or product is unknown. For simplicity, I focus primarily on the unilateral-care model, except for the discussion of comparative negligence in section 2.2.1.

2.1. Uncertainty by Injurers About the Due Standard

In the unilateral-care accident model from the previous chapter, we saw that a negligence rule with the due standard set equal to the optimal care level would induce efficient care by the injurer. This result relied on the assumption that the injurer could observe the due standard with certainty, and therefore knew when he had complied with it. In reality, however, injurers will *not* know the due standard with certainty; at best they will know its distribution. The question is what impact this uncertainty has on injurers' incentives to take care.

To answer this question, let the due standard, z, be a random variable with distribution $F(z)$, which is known by injurers ($F' > 0$).[13] Given this specification, when the injurer chooses a level of care, x, he only knows the *probability* that he will escape liability, given by $Pr(x \geq z) = F(x)$, whereas with probability $1 - F(x)$ he will be found liable (negligent). The fact that $F' > 0$ implies that greater care reduces his chances of being found negligent, but in general he cannot be certain of avoiding liability.[14]

The problem the injurer faces is therefore to

$$\underset{x}{\text{minimize}} \; x + [1 - F(x)]D(x). \tag{3.12}$$

The resulting first-order condition is

$$1 + [1 - F(x)]D'(x) - F'(x)D(x) = 0. \tag{3.13}$$

Comparing this to the condition for efficient care, $1 + D'(x) = 0$, shows that uncertainty creates two offsetting effects. First, the factor $[1 - F(x)]$ in the second term reduces the marginal benefit of care because the injurer expects to avoid liability for some accidents that he causes. This reduces his incentives for care. However, the second term, $-F'(x)D(x)$, increases his incentive to take care because, by taking greater care, he lowers the probability that he will be found negligent. Since it is not possible in theory to determine which of these effects dominates, we can say only that uncertainty about the due standard may result in either too much or too little care compared to the social optimum.[15]

2.2. Errors by the Court in Determining Compliance with the Negligence Standard

The second source of uncertainty concerns errors by the court in administering the negligence rule owing to evidentiary uncertainty. For example, suppose the court cannot perfectly observe the level of care by the injurer. It therefore may find an injurer nonnegligent when he truly violated the due standard, or it may find an injurer negligent when he truly complied with the due standard. Following the literature, I will refer to the first as a "'type I error" and the second as a "'type II error."[16]

The analysis of errors by the court is most easily done in the context of a model in which the injurer's care choice is dichotomous—that is, he either complies with the due standard $(x = z)$ or he does not comply $(x < z)$. I thus modify the simple unilateral-care model as follows: let x be the cost of complying with the due standard (the cost of noncompliance is zero), let p_c be the probability of an accident if the injurer complies, let p_n be the probability of an accident if he does not comply (where $p_c < p_n$), and let D be the (constant) damage resulting from an accident. Finally, let q_1 be the probability of a type I error and let q_2 be the probability of a type II error. For now, I assume both are constant and that $1 - q_1 > q_2$. That is, the probability of a correct finding of negligence $(1 - q_1)$ exceeds the probability of an incorrect finding of negligence (q_2). This assumption implies that trials, as procedures for determining negligence, are correct more often than not.

Care is socially desirable in this model if $x < (p_n - p_c)D$; that is, if the cost of care is less than the expected savings in accident costs. Thus, errors by the court do not affect the social desirability of care. They do affect the injurer's private decision, however. In particular, if the injurer takes care, his expected cost is $x + p_c q_2 D$. Note that this *exceeds* his cost in the absence of error, which is just x. In contrast, if he does not take care, his expected cost is $p_n(1 - q_1)D$, which is *less* than his expected cost in the absence of error, $p_n D$. Thus, in the absence of error, the injurer will take care if $x < p_n D$, which *always* holds if care is socially optimal; but with error, the injurer will take care if $x < [p_n(1 - q_1) - p_c q_2]D$, which *may or may not* hold if care is socially optimal. That is, legal error may result in either underdeterrence or overdeterrence.[17]

2.2.1. LEGAL ERROR AND COMPARATIVE NEGLIGENCE

Cooter and Ulen (1986, 1988, pp. 400–403) have argued that court error in administering negligence rules tends to make comparative negligence preferable to the other negligence rules (simple negligence and negligence with contributory negligence). This conclusion can be demonstrated by extending the above model to allow victim care. Suppose that the cost of care for victims is the same as for injurers, x. In addition, let p_{ij} be the probability of an accident, where i denotes the injurer's care decision $(i = c, n)$ and j denotes the victim's care decision $(j = c, n)$. I assume that[18]

$$p_{cc} < p_{cn} = p_{nc} < p_{nn} \tag{3.14}$$

and that

$$x < (p_{cn} - p_{cc})D. \tag{3.15}$$

Condition (3.15) says that it is socially desirable for one party to take care when the other is taking care.

The three negligence rules will be distinguished as follows. Let s be the injurer's share of liability under a given rule, and let $1 - s$ be the victim's share. Under all three rules, $s = 0$ when the injurer takes care regardless of the victim's choice, and $s = 1$ when the victim takes care but the injurer does not. The rules differ only in the case where both parties fail to take care. In that case, $s = 1$ under simple negligence, $s = 0$ under negligence with contributory negligence, and $0 < s < 1$ under comparative negligence. Using this representation and given (3.14) and (3.15), it is easy to show that, in the absence of legal error, all three negligence rules induce both parties to take care in a Nash equilibrium.[19]

Now consider legal error. To keep the notation as simple as possible, I assume that the probability of the two types of errors is the same for the injurer and victim.[20] That is, q_1 is the probability that a negligent injurer or victim will be found nonnegligent, and q_2 is the probability that a nonnegligent injurer or victim will be found negligent. As above, I assume that $1 - q_1 > q_2$.

Given this specification, consider the care decisions of the two parties. When both parties take care, the victim is fully liable under all three negligence rules (i.e., $s = 0$) if the court correctly finds that both parties took care (probability $= (1 - q_2)^2$), or if the court incorrectly finds that only the victim did not take care (probability $= (1 - q_2)q_2$). The injurer is fully liable ($s = 1$) under all three rules if the court incorrectly finds that only the injurer did not take care (probability $= (1 - q_2)q_2$). Finally, if the court incorrectly finds that both parties did not take care (probability $= q_2^2$), then the injurer bears a fraction $s \in [0, 1]$ of the liability, where s depends on the rule as described above. Combining these possibilities shows that the injurer's and victim's expected costs of taking care, given that the other party is taking care are, respectively,

$$x + p_{cc}Dq_2[(1 - q_2) + sq_2] \tag{3.16}$$

and

$$x + p_{cc}D[(1 - q_2)^2 + (1 - q_2)q_2 + (1 - s)q_2^2]. \tag{3.17}$$

A similar procedure can be used to derive the injurer's and victim's expected costs in the other possible cases. These are summarized in table 3.1, whose columns give the probabilities of the various outcomes, and table 3.2, whose rows give the resulting expected costs for the injurer and victim. Since I am interested in an equilibrium in which both parties take care, I focus on the care

TABLE 3.1 Probability of Court's Finding Given Actual Care Choices

Court's finding (injurer, victim)	Share of liability	Probability (injurer, victim)			
		c,c.	c,n	n,c	n,n
c,c	$s = 0$	$(1 - q_2)^2$	$(1 - q_2)q_1$	$q_1(1 - q_2)$	q_1^2
c,n	$s = 0$	$(1 - q_2)q_2$	$(1 - q_2)(1 - q_1)$	$q_1 q_2$	$q_1(1 - q_1)$
n,c	$s = 0$	$q_2(1 - q_2)$	$q_2 q_1$	$(1 - q_1)(1 - q_2)$	$(1 - q_1)q_1$
n,n	$0 < s < 1$	q_2^2	$q_2(1 - q_1)$	$(1 - q_1)q_2$	$(1 - q_1)^2$

Notes: c = care, n = no care; s = injurer's share of liability. Probabilities in each column sum to one.

TABLE 3.2 Expected Costs of Taking Care

Actual Care Choices (injurer, victim)	Injurer's costs	Victim's costs
c,c	$x + p_{cc}D[q_2(1 - q_2) + sq_2^2]$	$x + p_{cc}D[(1 - q_2)^2 + (1 - q_2)q_2 + (1 - s)q_2^2]$
c,n	$x + p_{cn}D[q_2 q_1 + sq_2(1 - q_1)]$	$p_{cn}D[(1 - q_2)q_1 + (1 - q_2)(1 - q_1) + (1 - s)q_2(1 - q_1)]$
n,c	$p_{nc}D[(1 - q_1)(1 - q_2) + s(1 - q_1)q_2]$	$x + p_{nc}D[q_1(1 - q_2) + q_1 q_2 + (1 - s)(1 - q_1)q_2]$
n,n	$p_{nn}D[(1 - q_1)q_1 + s(1 - q_1)^2]$	$p_{nn}D[q_1^2 + q_1(1 - q_1) + (1 - s)(1 - q_1)^2]$

Notes: c = care, n = no care; s = injurer's share of liability.

choice of each party, assuming that the other is taking care. In that case, rows one and two of table 3.2 show (after rearranging) that the injurer will take care if

$$x < [p_{\text{nc}}(1 - q_1) - p_{\text{cc}}q_2]D[1 - q_2 + sq_2]. \tag{3.18}$$

Similarly, lines one and two of table 3.2 show that the victim will take care if

$$x < (1 - q_2)(p_{\text{cn}} - p_{\text{cc}})D + (1 - s)q_2D[p_{\text{cn}}(1 - q_1) - p_{\text{cc}}q_2]. \tag{3.19}$$

Notice that the right-hand side of (3.18) is *increasing* in s, whereas the right-hand side of (3.19) is *decreasing* in s. Thus, among the three negligence rules, simple negligence ($s = 1$) is most likely to induce care by the injurer and least likely to induce care by the victim. At the other extreme, negligence with contributory negligence ($s = 0$) is most likely to induce care by the victim but least likely to induce care by the injurer. Comparative negligence ($0 < s < 1$) falls between these extremes. Thus, although it does not guarantee that (3.17) and (3.18) are simultaneously satisfied, it is more likely to do so because it shares the cost of legal error between the two parties rather than concentrating it on one.

2.2.2. LEGAL ERROR AND COSTLY LITIGATION WHEN VICTIMS OBSERVE THE CARE CHOICE OF INJURERS

In this section I will extend the legal error model a bit by including the cost of litigation along with legal error (for simplicity, I will do this in the context of the unilateral-care case). As in the previous chapter, let c_i be the cost of litigation for the injurer and let c_v the cost for the victim. In this context, I will consider two scenarios. In the first, victims observe the care choice of injurers, and in the second, they do not.

Consider first the case where the victim observes whether or not the injurer took care (though she cannot prove this in court). If the injurer was negligent, the victim will file suit if

$$(1 - q_1)D > c_v. \tag{3.20}$$

If we let D vary across victims according the distribution function $F(D)$, then the probability of a suit in this case is $1 - F(c_v/(1 - q_1))$. In contrast, if the injurer was not negligent, the victim will file suit if

$$q_2D > c_v, \tag{3.21}$$

in which case the probability of a lawsuit is $1 - F(c_v/q_2)$. The assumption that $1 - q_1 > q_2$ implies that $1 - F(c_v/(1 - q_1)) > 1 - F(c_v/q_2)$. That is, negligent injurers face a higher probability of a lawsuit than nonnegligent injurers. However, in contrast to the certainty model, nonnegligent injurers cannot avoid suits altogether.

Now consider the injurer's care decision, given the above probabilities of lawsuits. If the injurer takes care, his expected costs are

$$x + p_c \int_{\frac{c_v}{q_2}}^{\infty} (q_2 D + c_i) dF(D) \tag{3.22}$$

and if he does not take care, his expected costs are

$$p_n \int_{\frac{c_v}{1-q_1}}^{\infty} ((1 - q_1)D + c_i) dF(D). \tag{3.23}$$

Thus, he will take care if

$$x < (1 - q_1)p_n \int_{\frac{c_v}{1-q_1}}^{\infty} D dF(D) - q_2 p_c \int_{\frac{c_v}{q_2}}^{\infty} D dF(D)$$
$$+ \{p_n[1 - F(c_v/(1 - q_1))] - p_c[1 - F(c_v/q_2)]\}c_i \tag{3.24}$$

and not take care otherwise.

As in the litigation cost model, the condition for care to be socially optimal in the current model is[21]

$$x < (p_n - p_c)E(D) + \{p_n[1 - F(c_v/(1 - q_1))] - p_c[1 - F(c_v/q_2)]\}(c_i + c_v). \tag{3.25}$$

The efficiency of the injurer's actual care choice is found by comparing the right-hand sides of (3.24) and (3.25). Note that the first term on the right-hand side of (3.24) may be larger or smaller than the first term on the right-hand side of (3.25). The fact that damages are truncated by the litigation costs of victims reduces expected costs in (3.24) relative to (3.25), but the impact of legal error is ambiguous given that $p_n(1 - q_1) - p_c q_2 \gtrless p_n - p_c$. As for the second term, the fact that c_v is absent in (3.24) compared to (3.25) tends to result in too little care. On the whole, this comparison shows that injurers may take too much or too little care compared to the optimum.

2.2.3. LEGAL ERROR AND COSTLY LITIGATION WHEN VICTIMS DO NOT OBSERVE THE CARE CHOICE OF INJURERS

Consider next the case where victims do not observe the care choice of injurers. In that case, all injurers appear the same to victims. Thus, if a is the victim's assessment of the probability that the injurer is negligent, then the victim will file suit if

$$[a(1 - q_1) + (1 - a)q_2]D \equiv QD > c_v. \tag{3.26}$$

The probability that an injurer will face a lawsuit conditional on an accident is therefore $1 - F(c_v/Q)$, whether or not he takes care. As a result, the injurer will take care if

$$x < [(1 - q_1)p_n - q_2 p_c] \int_{\frac{c_v}{Q}}^{\infty} D \, dF(D) + (p_n - p_c)[1 - F(c_v/Q)]c_i. \qquad (3.27)$$

The corresponding social condition is

$$x < (p_n - p_c)E(D) + (p_n - p_c)[1 - F(c_v/Q)](c_i + c_v). \qquad (3.28)$$

Comparing these conditions shows that injurers have too little incentive to take care because (1) they ignore damages incurred by victims who do not file suit, and (2) they ignore the litigation costs of victims who do file suit. The impact of legal error is that some negligent injurers will avoid liability and some non-negligent injurers will face liability owing to legal error. Again, these errors have an ambiguous effect.

Note that the results for the negligence rule in this case are similar to those for the case of strict liability with costly litigation but no legal error. This is because uncertainty about injurers' care in the current model makes them all look alike to victims. Thus, victims file suit based on their expected return, QD, compared to their litigation costs, c_v. This differs from the corresponding condition under strict liability ($D > c_v$) only in that there is a chance they will lose the case, as captured by the factor Q. Thus, suits are less likely in the current model; that is, $1 - F(c_v) > 1 - F(c_v/Q)$ given $Q < 1$.

2.2.4. THE OPTIMAL STANDARD OF PROOF FOR DETERMINING NEGLIGENCE

To this point we have treated the probabilities of the two types of errors as fixed. In reality, however, they are functions of the standard of proof used by the court to judge whether a defendant is negligent under evidentiary uncertainty. In actual negligence cases (and generally, in most civil litigation), the standard of proof is *preponderance of the evidence*, which means that a defendant is judged negligent if it is more probable than not that he violated the due standard.

Formally, we can model this as follows. Let e be the probability, as assessed by the court, that the defendant is negligent ($e \in [0, 1]$), and let e_s be the minimum probability necessary for the court to find him negligent. Thus, the defendant is found negligent if $e \geq e_s$ and nonnegligent otherwise. The presence of evidentiary uncertainty implies that, in general, e will be a random variable, though one expects that higher realizations of e will tend to be associated with truly negligent defendants.[22] As shown in figure 3.1, this will be the case if the distribution of evidence for truly negligent defendants, f_G, is shifted to the right of the distribution of evidence against truly innocent defendants, f_I.

Figure 3.1 also shows the relationship between the standard of proof, e_s, and the two types of errors. Note that the probability of a type I error (false acquit-

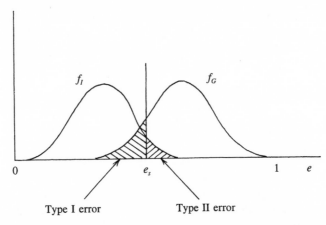

FIGURE 3.1 Distributions of evidence for innocent (f_I) and guilty (f_G) defendants.

tal) is shown by the shaded area to the left of e_s, and the probability of a type II error (false conviction) is shown by the shaded area to the right of e_s. Further, notice that if e_s is *increased*—that is, if it is made more difficult to find a defendant negligent—then q_1 *increases* (i.e., $\partial q_1/\partial e_s > 0$), and q_2 *decreases* (i.e., $\partial q_2/\partial e_s < 0$). Thus, the probabilities of the two errors move in opposite directions. This makes sense, since a higher standard of proof increases the number of acquittals (including false ones) and reduces the number of convictions (including false ones). Further, notice that

$$q_1(0) = 0, q_1(1) = 1, q_2(0) = 1, \text{ and } q_2(1) = 0.$$

Thus, when $e_s = 0$, which corresponds to strict liability (i.e., $e \geq e_s$ for all defendants), only type II errors occur since all defendants are held liable regardless of their care. In contrast, when $e_s = 1$, which corresponds to no liability (i.e., $e < e_s$ for all defendants), only type I errors occur since all defendants are absolved of liability regardless of their care.

We can use this specification in the context of the above error model to ask how the standard of proof affects the incentive of victims to file suit and for injurers to take care. I will begin by focusing on the second version of the model, in which the victim does not observe the injurer's care. In that context, victims will file suit if (3.26) holds. The model in the previous section implies that the probability of plaintiff victory, Q, is a function of the standard of proof as follows:

$$Q(e_s) = a[1 - q_1(e_s)] + (1 - a)q_2(e_s). \tag{3.29}$$

Furthermore,

$$\partial Q/\partial e_s = -a(\partial q_1/\partial e_s) + (1 - a)(\partial q_2/\partial e_s) < 0. \tag{3.30}$$

Thus, a higher standard of proof reduces the plaintiff's chances of victory. In addition, a victory is certain under strict liability ($Q(0) = 1$), and a loss is certain under no liability ($Q(1) = 0$). As a result, the defendant will face a suit with the highest probability under strict liability and no suits under no liability.

Now consider the incentives of injurers to take care as a function of the standard of proof. Recall that the condition for the injurer to take care is given by (3.27), which I abbreviate here as $x < G(e_s)$. When $e_s = 0$ (strict liability), this reduces to

$$x < G(0) = (p_n - p_c) \int_{c_v}^{\infty} (D + c_i) dF(D). \tag{3.31}$$

Alternatively, when $e_s = 1$ (no liability), no suits are filed so injurers never take care. The upper panel of figure 3.2 shows the general relationship between care and the standard of proof under the assumption that, for the injurer in question,

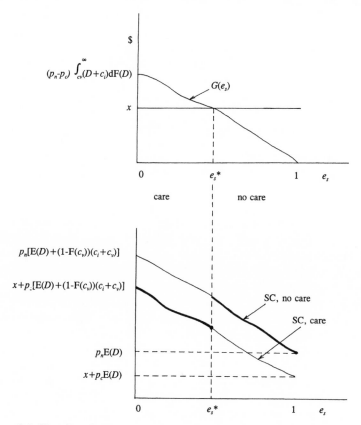

FIGURE 3.2 Choosing the optimal standard of proof in the presence of legal error.

(3.31) holds.[23] Thus, for $e_s \leq e_s^*$, the injurer takes care, and for $e_s > e_s^*$, he does not.[24]

The next question is whether care is socially desirable or not. To answer this question, compare social costs when care is taken,

$$x + p_c E(D) + p_c [1 - F(c_v/Q)](c_i + c_v),$$

to social costs when care is not taken

$$p_n E(D) + p_n [1 - F(c_v/Q)](c_i + c_v).$$

The condition for care to be desirable for any Q is thus given by (3.28). If we assume $x < (p_n - p_c)E(D)$, this condition always holds. The lower panel of figure 3.2 illustrates this case. Note that for all e_s, social costs are lower when care is taken. Also note that both cost curves are decreasing in e_s because as e_s increases, there are fewer lawsuits and hence lower litigation costs.

It does not follow, however, that care is necessarily desirable given that lawsuits are required to induce injurers to take care. In particular, the analysis of the injurer's problem showed that care is only taken for $e_s \leq e_s^*$. This fact is represented by the darkened segments of the social cost curves, which show the *feasible* levels of social costs given injurer behavior. Thus, the problem is to choose the lowest point on the darkened segments.

It should be apparent that two solutions are possible: $e_s = e_s^*$ or $e_s = 1$. The first possibility, which is an interior solution, corresponds to a negligence rule with a standard of proof equal to e_s^*. Social costs in this case are

$$x + p_c E(D) + p_c [1 - F(c_v/Q(e_s^*))](c_i + c_v).$$

The second possibility corresponds to a rule of no liability, which yields social costs of $p_n E(D)$. No liability may be desirable in this case because it avoids litigation costs altogether. Thus, it is preferable when litigation costs are high and care is not effective in reducing expected damages.

Notice that strict liability ($e_s = 0$) is never optimal. The reason is that a negligence rule is equally good at inducing injurer care and it results in fewer lawsuits. This, of course, is the same point we made earlier in the context of the litigation-cost model. The same qualification therefore applies—namely, that the greater administrative cost of employing a negligence rule may offset its advantage relative to strict liability. In terms of the current model, the administrative costs under negligence consist of the court's measuring e and then comparing it to e_s^*.

As a final point, note that if we want the preceding model to be consistent with rational expectations by plaintiffs, then under a negligence rule that succeeds in inducing care by all injurers, a must equal zero in equilibrium. (Recall that a is the plaintiff's prior probability that the injurer failed to take care.) As a result, Q reduces to $q_2(e_s^*)D$. This implies that, in a sense, all suits are "frivolous," in that plaintiffs' only hope of winning is an error by the court.[25] In addition, notice that in this case the model becomes equivalent to the one in which victims observe the care of injurers.

2.3. Uncertainty Over Causation

The analysis of uncertainty so far has focused solely on the determination of compliance with the negligence rule, but uncertainty can arise in the context of any factual inquiry by the court,[26] such as the determination of causation in accident cases. Uncertainty over causation occurs when more than one agent may be the true cause of an accident. An example is when consumption of a product increases the risk of contracting a disease that occurs naturally with some background probability. Another is when there is uncertainty over which of several human agents caused an accident, as when two hunters fire and only one bullet hits a third party.[27] For simplicity, the analysis here focuses on the first example, where "nature" provides the uncertainty.[28]

Consider a unilateral-care model in which the probability of an accident is given by $p(x) + q$, where $p(x)$ is the probability that it is caused by an injurer taking care of x, and q is the probability that it is caused by nature. Since q is additive and independent of x, the socially optimal level of care, x^*, solves $1 + p'(x)D = 0$, and therefore does not depend on q. Thus, holding the injurer strictly liable for the damages D *whenever* the accident occurs will result in optimal care. So will a standard negligence rule with due care set at x^*. In this sense, uncertainty over causation does not reduce efficiency, even though injurers are (potentially) held liable for accidents they did not cause.[29]

In reality, however, we saw earlier that courts typically limit an injurer's liability to those injuries for which he is judged to be the proximate cause. In the case of uncertainty over causation, this can be interpreted to mean that the relevant liability rule is applied if and only if the conditional probability that the injurer caused the accident (given that it occurred) exceeds a threshold. Since this conditional probability is given by $p(x)/[p(x) + q]$, the relevant liability rule is applied if and only if

$$p(x)/[p(x) + q] > T \tag{3.32}$$

where T is the threshold for proximate cause. Note that $p(x)/[p(x)+q]$ is decreasing in x, which implies that, for any T, (3.32) is more likely the smaller is x. This is shown in figure 3.3.

Suppose the relevant liability rule is strict liability. The injurer's problem in this case is to

$$\text{minimize} \quad \begin{array}{ll} x, & p(x)/[p(x) + q] \leq T \\ x + [p(x) + q]D, & p(x)/[p(x) + q] > T \end{array} \tag{3.33}$$

The question is, can we choose the value of T such that the solution to this problem is x^*? It turns out that the answer is yes, and the proper choice of T is

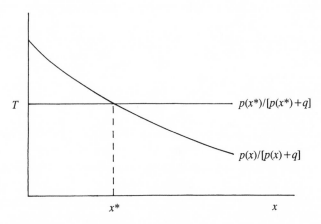

FIGURE 3.3 The efficient threshold for proximate cause when causation is uncertain.

$$T = p(x^*)/[p(x^*) + q]. \tag{3.34}$$

This is illustrated in figure 3.3, which shows that this choice of T in effect transforms strict liability with a proximate cause limitation into a negligence rule with the due standard set equal to x^*. In particular, by choosing $x = x^*$, the injurer avoids liability. This is another illustration of the conclusion reached in the previous chapter that proximate cause and negligence are redundant tests for liability. Of course, it follows immediately from this observation that the same choice of T will yield the efficient result when the liability rule is negligence.[30]

2.4. Uncertainty About Risk

The final form of uncertainty that I examine concerns uncertainty about the riskiness of an activity or product. As an example, consider a drug company that is uncertain about the possible harmful side effects that a particular drug might cause. The questions that I will address in this context are, When is it socially desirable to obtain information about the risk? and Which liability rules, if any, induce both the optimal acquisition of information and the optimal choice of care given that information?[31]

To answer these questions, I amend the simple unilateral-care accident model as follows. Assume that with probability p a risk is present that will result in expected damages of $D(x)$, and with probability $1 - p$ there is no risk (i.e., $D \equiv 0$), where x is the injurer's expenditure on care. Prior to making his care choice, assume that the injurer can ascertain the presence or absence of risk with certainty at a cost c. In the drug example, this may be thought of as expenditures on R&D to determine the drug's nature prior to marketing.

2.4.1. THE SOCIAL OPTIMUM

The social optimum involves first deriving optimal care given the information available and then determining whether it is efficient to acquire the information. In the case where information is not available, the optimal level of care solves

$$\underset{x}{\text{minimize}}\ x + pD(x) \tag{3.35}$$

which yields the first-order condition

$$1 + pD'(x) = 0. \tag{3.36}$$

Denote the resulting level of care x_0^*.

Now consider the case where information about risk is known. If there is no risk, the optimal level of care is obviously zero. If there is a risk, the optimal level of care solves

$$\underset{x}{\text{minimize}}\ x + D(x), \tag{3.37}$$

which yields the first-order condition

$$1 + D'(x) = 0. \tag{3.38}$$

Denote the resulting level of care x^*, where $x^* > x_0^* > 0$ given $0 < p < 1$.

To determine whether it is efficient to acquire information about risk, we need to calculate the value of information in this case.[32] This consists of the difference between expected social costs when the risk is unknown (in which case care of x_0^* is chosen) and expected social costs when the risk is known (in which case care of zero or x^* is chosen). Specifically,

$$
\begin{aligned}
V &= [x_0^* + pD(x_0^*)] - p[x^* + D(x^*)] \\
&= p\{[x_0^* + D(x_0^*)] - [x^* + D(x^*)]\} + (1 - p)x_0^*.
\end{aligned}
\tag{3.39}
$$

Note that V is positive, since $x + D(x)$ is by definition minimized at x^*. Thus, information is valuable. The question is whether it is more valuable than the cost of obtaining it. If it is—that is, if

$$V > c, \tag{3.40}$$

then it is socially optimal to acquire information.

2.4.2. EQUILIBRIUM BEHAVIOR UNDER VARIOUS
LIABILITY RULES

The next question is whether any of the standard liability rules induce the injurer to behave in a socially optimal manner. To begin, consider strict liability.

Since this rule imposes damages on the injurer in the event of an accident, he internalizes the full social costs and therefore will make the optimal decision regarding both information acquisition and care.

Under a negligence rule, the injurer's behavior will depend on how the due standard of care is defined. A negligence rule that holds the injurer liable if he failed either to choose the socially efficient level of care *or* to acquire information when it was efficient to do so will result in the socially optimal solution. A negligence rule that holds the injurer liable for failure to take efficient care, assuming optimal acquisition of information, will also lead to the optimal solution. Both of these forms of negligence work because they incorporate the optimal information acquisition decision into the definition of the due standard. In contrast, a negligence rule that sets the due standard at the efficient level of care given the information the injurer *actually* has will *not* lead to the optimal outcome. In particular, the injurer will tend to gather information too infrequently.

This analysis suggests that strict liability is the best rule, in that it achieves the efficient outcome in terms of information acquisition and care at the lowest administrative cost. Of course, this result may not hold in cases where victims as well as injurers can take care. Victim care also raises the question of information disclosure rules, given that it is presumably the injurer who is in the better position to learn about the risk. For example, Cooter (1985b) has argued that, in the context of products liability, manufacturers of dangerous products will issue adequate warnings to consumers under a rule that holds them liable only for inadequate warnings. As the above analysis showed, however, such a rule must also take account of the information-acquisition decision so as not to impair the incentives of manufacturers to learn about risks in the first place.

3. Sequential Care Torts and Strategic Behavior

Sequential care torts refer to accidents in which the injurer and victim act in sequence in choosing their care levels. This fact alone, however, does not distinguish these accidents from those we have examined up to now (i.e., simultaneous-care accidents). What is also necessary is that the party moving second be able to observe the first party's care choice and have an opportunity to react to it.[33] The old case of *Davies* v. *Mann* illustrates the situation.[34] The plaintiff Davies negligently left his donkey tethered in the street, and Mann struck the donkey, killing it. The general question that this case, and others like it, raises is what amount of compensating precaution (if any) does the party moving second owe to the party moving first, given that the first party acted negligently?

Under the doctrine of last clear chance, which arose out of *Davies* v. *Mann*, the second mover owes an increased duty to a negligent first mover. From an economic point of view, this rule appears designed to attain a second-best outcome (compensating precaution) in cases where the first party is inadvertently negligent, but we will see that it also creates an incentive for the first party to reduce his care strategically in the first place, thereby foreclosing attainment of the first-best outcome. In this section I will examine the efficiency of various liability rules, including last clear chance, in sequential accident cases, paying close attention to the trade-off just described. In general, the analysis does not depend on which party moves first, the injurer, or the victim, but I will restrict attention to cases where the victim moves first as this seems to be the most common scenario.

3.1. The Basic Model

I will continue to employ the bilateral-care accident model where $D(x,y)$ is expected damages, x is the injurer's expenditure on care, and y is the victim's expenditure on care.[35] The sequential nature of the problem does not change the derivation of the social optimum, which, as we saw in the previous chapter, solves

$$\underset{x,y}{\text{minimize}} \quad x + y + D(x,y). \tag{3.41}$$

Recall that the first-order conditions are given by

$$1 + D_x = 0 \tag{3.42}$$

and

$$1 + D_y = 0. \tag{3.43}$$

Also recall that equation (3.42) defines a function $x^*(y)$, which is the optimal care by the injurer for any choice of care by the victim, and equation (3.43) similarly defines a function $y^*(x)$. Given the properties of $D(x,y)$, we showed that

$$\partial x^* / \partial y = -D_{xy}/D_{xx} < 0 \tag{3.44}$$

and

$$\partial y^* / \partial x = -D_{xy}/D_{yy} < 0. \tag{3.45}$$

Figure 3.4 graphs $x^*(y)$ and $y^*(x)$ and shows the optimum (x^*, y^*) at the intersection of the two curves. I will refer to this intersection as the first-best outcome.

As noted, the derivation of the optimal (first-best) outcome does not depend on the sequential nature of the problem, but it does matter in the definition of the second-best outcome. Suppose the victim, moving first, chooses $y_0 < y^*$. What is the optimal choice of x, given y_0? The answer is $x^*(y_0)$, since this level of x minimizes (3.41) subject to the constraint that $y = y_0$. This outcome is shown in figure 3.4 by the point S, which is on the lowest isocost line that just touches y_0.

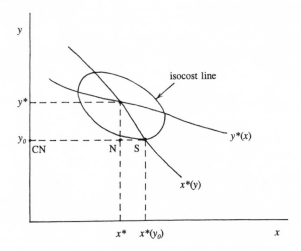

FIGURE 3.4 Reaction curves for the injurer and victim in a sequential-care accident.

3.2. Liability Rules

We are interested in determining if there are any liability rules among those we have studied, and/or any new ones (e.g., last clear chance) that have three properties: (1) they achieve the first-best outcome if the party moving first (the victim) chooses y^*; (2) they achieve the second-best outcome (i.e., compensating precaution) if the victim chooses $y < y^*$; and (3) they do not create an incentive for the victim to choose $y < y^*$ in the first place.[36] Note that properties 1 and 3 are the criteria we used to evaluate the efficiency of the Nash equilibrium in the simultaneous move model. They are also the criteria for the sequential-move model in which the first party is never inadvertently negligent. What I will show, however, is that it is quite difficult to design a rule that satisfies all three properties, given the desire for attainment of a second-best outcome in the event of inadvertent negligence by the first party (property 2). In particular, property 2 will generally conflict with property 3.

3.2.1. RULES WITH FIXED STANDARDS OF CARE

The first class of rules I consider are those with due standards of care fixed at x^* for the injurer and/or y^* for the victim. In this context, I consider negligence, negligence with contributory negligence, and strict liability with contributory negligence.[37] As was true for simultaneous-care accidents, all three rules satisfy properties 1 and 3. Specifically, if the injurer observes the victim choosing optimal care, y^*, he also chooses optimal care, and if the victim anticipates optimal care by the injurer, she chooses optimal care as well.[38]

The next question is, How do these rules fare with regard to property 2—that is, when the injurer confronts a victim choosing less than due care inadvertently ($y_0 < y^*$)? Under negligence with a due care standard of x^*, the injurer's problem in this case is to

$$\underset{x}{\text{minimize}} \quad \begin{matrix} x, & x \geq x^* \\ x + D(x, y_0), & x < x^* \end{matrix}. \tag{3.46}$$

It is easy to see that the injurer will choose x^*, since

$$x^* < x^*(y_0) < \min_{x} x + D(x, y_0) \leq \min_{x < x^*} x + D(x, y_0) \tag{3.47}$$

where the first inequality follows from (3.44). Thus, the injurer has no incentive to compensate for the victim's underprecaution because the rule allows him to avoid liability at a lower standard. The outcome in this case is shown by point N in figure 3.4.

Next, consider negligence with contributory negligence. In this case, if the injurer observes $y_0 < y^*$, he knows the victim will be found contributorily negligent regardless of the level of care he chooses. Thus, he will choose $x = 0$. This outcome is shown by point CN in figure 3.4. Strict liability with contributory negligence yields the same outcome for the same reason.

Thus, none of the standard rules with fixed care levels satisfies property 2; of the three, negligence results in the lowest cost when the victim is negligent. At the same time, none of the rules creates an incentive for the victim to choose to be negligent strategically (that is, they all satisfy property 3). The next section examines in more detail the nature of the trade off between properties 2 and 3 in sequential-care accidents.

3.2.2. RULES COMPELLING COMPENSATING PRECAUTION

In this section I consider liability rules where the standard of care for the party moving second (the injurer) is not fixed at x^* but instead is conditional on the actual care he observed the first party (the victim) taking. In particular, let the due standard for the injurer be $x^*(y)$ for any y.[39] (Assume that the due standard for the victim, when relevant, remains fixed at y^*.) Notice that, in contrast to the fixed standard, this new standard for the injurer compels compensating precaution in the event of prior negligence by the victim because $x^*(y) > x^*$ for $y < y^*$ (see figure 3.4). It is thus explicitly aimed at achieving property 2 above.

Given this new standard, I consider only negligence, with and without contributory negligence, since strict liability rules impose no due standard on the injurer.[40] Notice first that under both rules, the first-best solution is achieved if the victim chooses y^* (property 1), given that $x^*(y^*) = x^*$. In this case, the liability rules are identical to the fixed standard case from the injurer's perspective. It does not follow, however, that it is rational for the victim in fact to choose y^* in equilibrium (that is, it does not follow that property 3 holds).

Before considering the victim's incentives, consider the reaction of injurers to victims who have chosen $y_0 < y^*$. Under simple negligence, the injurer's problem is to

$$\underset{x}{\text{minimize}} \quad \begin{array}{ll} x, & x \geq x^*(y_0) \\ x + D(x,y_0), & x < x^*(y_0). \end{array} \qquad (3.48)$$

By the standard argument, the solution to this problem is $x^*(y_0)$, given that $x^*(y_0)$ by definition minimizes $x + D(x,y_0)$. In contrast, when contributory negligence is added as a defense for the injurer, the latter will choose $x = 0$ whenever he observes $y_0 < y^*$. Thus, only simple negligence achieves the second-best outcome in this case (property 2).

Given this result, let us now consider the incentives the rules create for victim care among those victims who make a rational choice, referred to as *strategic victims* (i.e., those who are not inadvertently negligent), assuming that they correctly anticipate the behavior of injurers under the applicable rule. Since we have shown that simple negligence induces the injurer to choose $x^*(y)$ for any $y \leq y^*$ the strategic victim expects to bear her own costs and will choose y to

$$\text{minimize } y + D(x^*(y),y). \qquad (3.49)$$

The first-order condition for this problem is

$$1 + D_y + D_x(\partial x^*/\partial y) = 0. \qquad (3.50)$$

Since the final term is positive, it must be true that $1 + D_y < 0$, which implies that $y < y^*$. That is, the victim chooses too little care. Intuitively, since the strategic victim anticipates compensating precaution by the injurer, and she knows she will be liable in the event of an accident, she underinvests in precaution at the margin in order to shift some of the costs of precaution to the injurer. Thus, negligence with a conditional standard of care does not satisfy property 3.

If we add a contributory negligence defense with a due standard of y^*, the strategic victim's problem becomes

$$\underset{y}{\text{minimize}} \quad \begin{array}{ll} y + D(x^*(y),y), & y \geq y^* \\ y + D(0,y), & y < y^*. \end{array} \qquad (3.51)$$

The solution to this problem is y^* given that

$$\underset{y < y^*}{\text{minimize }} y + D(0,y) > y^* + D(x^*(y^*),y^*). \qquad (3.52)$$

Thus, the victim does not have an incentive to be negligent, and property 3 is satisfied.

The preceding analysis demonstrates the fundamental conflict between properties 2 and 3: if the rule creates an incentive for the injurer to compensate for *inadvertent* negligence by the strategic victim, it also creates an incentive for victims to be negligent in a *strategic* manner (as under simple negligence). In contrast, if the rule does not create an incentive for compensating precaution, it also does not create an incentive for strategic negligence (as under negligence with contributory negligence). One solution is to compel compensating precaution only when the victim's negligence was inadvertent. The problem this creates, however, is that it is not generally possible for injurers or the court to distinguish inadvertent negligence from strategic negligence. The next section pursues this point in the context of the doctrine of last clear chance.

3.2.3. LAST CLEAR CHANCE

As noted above, the common law doctrine of last clear chance imposes an additional duty of care beyond that normally required under negligence on the last party who could have reasonably avoided an accident. Although this doctrine has faded in importance with the emergence of comparative negligence,[41] it seems on its face to be an attempt to induce compensating precaution by injurers (victims) confronting a negligent victim (injurer).[42] Indeed, one way to interpret the conditional standard for injurers in the preceding section, $x^*(y)$, is as a last clear chance doctrine.

The actual application of last clear chance, however, differs from this interpretation in one respect. In general, courts have held that last clear chance *defeats* a contributory negligence defense for the injurer when it is available.[43] That is, if a contributorily negligent victim can prove that the injurer observed her negligence, and had time to react, the injurer is liable if he failed to exercise compensating precaution (i.e, if he chose $x < x^*(y)$). If this feature were added to the two rules with contributory negligence defenses (negligence and strict liability), it is easy to show that the injurer will be induced to choose $x^*(y)$ rather than $x = 0$ under both. That is, the outcome is equivalent to that under simple negligence (i.e., the injurer's problem is identical to (3.48) for both rules).[44]

The strategic victim's problem under negligence with contributory negligence (augmented by last clear chance) is also the same as under simple negligence (the problem in (3.49)), resulting in $y < y^*$. However, under strict liability with contributory negligence and last clear chance, note that the strategic victim can avoid liability altogether by choosing $y \geq y^*$ up front, or she can solve (3.49) subject to $y < y^*$ (knowing that the injurer will respond with $x^*(y)$). Since the solution to (3.49) yields $y < y^*$, the victim may or may not choose y^* in this case, depending on the following comparison:

$$y^* \gtrless \min_{y < y^*} y + D(x^*(y),y).$$

If she chooses y^*, then strict liability with contributory negligence and last clear chance satisfies all 3 properties. Despite this possibility, this rule has rarely (if ever) been applied by courts.

Grady (1988) has examined last clear chance explicitly with the tradeoff between properties 2 and 3 in mind:

> When someone has been negligent in the first place—one hopes, through inadvertence—the best thing left to do is to get the other party to make up for it. But there is a flip side to the coin. If the second party must compensate for errors, the first party may think about the payoff from being deliberately negligent (p. 19).

He argues that courts are sensitive to this problem, and have limited the duty of compensating precaution to those cases where strategic behavior is not a serious threat. In order for strategic negligence to be profitable for a potential victim ('trapper'), Grady argues, the following conditions must be met: (1) the victim's negligence must be easily observed by the injurer so that the latter will face a duty of compensating precaution; (2) the injurer must have ample time to react (i.e., the reaction period must be sufficiently long); and (3) the strategic victim must be able to conceal the "willful and wanton" nature of her negligence. If these conditions are not frequently satisfied, then *trap-setting* (or strategic negligence) will not be a serious problem, and courts can concentrate on second-best outcomes. The problem with dismissing strategic behavior as unlikely based on these conditions is that the third condition relies on the court's selectively invoking last clear chance based on its ability to discern the mental state of the victim at the time she was negligent. This will generally be very difficult to do. Given this uncertainty, it may be preferable to apply last clear chance selectively based on a more easily observed feature of a case. A candidate for such a feature emerges from an examination of the types of cases to which last clear chance has been applied by the courts.

Historically, courts have applied last clear chance in two types of cases, those in which the plaintiff (victim) was *helpless,* and those in which the plaintiff was *inattentive.*[45] A plaintiff is helpless if her negligence places her in a position of danger from which she cannot extricate herself, and a plaintiff is inattentive if she merely fails to notice her peril. Both types of plaintiffs have recovered provided that (1) the defendant discovered the plaintiff's situation, (2) he had time to react, and (3) he failed to take reasonable care.

Given these two categories of cases, I will argue that a good candidate for cases in which strategic negligence is unlikely is the set of cases involving helpless plaintiffs. The reason is that one supposes that victims acting strategically would not consciously put themselves into a position of not being able to react to injurers who, for whatever reason (inadvertance?), do not take compensating precaution. Alternatively, inattentive plaintiffs are more likely to be feigning inattention in an effort to "trap" injurers. Moreover, it is much easier for a negligent victim to plead inattentiveness—as opposed to helplessness—ex post in an effort to avoid liability. The greater threat of (concealed) strategic behavior in this case suggests that the cost of last clear chance may outweigh its benefits.

Examination of some last clear chance cases helps to illustrate this argument. The case of *New York Cent. R. Co.* v. *Thompson*[46] concerned a woman who, while walking home one night, caught her foot in some railroad tracks in such a way that she could not get it loose. An approaching train saw her predicament, but did not brake in time and injured her. The court held the railroad liable under last clear chance because it found that the train could have stopped in time to avoid the accident. Since this is clearly a helpless plaintiff case, according to the above argument the benefits of last clear chance in terms of accident avoidance outweigh the risks of strategic behavior, for it is hard to imagine a victim acting in this way merely to shift the costs of taking care to the injurer.

In a second case, *Greear* v. *Noland*,[47] a man was hit by a passing truck while he was standing by the side of the road. In this case, the man was merely inattentive, but the court nevertheless allowed recovery against the truck driver under last clear chance. This represents a much more questionable invocation of the doctrine since, as argued above, "casualness" by potential victims is much more likely to be a deliberate strategic choice. In another similar case, the court seemed to recognize this fact. In denying the plaintiff recovery under last clear chance, the court said:

> The plaintiff, possessing full use of her faculties, was at all times able to prevent the mishap by the exercise of ordinary prudence. Instead of doing so, she deliberately and knowingly elected to walk on the forbidden side of the road and thus actively exposed herself to danger.[48]

3.2.4. COMPARATIVE NEGLIGENCE

As noted above, most states have adopted some form of comparative negligence in place of contributory negligence (Curran, 1992), a development that has also greatly reduced the use of last clear chance. The reason appears to be a general dissatisfaction with "all-or-nothing" liability rules such as contributory negligence and last clear chance.[49] While this may be a desirable development from a fairness perspective, we saw above that all-or-nothing rules have desirable incentive effects in bilateral-care situations.[50] Indeed, we saw that comparative negligence rules that retain the threshold feature can induce efficient care in equilibrium, but when they do, they end up not sharing damages—a result seemingly contrary to their intended goal of greater fairness.

More to the point of the current discussion, Rea (1987) has suggested that comparative negligence often has an advantage over ordinary negligence rules in terms of inducing compensating precaution in sequential torts. If this is true, it may help to explain (along with the fairness argument) why the doctrine of last clear chance has declined with the onset of comparative negligence. In evaluating this possibility, I consider the same basic version of comparative negligence from the previous chapter. In particular, recall that $\beta(x,y)$ is defined to be the fraction of damages borne by the injurer in the event of an accident, where

$$
\begin{aligned}
&\beta = 0 && \text{when } x \geq x^* \text{ and } y < y^* \\
&\beta = 1 && \text{when } x < x^* \text{ and } y \geq y^* \\
&0 \leq \beta \leq 1 && \text{when } x < x^* \text{ and } y < y^*, \text{ or } x \geq x^* \text{ and } y \geq y^* \\
&\beta_x < 0, \beta_y > 0.
\end{aligned}
$$

As shown above, this form of comparative negligence results in efficient care by both parties in simultaneous-move accidents. In addition, Rea (1987) has shown that it leads to efficiency in sequential-move accidents. I will prove it here for the simple case where $\beta(x^*, y^*) = 0$ (i.e., the victim bears the loss when both meet the threshold).[51] Suppose first that the injurer observes the victim choosing $y = y^*$. In that case, $\beta = 1$ if he chooses $x < x^*$, and $\beta = 0$ if he chooses

$x \geq x^*$. He therefore chooses x^* based on the efficiency of a standard negligence rule. Suppose, on the other hand, the injurer observes $y_0 < y^*$. In that case, $\beta = 0$ if he chooses $x \geq x^*$, and $0 \leq \beta(x,y) \leq 1$ if he chooses $x < x^*$. He therefore will choose $x < x^*$ if and only if

$$x^* > \min_{x < x^*} x + \beta(x,y_0)D(x,y_0), \tag{3.53}$$

which may or may not hold, depending on the magnitude and characteristics of β. Let x_0 denote the solution to (3.53) if $x < x^*$ is optimal and let $\beta_0 \equiv \beta(x_0,y_0)$.

Now consider the victim moving first. Suppose first that the solution to (3.53) is x^*. In that case, $\beta = 0$ since the injurer takes due care regardless of the victim's prior behavior. Thus, the victim's problem is

$$\underset{y}{\text{minimize}} \; y + D(x^*,y), \tag{3.54}$$

which clearly results in efficient care, y^*. Alternatively, suppose that the solution to (3.53) is $x_0 < x^*$. In this case, the victim's problem is to

$$\text{minimize} \; \begin{array}{ll} y + D(x^*,y) & y \geq y^* \\ y + [1 - \beta(x_0,y)]D(x_0,y) & y < y^* \end{array}. \tag{3.55}$$

The solution to this problem is $y_0 < y^*$ if

$$y_0 + (1 - \beta_0)D(x_0,y_0) < y^* + D(x^*,y^*). \tag{3.56}$$

Thus, (x_0,y_0) is an equilibrium if both (3.53) and (3.56) hold. I will show, however, that this can never happen.

First, by definition,

$$x_0 + y_0 + D(x_0,y_0) > x^* + y^* + D(x^*,y^*). \tag{3.57}$$

Now, combine this with (3.53) to obtain

$$x^* + x_0 + y_0 + D(x_0,y_0) > x_0 + \beta_0 D(x_0,y_0) + x^* + y^* + D(x^*,y^*). \tag{3.58}$$

After canceling terms and rearranging, this becomes

$$y_0 + (1 - \beta_0)D(x_0,y_0) > y^* + D(x^*,y^*), \tag{3.59}$$

which contradicts (3.56). It therefore follows that if the victim expects the injurer to respond to y_0 by choosing $x_0 < x^*$, then she will choose y^*. Thus, the only equilibrium can be (x^*,y^*).

The foregoing shows that a comparative negligence rule satisfies properties 1 and 3 in sequential-accident cases when victims are not inadvertently negligent. The next question is whether it can achieve the second-best outcome when some victims *are* inadvertently negligent. Recall that to satisfy property 2, the liability rule must induce an injurer confronting a negligent victim to choose compensating precaution of $x^*(y) > x^*$ for $y < y^*$. Note that the above formulation of the comparative negligence rule will *not* do this since, if an injurer confronts a negligent victim, he can avoid all liability (i.e., $\beta = 0$) if he chooses x^*. Thus, in order to induce compensating precaution, the threshold, or minimum, level of care for $\beta = 0$ for the injurer in this setting must be adjusted upward to $x^*(y)$ for any $y < y^*$, and the value of β when the injurer *fails* to meet the threshold must be chosen so that the following inequality is satisfied

$$x^*(y_0) < x^n + \beta(x^n, y_0)D(x^n, y_0) \tag{3.60}$$

for some $y_0 < y^*$, where x^n is defined to be the choice of care by the injurer that minimizes the right-hand side of (3.53).

Although $x^n < x^*(y_0)$ (by assumption), it is possible that $x^n \geq x^*$. Thus, in order for (3.60) to hold, β *cannot* equal zero at x^*, as was true in the case where the victim was not negligent. This shows that, in order to satisfy property 2, comparative negligence must incorporate (possibly implicitly) a requirement for compensating precaution. By doing so, it in effect replicates the function of the last clear chance doctrine combined with standard negligence rules. At the same time, however, it potentially creates the same conflict between properties 2 and 3 that arose with last clear chance. Specifically, if victims anticipate compensating precaution from all injurers, then they expect $\beta = 0$ and their problem is identical to (3.49). Thus, they would choose $y < y^*$.

The only way that victims might not choose strategic negligence is if some injurers are not expected to respond to victims' prior negligence with compensating precaution. In that case, victims would perceive a chance that, if they chose y^*, $\beta = 1$ and they would avoid liability altogether. Thus, the greater the chance that some injurers will *not* respond, the lower the incentive for victims to behave strategically and the more likely the first-best is attained. However, the tradeoff is that, if there is a large fraction of inadvertently negligent victims, the existence of unresponsive injurers reduces the chances of attaining the second-best.

Of course, this just illustrates the apparently fundamental conflict between the first-best and second-best outcomes that courts must face in designing a liability rule in sequential accidents. It seems that the rule must favor one outcome at the expense of the other (with the possible exception of strict liability with contributory negligence augmented by last clear chance). It turns out, however, that there does exist a liability rule that always satisfies properties 1 to 3 regardless of the fraction of unresponsive agents in the population. I turn to that rule next.

3.2.5. MARGINAL COST LIABILITY

Wittman (1981) has proposed a rule for sequential move accidents that he refers to as *marginal cost liability* (LMC). Before defining marginal cost liability, it is useful to distinguish it from rules based on liability for *actual damages* or *actual costs.* All of the rules we have examined to this point are based on liability for actual damages, $D(x,y)$,[52] according to either strict liability or negligence principles.[53] Liability for actual cost holds the responsible party liable for actual damages plus the other party's costs of precaution, again according to strict liability or negligence. For example, a strictly liable injurer would be liable for $D(x,y) + y$ in addition to his own costs of care x.

In contrast to these rules, LMC rules hold the responsible party liable for cost-effective precaution the other party *should* have taken (based on the efficient solution), plus any damages occurring at that cost-effective level of precaution. In the sequential-move case, this rule applies to the *first* mover, or, in our model, the victim. Thus, under *strict* LMC, the victim is liable for $y + x^*(y) + D(x^*(y),y)$, whereas the injurer is liable for the excess of his actual care, x, and actual damages, $D(x,y)$, beyond the victim's liability.

Formally, the injurer's problem, after observing the actual y chosen by the victim, is to

$$\underset{x}{\text{minimize}}\ x + D(x,y) - x^*(y) - D(x^*(y),y) \tag{3.61}$$

where the last two terms represent the victim's LMC.[54] The first-order condition for (3.61) is $1 + D_x = 0$, given that the final two terms are constants from the injurer's viewpoint. The injurer thus chooses $x^*(y)$ for any y, the efficient choice. The victim, moving first, solves the following problem:

$$\underset{y}{\text{minimize}}\ y + x^*(y) + D(x^*(y),y) \tag{3.62}$$

which yields the first-order condition:

$$1 + D_y + (1 + D_x)(\partial x^*/\partial y) = 0. \tag{3.63}$$

Notice that, since $1 + D_x = 0$ from the injurer's problem, the final term drops out, in which case $1 + D_y = 0$. Thus, the solution to (3.63) is y^*.

This shows that the LMC rule satisfies all three properties. Specifically, because the solution to the injurer's problem is $x^*(y)$ for all y, he will choose x^* in response to y^* (given that $x^*(y^*) \equiv x^*$) (property 1), and he will choose compensating precaution when $y < y^*$ (property 2). Finally, the solution to (3.63) shows that there is no incentive for the victim to be strategically negligent (property 3).

It is worth comparing the victim's problem in (3.62) to (3.49) to see why LMC does not induce strategic negligence, whereas simple negligence coupled with last clear chance does. The only difference is the extra term in (3.62), $x^*(y)$, which does not appear in (3.49). The absence of this term allows the victim to ignore the additional precaution the injurer takes in response to the victim's negligence, thereby resulting in an externality. By holding the victim liable at the margin for the injurer's compensating actions, LMC internalizes the externality and removes the incentive for too little care.

LMC can also be formulated as a negligence rule.[55] In particular, the victim's expected liability is

$$\text{LMC} = \begin{array}{ll} 0, & y \geq y^* \\ x^*(y) + D(x^*(y),y), & y < y^* \end{array}. \tag{3.64}$$

In this case, if the injurer observes y^*, he is fully liable and minimizes $x + D(x,y^*)$, which yields x^*. If instead he observes $y < y^*$, his problem is identical to (3.61) and he chooses $x^*(y)$. As for the victim, she will choose y^* since

$$y^* < x^*(y^*) + y^* + D(x^*(y^*),y^*) < y + x^*(y) + D(x^*(y),y)$$

for any $y < y^*$. Thus, the outcome is identical to strict LMC.

Despite the benefits of LMC rules, they do not seem to have been employed by courts in accident cases. However, Wittman (1981, p. 80) notes that combining a criminal fine equal to the injurer's compensating precaution with liability for actual damages can, like a Pigouvian tax, internalize the externality, thereby leading to the efficient solution.[56]

3.2.6. PROXIMATE CAUSE AND SEQUENTIAL ACCIDENTS

The final approach I consider for dealing with the problems created by sequential-care accidents is the doctrine of proximate cause. Recall that, in order for an individual to be liable for the costs of an accident, he must be both cause in fact of the harm and proximate cause. Grady (1984) has recently argued that one theory of proximate cause that courts have invoked—the *direct consequences* doctrine—can be understood as an effort to address the compensating precaution issue (property 2) in sequential torts. In particular, Grady notes that

> The purpose of the direct-consequences doctrine of proximate cause is to increase the pecuniary incentives of persons other than the original wrongdoer, such as the last wrongdoer, to take precautions that compensate for the original wrongdoer's lack of care. (pp. 416–417).

The doctrine accomplishes this objective by finding the last wrongdoer the proximate cause of the harm, and hence liable for the full damages, even though the original wrongdoer's negligence is also a cause in fact. In this way, it functions much like last clear chance by inducing parties, under the threat of liability, to compensate for the negligence of previous wrongdoers.[57] Of course, as Grady recognizes, it has the same drawback as last clear chance in that it is an all-or-nothing rule, and possible immunity from liability may reduce the incentives of previous actors to take care in the first place. Thus, as the discussion of last clear chance indicated, courts are faced with the difficult task of selectively invoking the doctrine in an effort to balance the desire for compensating precaution from subsequent actors against the possibly adverse effects on the incentives of previous actors (properties 2 and 3). Grady proposes some guidelines for doing this, but in general it can be done imperfectly at best.

4. Summary

In this chapter I extended the basic accident model from chapter 2 to consider three topics. The first was the impact of litigation costs. These costs include the victim's cost of filing suit and pursuing a claim for damages, and the injurer's cost of defending himself against such a claim. We saw that litigation costs matter for at least two reasons: first, they introduce a cost of using the tort system to internalize accident costs; second, they tend to reduce the incentives of injurers to take precaution compared to the social optimum.

The second extension I examined was the impact of uncertainty. I considered uncertainty by injurers about the due standard under negligence, uncertainty by the court about whether an injurer was negligent or was the cause of an accident, and uncertainty by injurers about the degree of risk caused by their activity. I showed how uncertainty affects incentives for injurers to take care, and what liability rules provide the most efficient incentives.

Finally, I considered sequential-care accidents, or accidents in which injurers and victims choose their care in sequence. In this context, I first demonstrated the potential for strategic behavior by the party moving first (usually the injurer), and then examined the ability of various liability rules to prevent it.

FOUR

THE ECONOMICS OF CONTRACT LAW

Remedies for Breach

In a world of perfect certainty and costless contracting, the parties to a contract will specify as part of the contract the manner in which they will react to all possible contingencies. That is, they will write fully contingent contracts. In reality, however, the parties will not be able to provide for all contingencies. Thus, there will occasionally arise circumstances in which one of the parties no longer values performance of the contract under the original terms. In this case, a dispute arises. Contract law provides rules for resolving disputes over nonperformance (or modified performance) that the parties are not able to resolve on their own. The two basic questions contract law addresses are: What contracts should be enforceable? and, What should be the remedies available to victims of broken but enforceable promises? (Cooter and Ulen, 1988, p. 213).

In this chapter, I focus on the second question by examining remedies for breach of contract. I begin by analyzing the impact that various court-imposed damage measures have on the breach decision, the decision of how much the parties invest in transaction-specific assets (i.e., "reliance"), and risk sharing. Although efficient breach requires that "victims" of breach receive full compensation for their expected gain from the contract (their expectation interest), other considerations argue for limiting damages in particular ways. For example, I show that the latter provide economic justifications for the famous *Hadley* v. *Baxendale* rule.

I next turn to the question of whether courts should enforce liquidated damages specified by the parties as part of the contract. The refusal of courts to enforce contract terms that both parties agreed to at first seems puzzling, but I will suggest reasons why it may sometimes be efficient to do so. Finally, I examine the merits of specific performance, or enforcement of the contract as written, as an alternative to money damages.

1. Court-Imposed Damage Remedies

The basic contract model[1] that I will employ in this and the next chapter consists of a single buyer, B, who has contracted to purchase a good from a single seller, S. With the exception of section 2, I will assume in this chapter that the parties are risk neutral. After the contract is signed, the seller will produce the good and deliver it at some specified future date. The uncertainty in the contract is over the seller's production cost, C, which is assumed to be a random variable whose value is realized only *after* the contract is signed but before delivery is due. Let $F(C)$ be the distribution function of C that is known by both parties $(F' \equiv f > 0)$, and let $E(C)$ be its expected value. The price of the good, P, is set when the contract is signed, but is payable only on delivery of the good.[2] I assume that the parties are unable to specify a *price schedule*, $P(C)$, which would set a price for each realization of C.

The value of the good to the buyer is denoted $V(r)$, where r is the buyer's (dollar) investment in transaction-specific capital, or reliance.[3] I assume that $V' > 0$, indicating that greater reliance increases the value of performance to the buyer. I also assume that the value of r in the event of nonperformance is zero—that is, it has no salvage value. This assumption is inessential; all that matters is that reliance be partially nonsalvageable in the event of nonperformance.[4]

The sequence of events is as follows: (1) the parties sign a contract and specify the price P; (2) the buyer invests r; (3) the seller realizes his cost of production C and decides whether to perform or breach; and (4) if the seller breaches, the buyer files suit (at no cost), and the court awards damages, $D \geq 0$, which may be a function of r and P.

1.1. The Socially Optimal Solution

In order to examine the efficiency of the various damage measures, I first derive the socially optimal solution. This consists of the optimal reliance decision by the buyer, and the optimal breach decision by the seller. The optimum is found by examining these decisions in reverse sequence of time. Thus, I first consider the optimal breach decision, given the level of reliance, r.

Breach of the contract is socially desirable when nonperformance yields a greater net value than performance, given the buyer's sunk investment in reliance. Thus, when the seller realizes the cost of performance C, performance is efficient if $V(r) \geq C$, and breach is efficient if $V(r) < C$. The set of realizations of C such that the latter inequality holds is termed the *breach set* (Shavell, 1980a). Prior to the realization of C, the probability of an efficient breach is therefore given by $1 - F(V(r))$, and the probability of efficient performance is $F(V(r))$.

Given these probabilities, the optimal investment in reliance by the buyer is made to maximize the joint expected value of the contract. Thus, the optimal choice of r, denoted r^*, maximizes

$$F(V(r))\{V(r) - E[C|C \leq V(r)]\} - r = F(V(r))V(r) - \int_0^{V(r)} CdF(C) - r. \quad (4.1)$$

The resulting first-order condition is

$$F(V(r))V'(r) - 1 = 0 \quad (4.2)$$

It follows from (4.2) that $V'(r) > 1$. Thus, r^* is smaller than the value that would maximize $V(r) - r$. This reflects the fact that, because breach is efficient for high realizations of C, r should be set below the level that would be efficient if performance were certain.

1.2. The Efficiency of Various Damage Measures

I now consider whether various court-imposed damage measures can achieve the efficient solution just described. The sequence of moves is as follows. The buyer moves first by choosing the level of reliance to maximize her expected return from the contract, given the price and the probability of breach as determined by the damage measure. The seller then decides whether or not to breach to maximize his expected return, given the price, the buyer's reliance, and the damage measure. The damage measures I examine are expectation damages, reliance damages, and restitution damages.

1.2.1. EXPECTATION DAMAGES

The expectation-damage measure is defined to be the amount of money that the victim of a breach (the buyer) must receive to be as well off as if the contract were performed. To calculate this amount, note that the buyer's position in the event of performance is $V(r) - P - r$, and her position in the event of non-performance is $-r$. The expectation damage measure is the difference between these, or

$$D_e = V(r) - P. \quad (4.3)$$

It thus corresponds to the buyer's surplus given r.[5]

Consider first the breach decision of the seller under expectation damages. Once C is realized, the seller will perform if $P - C \geq -D_e$, or substituting from (4.3), if $C \leq V(r)$, which is the efficient condition. Thus, expectation damages induce efficient breach, given the buyer's choice of r, because the seller fully internalizes the cost of breach to the buyer.

Now consider the buyer's choice of reliance under expectation damages, denoted r_e. Given efficient breach by the seller, the buyer will choose r to maximize

$$F(V(r))[V(r) - P] + [1 - F(V(r))]D_e - r = V(r) - P - r \quad (4.4)$$

which yields the first-order condition $V'(r) - 1 = 0$. Thus, the buyer will over-rely, or $r_e > r^*$, The reason is that expectation damages fully insure the buyer against breach, which creates a moral hazard problem.

1.2.2. RELIANCE DAMAGES

The reliance-damage measure is defined to be the amount of money that leaves the buyer as well off as if the contract were never made. It thus differs from expectation damages by the baseline against which damages are measured. The buyer's position if the contract were never made is zero, and her position in the event of breach is $-r$. Thus, $D_r = r$, or the seller must refund the buyer's reliance.[6]

Under reliance damages, the seller performs if $P - C \geq -D_r$, or if $C \leq P + r$. Since we assume that $V(r) > P + r$ (otherwise, the buyer would never enter the contract), it follows that the seller will perform too infrequently or breach too often.[7] Intuitively, reliance damages undercompensate the buyer in the event of breach (given $r < V(r) - P$), and therefore charges the seller a "price of breach" that is too low.

Given that the equilibrium probability of breach under reliance damages is $1 - F(P + r)$, the buyer chooses r_r to maximize $F(P + r)[V(r) - P - r]$. The resulting first-order condition, after rearranging, is

$$V'(r) - 1 = \frac{-[V(r) - P - r]f(P + r)}{F(P + r)}. \tag{4.5}$$

Since the right-hand side is negative, $V'(r) - 1 < 0$, implying that the buyer overinvests in reliance. In fact, it follows from (4.5) that the buyer invests more than under expectation damages; that is $r_r > r_e > r^*$. Reliance damages cause the buyer to overinvest for two reasons. First, because r is returned in the event of breach, the buyer ignores the loss of r in nonperformance states (this again is a moral hazard problem). Second, because reliance damages undercompensate the buyer relative to performance, she increases r to reduce the probability of a breach (this is reflected by the term $f(P + r)$ in (4.5)).

1.2.3. RESTITUTION DAMAGES

The final measure of damages, restitution damages, restores to the buyer any payments she made to the seller prior to breach. Thus, if the buyer prepaid the price, $D_s = P$; however, if the buyer did not prepay any part of the price, as in the case we are considering, $D_s = 0$, and restitution damages coincide with no damages. In the latter case, the seller will perform if $P - C \geq 0$, or if $C \leq P$.[8] Again, since $V(r) > P$, the seller will breach too often.

As for the buyer's choice of reliance, she will choose r to maximize $F(P)[V(r) - P] - r$, which yields the first-order condition

$$F(P)V'(r) - 1 = 0. \tag{4.6}$$

Thus, under either restitution damages or no damages, the buyer chooses the efficient level of reliance, given the equilibrium breach set. The reason is that the buyer fully internalizes the social cost of breach, and therefore does not over-invest in reliance. In other words, there is no moral hazard problem.

1.2.4. LIMITED EXPECTATION DAMAGES AND MITIGATION

The preceding analysis of the three damage measures showed that none was able to achieve efficiency of both the breach and the reliance decision. An analogy with bilateral-care torts suggests why this happened. Recall that strict liability (without a contributory negligence defense) could only induce efficient care by injurers because victims were fully compensated for their injuries and could therefore ignore the risk of an accident. No liability similarly allowed injurers to ignore the risk.

The current model of contract breach is also a bilateral-care model in that both parties make choices that affect the probability of breach. Thus, a strict liability rule like expectation damages will only induce efficient behavior by the "injurer" (the seller) but will fully insure the "victim" (the buyer). Likewise, a no-liability rule (or restitution damages) will only induce efficient behavior by the victim and not by the injurer. In order to induce both parties to behave efficiently, we need to design a rule that holds both parties responsible at the margin for the costs of their actions.[9] One possibility is a negligence-type rule. For example, the seller's liability to pay expectation damages could be conditioned on whether he breached efficiently, or the buyer's right to expectation damages could be conditioned on whether she invested in the efficient level of reliance (Sykes, 1990, p. 61). In general, rules of this sort do not seem to be used in contract law.

Alternatively, consider an expectation-damages remedy that specifies a constant level of damages based on the buyer's expectation interest evaluated at her efficient level of reliance; that is $D_e^* = V(r^*) - P$. Clearly, this measure of damages will continue to induce efficient breach by the seller, since he regarded r as fixed anyway. As for the buyer, her choice of r maximizes the left side of (4.4), except that the probabilities are replaced by $F(V(r^*))$ and $1 - F(V(r^*))$, and D_e is replaced by D_e^* all of which are now constants. The first-order condition of this problem is $F(V(r^*))V'(r) - 1 = 0$, which yields r^* as the solution. Thus, the buyer chooses the efficient level of reliance.[10]

An important case in the law of contracts, *Hadley* v. *Baxendale*,[11] held that victims of breach are only entitled to damages that were reasonably foreseeable to the breaching party. If we interpret "reasonably foreseeable damages" to mean "damages at the efficient level of reliance," then the *Hadley* v. *Baxendale* rule corresponds to the limited expectation damage rule just defined.[12] I shall return in the next chapter to the problem of designing contract rules that simultaneously induce efficient breach by the promisor (seller) and efficient reliance by the promisee (buyer). I shall also revisit the *Hadley* v. *Baxendale* rule in section 3 below in the context of information asymmetries between the promisor and promisee.

Limiting expectation damages to prevent overreliance is related to the general principle of mitigation of damages.[13] Because unforeseen events make breach unavoidable in some circumstances, it is desirable for the parties to take all reasonable steps to minimize the resulting losses. Courts employ various doctrines to encourage such steps. The example of limiting damages to prevent overreliance by promisees resembles rules that encourage victim precaution *before* an accident. Other rules encourage actions to minimize losses *after* breach. For example, when a promisor fails to deliver promised goods, the replacement-price rule limits the promisee's recovery to the difference between the contract price and the best price at which a substitute can be purchased on the spot market. This limitation encourages the promisee to mitigate the loss, given that she is in the best position to do so once the breach has occurred. Note that this rule resembles the tort doctrine that bars victims from recovering losses that they could have avoided with reasonable efforts after an accident occurs.[14]

2. Risk Sharing and Remedies for Breach

If one or both of the parties to a contract are risk averse, then some remedies for breach may be better than others in terms of allocating the risk from changed circumstances.[15] In this section, I will therefore examine the risk-sharing properties of the three breach remedies: expectation damages, reliance damages, and restitution damages. I will continue to employ the model from the previous section in which the source of risk was the cost of production.[16]

In order to focus on risk sharing as distinct from breach and reliance, the current model abstracts from those decisions.[17] Specifically, the buyer's investment in reliance, r, is treated as exogenous, and the buyer's dollar value of performance is simply a constant, V. The model abstracts from the breach decision by assuming that the seller's costs can take only two values: low (C_l) and high (C_h), where q is the probability of C_l and $1 - q$ is the probability of C_h. Further, let $C_l < V < C_h$, which implies that performance is efficient when costs are low, but breach is efficient when costs are high. As for actual performance, we know from the previous section that, given damages of D and a prepaid price of P,[18] the seller will actually perform if $P - C \geq P - D$ or if $C \leq D$. Thus, actual behavior will coincide with efficient behavior if $C_l \leq D < C_h$. Since this range for D turns out to be consistent with optimal risk sharing, we can ignore efficiency of the breach decision. As a result, q becomes the probability of performance and $1 - q$ is the probability of breach.

2.1. Optimal Risk Sharing

When the parties are risk averse, they care about utility rather than wealth. Thus, let $U_s(\cdot)$ be the seller's utility $(U_s' > 0, U_s'' \leq 0)$, and let $U_b(\cdot)$ be the buyer's utility $(U_b' > 0, U_b'' \leq 0)$. At the time the contract is made, the seller's expected utility is

$$EU_s = qU_s(P - C_1) + (1 - q)U_s(P - D) \qquad (4.7)$$

where D is the damage payment in the event of breach. Similarly, the buyer's expected utility is

$$EU_b = qU_b(V - P - r) + (1 - q)U_b(D - P - r). \qquad (4.8)$$

Optimal risk sharing is achieved by choosing P and D to maximize the expected utility of one party (e.g., the buyer) subject to a minimum expected utility for the other party (the seller). The resulting first-order condition is given by[19]

$$\frac{U_b'(V - P - r)}{U_b'(D - P - r)} = \frac{U_s'(P - C_1)}{U_s'(P - D)} \qquad (4.9)$$

This condition, along with the seller's utility constraint, determine the optimal damage payment and contract price.

There are four possible cases to examine, depending on the risk attitudes of the two parties. First, if both are risk neutral ($U_s'' = U_b'' = 0$), then the value of D that shares risk optimally is indeterminate. In this case, considerations other than risk sharing (for example, ensuring efficient breach) can be used to determine D.

If the buyer is risk averse and the seller is risk neutral (i.e., $U_s'' = 0, U_b'' < 0$), then the right-hand side of (4.9) equals 1 (i.e., the seller's marginal utility of income is the same regardless of the state). It follows immediately that $D^* = V$. In this case, the buyer's income is state-independent ($V - P - r$), and the seller bears all of the risk. If the buyer is risk neutral and the seller risk averse (i.e., $U_s'' < 0, U_b'' = 0$), the left-hand side of (4.9) equals 1 and, as a result, $D^* = C_1$. Thus, the seller's income is state-independent ($P - C_1$), and the buyer bears all the risk.

Finally, if both parties are risk averse (i.e., $U_s'' < 0, U_b'' < 0$), they share the risk. This is achieved by setting $C_1 < D^* < V$.[20] To see why, note that if $D = C_1$, the right-hand side of (4.9) equals one but, given $U_b'' < 0$ and $V > C_1$, the left-hand side is less than 1. Thus, D must be increased to achieve equality. The reverse is true if we begin with $D = V$.[21]

2.2. Breach Remedies

I now consider the risk-sharing properties of the actual breach remedies from the previous section. First, the expectation-damages remedy when the price is prepaid is given by $D = V$. Thus, it allocates risk efficiently if and only if the buyer is risk averse and the seller is risk neutral. The reliance-damages remedy when the price is prepaid is given by $D = r + P$ (recall that the buyer must be restored to her precontract position). Since $V > P + r$ in order for the contract to be profitable to the buyer, $D < V$ under reliance damages. Further, since $P > C_1$ for performance to be profitable for the seller, $D = r + P > C_1$. Thus, risks *may* be shared optimally in case four, though this would only be by coincidence since there is no reason to expect $D = P + r$ to solve (4.9) in that case. Finally, under restitution damages, $C_1 < D = P < V$, thus leading to the same conclusions as obtained for reliance damages.

The preceding analysis has shown that none of the court-imposed damage remedies will generally result in optimal risk sharing between the parties to a contract. We have also seen that none was capable of simultaneously inducing efficient breach and investment in reliance (with the exception of limited expectation damages). Given these deficiencies, I later consider two alternative remedies for breach that rely on the parties to resolve disputes—namely, liquidated damages and specific performance. Before doing that, however, I reconsider the *Hadley* v. *Baxendale* rule.

3. Asymmetric Information and Limited Liability for Breach

In section 1.2.4 I examined the limited-liability (or remoteness of damages) rule arising from the case of *Hadley* v. *Baxendale* as a way of preventing promisees from overinvesting in reliance. In this section will argue that it can also serve to facilitate information exchange prior to contracting. Specifically, I will show that it can induce promisees to reveal private information about the value of performance to promisors such that breach occurs only when it is efficient.[22] Since uncertainty may result in inefficient breach, this information is socially valuable. Thus, the efficient rule would induce the promisees to reveal their information when the social benefits exceed the cost of revelation.

The case of *Hadley* v. *Baxendale* concerned a mill owner who hired a carrier company to transport a broken shaft to the original manufacturer for the purpose of having a new one made. Since the mill did not have a spare shaft, it had to shut down during the repair process. It turned out that the carrier was delayed in returning the shaft through its own negligence, which constituted a breach of contract. The court held, however, that the damages it owed should not include the mill's lost profits because it was not reasonable for the carrier to anticipate that the mill would have to shut down. In order to recover such damages, the court held, the mill owner would have had to convey its special circumstances (i.e., the fact that it had to shut down) to the carrier. The general rule, therefore, is that only those losses that promisors can reasonably foresee arising from breach are recoverable, unless the promisee informs them of the possibility of greater losses.

3.1. Limited Liability and Information Revelation

This section develops a formal model of asymmetric information in contract settings and derives the conditions under which the limited liability rule described in *Hadley* v. *Baxendale* will elicit private information about the value of performance to promisees.[23] Consider a situation in which some promisees place a high value on performance, V_h, and some a low value, V_l.[24] Promisors, however, only know the average value of performance, $V^e = \alpha V_h + (1 - \alpha)V_l$, where α is the fraction of high types. Assume that the high types are the minority, $\alpha < 1/2$.

Private information affects efficiency in this setting because the value of performance determines when the promisor should and should not breach. In particular, if the value of performance were known, recall that breach is efficient if and only if $C > V_j(j = h, l)$, where C is the promisor's cost of performance. I assume, however, that it is costly for the promisee to reveal her type, so that in some circumstances, it may be preferable from a social point of view for her to remain silent. In that case, breach is efficient if $C < V^e$.

3.1.1. SOCIALLY OPTIMAL REVELATION

To determine when revelation by the promisee is efficient, we need to calculate the expected value of the contract under full information and under uncertainty, given efficient breach in both cases. The expected value of the contract given full information is

$$EV^F = \alpha \int_0^{V_h} (V_h - C)dF(C) + (1 - \alpha) \int_0^{V_l} (V_l - C)dF(C) \tag{4.10}$$

and the expected value given uncertainty is

$$EV^U = \int_0^{V^e} (V^e - C)dF(C). \tag{4.11}$$

The value of information in this case, denoted I, is the difference between EV^F and EV^U, or the gain when promisors make the correct breach decision for each type of promisee rather than basing it on the average type.[25] Thus,

$$\begin{aligned} I &= EV^F - EV^U \\ &= (1 - \alpha) \int_{V_l}^{V^e} (C - V_l)dF(C) + \alpha \int_{V^e}^{V_h} (V_h - C)dF(C). \end{aligned} \tag{4.12}$$

The first term is the gain from avoiding excessive performance with low-value promisees, and the second term is the gain from avoiding excessive breach with high-value promisees.

Since only one type of promisee needs to communicate her type to achieve full information, revelation costs are minimized if high types alone reveal, given that they are assumed to be the minority (i.e., $\alpha < 1/2$). Let k be the promisee's cost of revelation. The social condition for revelation to be desirable is therefore

$$\alpha k < I. \tag{4.13}$$

The question is whether there exists a damage rule that replicates (4.13) in equilibrium. Two types of rules will be considered: an *unlimited liability* rule that awards promisees their actual expectation damages from breach regardless of whether they identify their type up front, and a *limited liability* rule that awards promisees the expectation interest of low types if they are silent and of high types if they identify themselves as such.[26] Note that this latter rule resembles the *Hadley* v. *Baxendale* rule. I examine it first.

3.1.2. EQUILIBRIUM UNDER LIMITED LIABILITY

I assume that the contract price is set up front but is payable on performance. I also assume that competition drives the promisor's (seller's) expected profits to zero, so the price reflects expected costs. Thus, if promisees (buyers) reveal themselves to be high types, the price will be different than if they remain silent, given that the promisor can treat silent promisees as low types under the limited liability rule. Define P_R^j as the price if the promisee reveals herself to be of type j $j(j = h, l)$, and P_S as the price if the promisee is silent. Thus, damages in the event of breach are $V_1 - P_S$ if the promisee is silent, and $V_j - P_R^j$ if the promisee reveals that she is type j. After the price has been set, the promisor realizes C and makes his breach decision.

As usual, we solve for the equilibrium in reverse sequence. Consider first the case where the promisee is silent. Under limited liability, the promisor treats her as a low type and breaches if $P_S - C < -(V_1 - P_S)$, or if $V_1 < C$. The expected profit of the contract for the promisor in this case is thus

$$\pi_S = F(V_1)P_S - \int_0^{V_1} C dF(C) - [1 - F(V_1)](V_1 - P_S). \tag{4.14}$$

Setting this equal to zero and solving for P_S yields

$$P_S = \int_0^{V_1} C dF(C) + [1 - F(V_1)]V_1 \tag{4.15}$$

The expected value of the contract for a promisee is

$$EV_S^l = V_1 - P_S, \tag{4.16}$$

for a low type, and

$$EV_S^h = F(V_1)V_h + [1 - F(V_1)]V_1 - P_S, \tag{4.17}$$

for a high type.

Substituting for P_S in each expression yields

$$EV_S^l = \int_0^{V_1} (V_1 - C) dF(C), \tag{4.18}$$

and

$$EV_S^h = \int_0^{V_1} (V_h - C)dF(C). \tag{4.19}$$

Now consider the case where the promisee reveals her type. Note first that if she reveals herself to be a low type, expressions (4.14) and (4.15) remain the same, so the contract price is P_S. Thus, (4.16) and (4.18) are also unchanged except that a cost of revelation, k, is incurred by the promisee. Consequently, revelation offers no benefits for low types, so they will always remain silent. This is consistent with efficiency given that low types are the majority group.

In contrast, high types may find it advantageous to reveal their type. If they do, the promisor's expected profit is

$$\pi_R^h = F(V_h)P_R^h - \int_0^{V_h} CdF(C) - [1 - F(V_h)](V_h - P_R^h). \tag{4.20}$$

Equating this to zero yields

$$P_R^h = \int_0^{V_h} CdF(C) + [1 - F(V_h)]V_h. \tag{4.21}$$

The expected value of the contract to a high-type promisee is $V_h - P_R^h$ regardless of whether a breach occurs. After substituting for P_R^h, this becomes

$$EV_R^h = \int_0^{V_h} (V_h - C)dF(C). \tag{4.22}$$

A high-type promisee will therefore reveal if $EV_R^h - k \geq EV_S^h$, or, using (4.19), if

$$\int_{V_1}^{V_h} (V_h - C)dF(C) \geq k. \tag{4.23}$$

The benefit of revelation to high types is therefore the net value of performance on the interval $[V_1, V_h]$, given that breach would have occurred over this range if the promisee had remained silent.[27]

A comparison of (4.23) to the social condition for revelation by high types (4.13) shows that they are not in general the same. It can be shown, however, that the left-hand side of (4.23) is strictly greater than I/α.[28] Thus, whenever revelation by high types is socially desirable, the limited liability rule will yield the efficient result. However, the reverse is not true; that is, the limited liability rule may result in revelation when it is not socially desirable.

3.2. Equilibrium Under Unlimited Liability

The results are different under unlimited liability because now promisors cannot treat silent promisees as if they were low types. In this case, it can be shown that high-type promisees never reveal their type. This is because they pay a price based on the average type, which is lower than they would pay if they revealed. And since they receive their true valuation in the event of breach, they have no incentive to reveal. On the other hand, low types will reveal if the following condition holds

$$\int_{V_1}^{V^e} (C - V_1)dF(C) + \int_{V^e}^{\infty} (V^e - V_1)dF(C) > k. \qquad (4.24)$$

Low types benefit from revelation by obtaining a lower price—this is the left-hand side of (4.24). They thus do so if the benefit exceeds the cost of revelation.

In terms of efficiency, the unlimited liability rule yields the efficient result if revelation is *not* socially desirable (i.e., if (4.13) does not hold), and (4.24) also does not hold. However, if communication by high types is efficient, the unlimited liability rule clearly will not yield the optimal result, since high types will remain silent (though information may still be conveyed by low types). Combining this with the results regarding the limited liability rule suggests that the latter is desirable as a way of eliciting information if communication is desirable and *high types* constitute the *minority* of promisees. The real advantage of the limited liability rule therefore appears to reside in the savings of communication costs from inducing revelation only in "exceptional" cases (Bebchuk and Shavell, 1991).

3.3. The Use of Limited Liability for Inducing Revelation of Information and Preventing Overreliance: A Comparison

We have now examined the limited liability rule from *Hadley* v. *Baxendale* as serving two possible functions: preventing promisees from overrelying on the contract (section 1.2.4) and inducing promisees to reveal exceptional circumstances. The relationship between these two functions is essentially the relationship between *moral hazard* and *adverse selection*, respectively. Both problems center on information asymmetries between parties to an economic relationship—moral hazard arises in situations where a party chooses an unobservable *action* (reliance), and adverse selection arises when a party has an unobservable *characteristic* (high or low value of the contract).

It is well known that both moral hazard and adverse selection can lead to inefficiencies, and economists have devoted much effort to devising incentive schemes to induce the party with the informational advantage to act in an efficient manner to eliminate them.[29] Much of this literature has been in the context of insurance, where one of the key insights has been that *limited coverage* is an effective way to mitigate both moral hazard and adverse selection.[30] The limited liability rule of *Hadley* v. *Baxendale* relies on this result to address both moral hazard and adverse selection problems in contract settings.

4. Liquidated Damages

Occasionally, the parties to a contract will provide for breach by including a liquidated damage clause that stipulates an amount of money the breaching party will pay to the other party in the event of breach. In this section, I examine the ability of liquidated damage remedies to achieve efficient breach, investment in reliance, and risk sharing. In light of the results, I will address the question of why courts often do not enforce liquidated damage clauses if the amount is judged to be excessive.

4.1. Breach and Reliance Under Liquidated Damages

Consider the case where both the buyer and seller are risk neutral. Thus, the relevant issues are breach and reliance. Recall from section 1.1 that, in the model of production-cost uncertainty, optimal reliance solves the equation $F(V(r))V'(r) - 1 = 0$, and given r, efficient breach occurs when $V(r) < C$ and efficient performance occurs when $V(r) \geq C$.

The analysis of a liquidated damage remedy is based on the following sequence of events: first, the parties specify the liquidated damage payment, D, along with the contract price, P, at the start of the contract; second, the buyer chooses a level of reliance given P and D; finally, the seller realizes his cost of production, and, given P, D, and r, chooses whether to breach or perform.

The derivation of the equilibrium proceeds in reverse sequence. Consider first the seller's breach decision. If the price is payable on performance, the seller will perform the contract if $P - C \geq -D$ and breach if $P - C < -D$. Thus, prior to the realization of C, the probability of performance is $F(P + D)$ and the probability of breach is $1 - F(P + D)$. The buyer therefore chooses her level of reliance at the previous stage to maximize

$$V_b = F(P + D)[V(r) - P] + [1 - F(P + D)]D - r. \qquad (4.25)$$

The resulting first-order condition is

$$F(P + D)V'(r) - 1 = 0. \qquad (4.26)$$

Denote the solution to (4.26) by $r(P, D)$.

Finally, consider the choice of P and D at the start of the contract. Assume that the buyer makes the choice to maximize his expected return from the contract, as given by (4.25), subject to $r = r(P, D)$ and to the constraint that the seller achieve a minimum level of expected utility,[31] i.e., that

$$V_s = F(P+D)P - \int_0^{P+D} CdF(C) - [1 - F(P+D)]D \geq V_s^0. \qquad (4.27)$$

The choices of P and D will thus be Pareto optimal given the absence of third-party effects. The constraint in (4.27) ensures that the seller is willing to participate in the contract given his next best alternative, and $r(P, D)$ recognizes that the buyer will choose r to maximize (4.25) once P and D are set.

After simplification, the first-order conditions for P and D arising from the above problem are, respectively,

$$F'(P+D)[V(r) - P - D] = F(P+D)(1 - \lambda) \qquad (4.28)$$

and

$$F'(P+D)[V(r) - P - D] = [1 - F(P+D)](\lambda - 1) \qquad (4.29)$$

where λ is the multiplier on (4.27).[32] Combining these conditions yields the results that $\lambda = 1$ and $V(r) - P - D = 0$, or

$$D = V(r) - P. \qquad (4.30)$$

This, of course, is simply expectation damages. Substituting (4.30) into (4.26) and the condition for seller breach shows that both reliance and breach are chosen efficiently. Thus, a liquidated damage remedy yields the socially optimal solution (Chung, 1992).

4.2. Risk Sharing Under Liquidated Damages

If the parties are risk averse rather than risk neutral and they care only about risk sharing, then in principle they can choose P and D to allocate production-cost risk optimally (Polinsky, 1983b). Indeed, notice that the manner in which the parties chose liquidated damages in the previous section coincides with the problem for optimal risk sharing in section 2.1. In practice, however, liquidated damages will not generally allocate risks optimally because risk sharing will conflict with the goals of optimal breach and reliance.

4.3. Court-Imposed Limits on Liquidated Damages

The analysis to this point does not explain the reluctance of courts to invalidate excessive liquidated damage, or "penalty" clauses. For one thing, the results in section 4.1. suggest that the parties will set D equal to expectation damages, which is surely not excessive. Nor do risk-sharing considerations ever imply that D will exceed expectation damages (Polinsky, 1983b). Thus, in order to examine the enforceability question, we first have to explain why the parties would ever choose D larger than expectation damages. Then we can ask whether these reasons ever justify a court-imposed limitation.

4.3.1. ECONOMIC ARGUMENTS FOR LIMITING
LIQUIDATED DAMAGES

I first consider economically justifiable explanations for limiting excessive liquidated damage amounts (i.e., amounts greater than expectation damages). One
such reason is provided by Chung (1992). The situation he considers is one in
which the uncertainty is not over the seller's production costs, but over the
amount that a second buyer (referred to as the entrant) will offer to purchase
the good promised to the first buyer (the incumbent). Assume that the entrant
arrives after the contract is signed, so the seller must breach in order to accept his
offer.

Let Y be the value the entrant places on the good, which, prior to his arrival,
is a random variable with distribution $G(Y)$. Assume, however, that only the
entrant observes his realization of Y, though the incumbent buyer and seller
know its distribution. The seller's cost of production is fixed at C in the current
model, and the incumbent buyer's valuation is also fixed at V. For simplicity, I
ignore reliance and focus on efficiency of the breach decision.[33] Optimal breach
occurs when the realized value of the entrant's valuation exceeds the incumbent's valuation—that is, when $Y > V$.

Since the entrant's valuation of the good is private information, we need to
specify his offer to the seller. Obviously, The maximum he would offer is his
valuation Y, in which case the seller would receive all of the surplus from the sale
(which he may end up sharing with the incumbent buyer via the liquidated
damage payment, D). At the other extreme, he would offer the lowest amount
the seller would accept in order to breach the original contract. That amount is
given by $P + D$, the sum of the foregone price from the incumbent buyer and the
liquidated damage payment.[34] In this case, the entrant obtains all of the surplus
from the sale. Suppose in general that the entrant's offer lies between these two
extremes. Thus, if R is his offer,

$$R(Y) = \alpha(P + D) + (1 - \alpha)Y. \tag{4.31}$$

Given (4.31), the seller will breach the original contract if $R > P + D$, or, substituting from (4.31), if $Y > P + D$. Thus, when the seller and initial buyer write
their contract, the probability of performance is $G(P + D)$, and the probability
of breach is $1 - G(P + D)$. Using these we can write the expected values of the
contract to the seller and incumbent buyer, respectively, as

$$V_s = G(P + D)P - [1 - G(P + D)]D + \int_{P+D}^{\infty} R(Y)dG(Y) - C \tag{4.32}$$

and

$$V_b = G(P + D)(V - P) + [1 - G(P + D)]D. \tag{4.33}$$

As above, I assume that the parties choose the contract terms, P and D, to maximize V_b subject to $V_s \geq V_s^0$.[35] In this case, the first-order conditions yield the result

$$D = V - P + \alpha[1 - G(P + D)]/G'(P + D). \qquad (4.34)$$

Thus, liquidated damages exceed expectation damages whenever $\alpha > 0$; that is, whenever the entrant has some market power and is therefore able to acquire the good for an amount below his true valuation. Moreover, the "excess" damage amount increases as the entrant's offer falls further below his valuation (i.e., as α increases). The impact is to reduce the probability that the seller will breach the contract.

Intuitively, the original parties use a higher liquidated damage payment as a way to "precommit" to the original contract when they expect the entrant to obtain some of the surplus created by his higher valuation. This strategy is inefficient from a social perspective, however, because it results in too little breach of the contract. That is, in some cases where $\Upsilon > V$, the seller will not breach the contract, even though the entrant values the good more than the incumbent. The excessive damage payment serves only to increase the expected surplus of the original contractors relative to the incumbent; it does not increase the overall expected surplus. Thus, a limit on liquidated damages in this case enhances efficiency by preventing the parties from overcommitting (from a social perspective) to the original contract.[36]

Other economic justifications for limiting liquidated damages that are "unreasonably large" are, first, situations in which one party did not realize the implications of the damage clause at the time the contract was formed; and second, when one or both of the parties made a mistake in estimating the losses from breach. These two justifications overlap with the contract doctrines of *unconscionability* and *mistake*, respectively, both of which are also potential reasons for nonenforcement of the contract (Rea, 1984).[37]

4.3.2. ECONOMIC ARGUMENTS AGAINST LIMITING LIQUIDATED DAMAGES

In contrast to the preceding argument, liquidated damages in excess of expectation damages may in some cases enhance the efficiency of contracting and therefore should be enforced by the courts. I will give several examples from the literature.[38] First, suppose one of the parties to the contract has such a high subjective value of performance that expectation damages would not leave him indifferent between performance and breach. In that case, economic efficiency, which is properly concerned with subjective valuations, may dictate that the parties provide for a lower probability of breach than would consideration of expected wealth alone.[39]

The way the parties can do this is by increasing the cost of breach to the seller to reflect the buyer's true valuation. Since the optimal liquidated damage amount was shown earlier to satisfy the condition $V = P + D$ (or $V = D$ if the price is payable up front), where V is the buyer's subjective valuation, we expect both P and D to increase with V (both must increase in order to keep the seller at his reservation profit).[40] If a court-imposed remedy that makes breach more frequent were substituted for D (for example, a remedy that understated V), then the value of the contract to the parties would be reduced.

A second economic reason for enforcing seemingly excessive liquidated damage clauses is that one of the parties may be using it to signal his commitment to performing the contract, which he cannot credibly do by alternative means. In a sense, the high damage payment in this case functions as a bond to ensure performance.

Finally, enforcement of damages judged to be excessive ex post (i.e., at the time of breach) may be desirable if they were reasonable ex ante (i.e., at the time of formation). This divergence between ex ante and ex post estimates can happen if losses are random ex ante, and are set equal to their expected value, or if circumstances change in the interval between contract formation and breach. Some jurisdictions actually follow this rule and enforce damages that are reasonable ex ante, even if they are unreasonable ex post, whereas other jurisdictions never enforce unreasonable damages, whether evaluated ex ante or ex post (Rea, 1984).

The key difference between the examples of excessive liquidated damages in the previous section, where a limit was consistent with efficiency, and those in this section, where it is not, is that an external effect or a defect in formation of the contract was present in the former but not in the latter. When an externality or other defect is present, court-imposed restrictions on contract terms can enhance efficiency; otherwise, courts should generally enforce contract terms that are freely accepted by the contracting parties.

5. Specific Performance

Rather than requiring the payment of money damages, the remedy of *specific performance* is a court order requiring the party wishing to breach a contract to perform as promised. In practice, this remedy is rarely used, being limited to cases in which the court views money damages as an inadequate substitute for performance. For example, contracts for the purchase of land are subject to specific performance because land is seen as a "unique good" for which perfect substitutes are unavailable in the market. In contrast, economists have argued that there are good reasons for wider use of specific performance, even for nonunique goods.[41] In this section I will first review some of these arguments, which are based on transaction costs and the subjective valuation of performance. I will then formally examine the incentives specific performance creates for breach, reliance, and risk sharing in the context of the production uncertainty model.

5.1. Specific Performance versus Money Damages

5.1.1. TRANSACTION COSTS

For economists, the real issue in determining the optimal remedy for breach is what remedy achieves the most efficient allocation of resources, including in the calculation the transaction plus litigation costs of the alternative remedies. Presumably, transaction costs are low in most contract settings, given that the parties have already demonstrated an ability to bargain. This argues for minimal court involvement in resolving disputes, given the high costs of litigation. Moreover, the parties themselves are probably better able to fashion an efficient remedy compared to the court. For both of these reasons, specific performance is potentially a superior remedy compared to damages. First, because it requires less fact-finding activity by the court compared to a damage remedy, it involves lower litigation costs. Second, because the parties are better able to determine their respective costs and benefits of performance compared to the court, they will be more likely to set the correct price for performance. A further benefit of specific performance is that it will give the parties an incentive ex ante to stipulate a damage remedy, which will permit them to avoid the cost of court intervention altogether. Note that these arguments for limited court involvement in contract disputes contrast with the desirability for greater court involvement in accident cases due to the higher transaction costs in the latter.

5.1.2. PROTECTING SUBJECTIVE VALUATION

In addition to economizing on transaction costs, specific performance protects the promisee's subjective valuation of performance. The reason is that specific performance gives the promisee the right to demand performance (and therefore the right to discharge performance), whereas a damage remedy only gives her the right to *compensation* for the promisor's failure to perform.[42] Thus, under specific performance the promisor can get out of performing only by offering the promisee a payment that leaves the latter at least as well off as performance. On the one hand, this enhances the efficiency of contracting because it guarantees that breach will occur only when it is efficient. On the other hand, a damage remedy that undercompensates the promisor will lead to breach too often.

The risk of excessive breach under a damage remedy is dramatically illustrated by the case of *Peevyhouse* v. *Garland Coal Mining Company*.[43] The case concerned a contract between a private party, the Peevyhouses, and a strip-mining company. As part of the contract, the mining company agreed to repair the damage to the land after completing its mining operation. The company reneged on that promise, however, claiming that the cost of the repairs would have been $29,000, whereas the market value of the repairs (i.e., the amount that the repairs would have increased the value of the land) was only $300. The court agreed and discharged the company's obligation to perform the repairs while awarding damages of $300 to the Peevyhouses.

It seems clear in this case that $300 was a gross underestimate of the value of the repairs to the Peevyhouses (some evidence is that the Peevyhouses appealed an award of $5,000 granted at the trial). Thus, in awarding that amount, the court set the cost of breach for promisors too low. In contrast, specific performance would have required the mining company to negotiate with the Peevyhouses until a mutually beneficial outcome were reached. As a result, the efficient outcome (which may or may not have involved breach, depending on the Peevyhouses" valuation of the repairs relative to $29,000) would have been achieved.

In contracts where subjective value is not important, specific performance is not superior to expectation damages in terms of inducing efficient breach, but there is another reason to prefer it based on fairness. Because expectation damages require the promisor (breacher) to pay the promisee the value of performance, they award the promisor all of the surplus arising from breach (recall that under expectation damages, breach occurs only when it is more valuable than performance). In contrast, specific performance allows the promisee to obtain at least some of the surplus according to the bargaining abilities of the parties. Again, this is because specific performance awards the promisee the right to performance whereas damages only awards her the right to compensation.[44]

5.1.3. SITUATIONS WHEN SPECIFIC PERFORMANCE IS NOT DESIRABLE

Cooter and Ulen (1988, pp. 323–324) note two situations in which specific performance is not a desirable (or feasible) remedy. The first is when performance is physically impossible, though we shall see in the next chapter that in this case, the breacher may be able to avoid paying damages altogether. The second is when performance would require monitoring by the court, and the cost of such monitoring is high.

5.2. Breach and Reliance Under Specific Performance

In this section I examine in a more rigorous manner the incentives for breach and reliance under specific performance.[45] To do so, I modify the above model of contracting under production uncertainty as follows. Suppose that once the seller realizes his production cost, he must either perform or negotiate with the buyer to cancel performance for a mutually agreeable payment, denoted S. Note that this situation resembles liquidated damages, in that the "damage" payment is determined by the parties rather than being court imposed, but it differs in that here, the amount of the payment is determined *after* the production cost is realized rather than before.[46]

Consider first the parties' decision to perform or cancel performance (breach). Clearly, the seller will always perform if $P - C \geq 0$, and if $P - C < 0$, the most he will pay to get out of performing is $C - P$. At the same time, the minimum amount the buyer will accept to cancel performance is $V(r) - P$, given her sunk reliance r.[47] If there are no barriers to bargaining, cancellation will therefore occur whenever $C - P > V(r) - P$, or whenever $C > V(r)$, which is the condition for efficient breach given r. Thus, as we concluded above, the breach decision will generally be efficient under specific performance.

Now consider the buyer's choice of reliance. In order to examine this choice, we have to specify the value of S anticipated by the buyer, given that it is determined after C is realized. Suppose S divides the surplus from cancellation as follows (Rogerson, 1984):

$$
\begin{aligned}
S &= \alpha(V(r) - P) + (1 - \alpha)(C - P) \\
&= V(r) - P + (1 - \alpha)(C - V(r)).
\end{aligned}
\tag{4.35}
$$

Thus, the buyer gets a fraction $(1 - \alpha)$ of the surplus $C - V(r)$.

Given (4.35), we can write the buyer's expected return from the contract, at the time it is written, as

$$
\begin{aligned}
V_b &= F(V(r))[V(r) - P] + [1 - F(V(r))]E[S|C > V(r)] - r \\
&= V(r) - P + (1 + \alpha)\int_{V(r)}^{\infty}[C - V(r)]dF(C) - r.
\end{aligned}
\tag{4.36}
$$

Taking the derivative of (4.36) with respect to r and rearranging yields the condition for the buyer's optimal investment in reliance:

$$
F(V(r))V'(r) - 1 + \alpha[1 - F(V(r))]V'(r) = 0.
\tag{4.37}
$$

Comparing this to (4.2) shows that $r = r^*$ (optimal reliance) when $\alpha = 0$, and $r > r^*$ when $\alpha > 0$. Moreover, when $\alpha = 1$, (4.37) reduces to $V'(r) - 1 = 0$, the condition for reliance under expectation damages.

These results show that the buyer chooses optimal reliance under specific performance only when she expects to extract all of the surplus from bargaining over cancellation. Otherwise, she overinvests in reliance. Intuitively, if the buyer expects to obtain all of the surplus, she internalizes the joint value of contract, including the social benefit of cancellation, and therefore makes the right reliance decision. On the other hand, if the seller expects to obtain some of the surplus, the buyer overinvests in order to reduce the probability of cancellation.

5.3. Risk Sharing Under Specific Performance

Equation (4.35) shows that the payment the seller must make to cancel performance will be greater than or equal to the buyer's expectation interest, and less than or equal to the seller's (net) cost of performing in states where breach is efficient (i.e., where $C > V(r)$). Although the actual amount of this payment depends on α, and is therefore indeterminate, it generally will not allocate risk optimally because, as shown in section 2.1, the optimal damage payment is less than or equal to the buyer's expectation interest (Polinsky, 1983b).[48]

6. Summary

This chapter has examined various remedies for breach of contract. The basic theme was that courts should impose remedies that enhance the efficiency of contracting, given that parties are generally unable, owing to information costs, to write contracts that provide for all possible contingencies. The economic problems that the analysis focused on were efficient breach, efficient investment in transaction-specific assets (reliance), and risk sharing. Of the court-imposed damage remedies, only expectation damages led to efficient breach, but in doing so it gave promisees an incentive to overrely on the contract. Efficient breach and reliance could be achieved only by limiting expectation damages to the promisee's expectation interest at the efficient level of reliance. In general, no breach remedies simultaneously achieved efficient breach, reliance, and risk sharing.

Court-imposed remedies are desirable when the parties are unable to specify efficient contract terms on their own, either ex ante or ex post. However, when the parties have specified the terms under which breach can occur as part of the contract, or if there is reason to believe that they can do so at low cost after breach, economists have argued that courts should refrain from imposing terms. In particular, courts should enforce liquidated damage clauses unless there is reason to believe that an externality (third-party effect) is present, and specific performance should be more widely used as an alternative to money damages in cases of breach.

FIVE

THE ECONOMICS OF CONTRACT LAW

Mistake, Impossibility, and Other Doctrines

The preceding chapter was primarily concerned with various remedies for breach of contract, taking as a given that the contracts in question were judged to be enforceable. This chapter is largely concerned with the prior question of what contracts are enforceable. It therefore begins with a brief description of the elements that courts have traditionally required to be present in an enforceable promise, the most interesting of which is the doctrine of consideration. It then goes on to examine formation defenses, which argue that a contract is unenforceable because it was not legitimately formed, and performance excuses, which argue that a contract was legitimately formed but that the promisor's obligation to perform should nevertheless be discharged without damages.

It is important to point out that an economic analysis of the question of what contracts are enforceable is not independent of the question of what is the optimal remedy for breaching an enforceable contract. For example, if a court ruled that a given contract is unenforceable, and therefore that the promisor is not obliged to perform his promise, this would be essentially equivalent to ruling that the contract is enforceable, but that the appropriate remedy for the promisee is zero damages. The analysis of formation and performance defenses in this chapter adopts this unified view by examining them as alternative solutions to the general economic problems discussed in the previous chapter—namely, providing incentives for efficient breach, reliance, and risk sharing. I retain the basic model of contracting from the previous chapter as well.

In addition to formation defenses and performance excuses, this chapter examines the question of when contract modification should be enforced by the court. Contract modification represents an effort by the parties to adjust the terms of a contract after it has been signed but before it is performed, generally in response to changed circumstances. Thus, it represents an alternative to breach that will often involve lower transaction costs. However, it can also signify an attempt by one party to behave opportunistically as a result of a change in the relative bargaining powers of the parties. Thus, from an economic perspective, a key issue regarding enforcement is whether the proposed modifications are genuine responses to changed economic circumstances, in which case they enhance value, or are purely opportunistic attempts at redistribution.

1. Offer, Acceptance, and Consideration

Under the classic theory of contracts, an enforceable promise must constitute a "bargain," which consists of three elements: offer, acceptance, and considera-tion.[1] The first two elements are straightforward: one party must make an offer and the other party must accept it. That is, there must be a "meeting of the minds." The third element, consideration, is what makes the contract an exchange. Consideration represents that which the promisee offers in return for the promise made by the promisor. Although it typically takes the form of a promise to pay for the promisor's performance, it need not be monetary or even material. For example, in the famous case of *Hamer* v. *Sidway*,[2] an uncle promised to pay his nephew $5,000 if the nephew refrained from drinking and smoking until his twenty-first birthday. The court found that this was a valid contract because consideration was present in the nephew's promise to give up something of value in return for the uncle's promise of money. A key aspect of the treatment of consideration revealed by this case is that courts will generally not inquire into the *adequacy* of consideration, only whether it is *present*. This makes economic sense because it reflects the general principle that the parties are in a better position than the court to judge their valuation of the terms of a contract.[3]

2. Formation Defenses

Formation defenses permit the promisor to escape performance based on the argument that the contract was not validly formed. From an economic point of view, the purpose of formation defenses is to invalidate contracts that were formed under conditions inconsistent with a competitive environment, which is the paradigm for efficient exchange.[4] The standard formation defenses include fraud, duress, incompetence, unconscionability, and mistake. In the next section, I will briefly discuss the first four of these defenses, and in the following section, I will undertake a more detailed examination of the defense of mistake, which has received the most attention from economists.

2.1. Fraud, Duress, Incompetence, and Unconscionability

Fraud concerns the use of deceit or misrepresentation by one of the parties to secure more favorable contract terms. Since provision of false information can lead to inefficient (and unfair) contracts, it makes economic sense for the court to overturn contracts formed on this basis. It is less obvious, however, that con-tracts should be overturned if one of the parties failed to disclose known infor-mation. Indeed, the desirability of disclosure duties is one of the more interesting questions in the economic analysis of contracts. I will therefore address it in detail in the context of the doctrine of mistake.

The presence of duress or coercion also violates one of the crucial conditions for the formation of efficient contracts—namely, mutual consent. Thus, contracts formed under duress should not be enforced. Although duress can be the result of a threat of force, it need not be. Suppose, for example, that party A agrees to perform a service for party B for a specified price, but later, after B has committed to A's performance, A threatens not to perform unless B agrees to a price increase. In this case, A takes advantage of B's commitment to the contract, which has caused a shift in the bargaining power between the parties in A's favor (perhaps B has foregone other options or has relied on the performance).[5] Note, however, that this form of duress, which is generally grounds for overturning the contract, is quite different from the following threat made before a contract is formed: "Lower your price or I'll take my business elsewhere." The latter threat does not depend on any monopoly power acquired by the threatener as a result of a change in bargaining power within an existing contract; in fact, it works in the direction of *promoting* competition. Thus, from an economic perspective, it should not be grounds for overturning a contract.

The defense of incompetence is based on the notion that a minimal degree of rationality is necessary for a party to enter into a contract. Clearly, this conforms with the presumption of rationality that forms the basis for a mutually beneficial exchange.

The most recently accepted formation defense is unconscionability, which allows the court to nullify any contract whose terms appear to be especially one-sided or unfair.[6] In general, this is a "catchall" defense that serves a similar purpose as the doctrines of fraud, duress, and incompetence, but it allows discharge of a contract without specific proof of the existence of any of these conditions. Rather, the court infers their presence from the terms of the contract (Epstein, 1975).[7] Although this feature of unconscionability may save on litigation costs, it also runs the risk of "overinclusiveness"—that is, the risk that contracts not involving fraud, duress, or incompetence will nevertheless be overturned based solely on their appearance of unfairness (Schwartz, 1977). Clearly, this can work against efficiency to the extent that the parties are better judges of their valuations of a contract than is the court (absent specific proof of the existence of fraud, duress, or incompetence). Note finally that this defense also runs contrary to the traditional treatment of consideration by courts, which involves inquiry only into its existence, not its adequacy. Thus, it conflicts with the notion that the parties themselves are the best judges of whether the terms of a contract are mutually beneficial.

2.2. Imperfect Information and Mistake

The final type of formation defense is mistake. In order to motivate the economic analysis of this defense, I will describe two cases in which the question arose, one classic and one recent. The classic case is *Sherwood* v. *Walker*,[8] which concerned a contract for the sale of a cow. The buyer and the sellers had agreed on a price for the cow based on its value for slaughter, but prior to delivery, the sellers discovered that the cow was fertile, which greatly increased its value. They therefore refused to make delivery, which precipitated a lawsuit by the buyer. The court found for the defendants (sellers) based on the doctrine of mutual mistake, arguing that "it appear[ed] from the record that both parties supposed [the] cow was bárren and would not breed . . . " In contrast, a dissenting judge argued that the contract should have been enforced because he believed that the buyer knew the cow would breed. That is, the mistake was unilateral and therefore was not grounds for invalidating the contract.

The second case concerned the sale of a baseball card for $12, when in fact it was worth $1,200. The mistake was made by a clerk of the store who misinterpreted the price, which was marked "1200." The store owner filed suit in small claims court to recover the card, but the parties settled before a decision was rendered (Kull, 1992). This case represents an example of unilateral mistake, since the buyer, a twelve-year-old collector, almost certainly knew the card's true value at the time of purchase.

Traditionally, the law of contracts has distinguished between *mutual mistakes*, cases where both parties misunderstand the nature of the contract, and *unilateral mistakes*, where only one party misunderstands—the former being more likely to result in a voided contract. For example, the Restatement (Second) of Contracts states that, for a contract to be voidable owing to mutual mistake, (1) both parties must be mistaken about a basic assumption of the contract; (2) the mistake must have a material effect on performance; and (3) neither party must have assumed the risk, explicitly or implicitly.[9] For a contract to be voidable due to unilateral mistake, (1) one party must be mistaken about a basic assumption of the contract; (2) the mistake must have a material effect on performance; and (3) the mistaken party must not have assumed the risk. In addition, enforcement of the contract must be unconscionable, or the unmistaken party must have either caused the mistake or have had reason to know of it.[10] In the following sections, I will review the principal economic arguments concerning the mistake doctrine. In particular, I will ask when mistake (mutual or unilateral) should be grounds for discharge of a contract.

2.3. Unilateral Mistake and Disclosure of Information

Most economic analyses have focused on the case of unilateral mistake. The basic question in these situations is whether a party with private information has a duty to disclose that information before contracting. For example, Kronman (1978) argued that the answer is yes if the private information was obtained casually, but no if it was obtained by deliberate search. This distinction provides an incentive for parties to produce information at a socially desirable level by giving them a property right in that information. Alternatively, Cooter and Ulen (1988, pp. 257–261) distinguished between socially productive and purely redistributive information, arguing that parties should be required to disclose only redistributive information. (Thus, they focused on the nature of the information rather than on the manner in which it was acquired.) Again, nondisclosure of productive information provides parties an incentive to acquire it in an efficient manner. Posner (1992, p. 102) argued that when the parties have not explicitly or implicitly assigned the risk from mistake, the seller should generally bear it because, having possession of the article, he or she can avoid mistakes at a lower cost than the buyer. That is, the seller is generally the better risk bearer. For example, in *Sherwood* v. *Walker*, the seller is probably in a better position than the buyer to determine the fertility of the cow, and in the baseball card case, the seller can be sure that prices are correctly and clearly marked. Thus, in both cases the sale should have been upheld.

Shavell (1994) examined in a more formal way the general question of when disclosure of private information, acquired at cost, should be mandatory or voluntary prior to exchange. His conclusions depend on whether the information has social value or is merely redistributive (Hirshleifer, 1971; Cooter and Ulen, 1988), and on whether it is the buyer or seller who can acquire it. When sellers can acquire the information, disclosure should be mandatory, since voluntary disclosure leads to excessive acquisition of information, both when the information is valuable and when it is not. When buyers can acquire the information, disclosure should also be mandatory when it is not socially valuable in order to discourage inefficient acquisition of nonvaluable information. However, when information is socially valuable, a voluntary disclosure rule may be a desirable way to encourage buyers to acquire valuable information. The asymmetry of the results for buyers and sellers in the case of valuable information apparently stems from the initial distribution of property rights over the article being exchanged, which lie with the seller. Specifically, buyers must be given rights over valuable information they acquire (the right to withhold it) in order to prevent sellers from profiting from it by simply raising the price.

The following section examines some of these issues in a more formal manner. I will not attempt to cover all possible economic aspects of the mistake doctrine, but rather suggest how economic theory can be used to evaluate its impact on efficiency and income distribution. In conducting the analysis, I will focus on the question of when performance should be excused as a result of mistake, whether it be mutual or unilateral.

2.4. A Formal Analysis of Mistake

Consider a contract for the exchange of a good of uncertain quality between a risk-neutral buyer and seller.[11] For example, consider a cow that may be fertile (F) or barren (B). Let V^F be the value of a fertile cow to a breeder, and let V^B be the value of a barren cow to a butcher, where $V^F > V^B$. Also, let q be the (known) frequency of barren cows. Thus, the expected value of a cow of uncertain type is $V^e = qV^B + (1 - q)V^F$.

2.4.1. INFORMATION IS CASUALLY ACQUIRED

Assume initially that information is casually acquired by the parties. For example, although they may be uncertain about the cow's type before exchange, the type is revealed with certainty afterwards regardless of who ends up with the cow. This scenario thus resembles the (apparent) facts of the *Sherwood* v. *Walker* case.

Once the cow's type is learned, two contract rules are possible. The first is *no excuse*, or enforcement of the contract, and the second is *excuse for mistake*. Under the latter, the seller can demand the cow back if it turns out to be fertile, and the buyer can return the cow if it turns out to be barren. Note, therefore, that mistake represents a type of court-imposed, two-way warranty: in the first case, the seller has a "guarantee" that the cow is barren, and in the second, the buyer has a "guarantee" that the cow is fertile (Smith and Smith, 1990). In the case where information about the cow's type is acquired casually, the only efficiency issue is whether the cow ends up with its highest valuing user.

Consider first the case where both parties are uncertain about the cow's type (but they agree on V^e). Assume for simplicity that the contract price reflects the value of the cow to the buyer given the excuse rule (i.e., the seller obtains any surplus from a transaction).[12] Thus, under a rule of no excuse, the price of the cow is V^e. When the cow's type is determined, the buyer realizes either V^F or V^B. If the buyer is a breeder, he resells it to a butcher if the cow is barren; if he is a butcher, he resells it to a breeder if it is fertile. Notice, therefore, that if $q = 1/2$, then the expected number of transactions needed for the cow to reach its highest valued use is 1.5.[13]

Consider next the case where the seller sells the cow under a rule of excuse for mutual mistake. In this case there are two possibilities. On the one hand, if the buyer is a breeder, the price is V^F and the buyer can return the cow if it turns out to be barren. In this case, the seller will resell the cow to a butcher. On the other hand, if the buyer is a butcher, the price is V^B and the seller can reclaim the cow and sell it to a breeder if it turns out to be fertile. In both cases, if $q = 1/2$, the expected number of transactions is again 1.5 given that the probability of resale is 1/2.

In all of the above cases, the cow ends up in its most valuable use through recontracting. This is an example of the Coase theorem. Thus, the only efficiency issue is the cost of transacting (assuming it is costless to implement the mistake rule). Smith and Smith (1990) therefore conclude that, because the expected number of transactions is the same with and without excuse, the doctrine does not affect efficiency under symmetric (mutual) uncertainty.

Now suppose information may be asymmetric—that is, one party may know the cow's type prior to exchange. Since it is most likely that the seller will have superior knowledge about the quality of the article, I examine that case.[14] Thus, let α be the fraction of sellers who know the cow's type, and let $1 - \alpha$ be the fraction of sellers who, along with all buyers, are uncertain about the cow's type.

Observe first that sellers who know their cow is fertile will reveal that fact and charge a price of V^F, regardless of the legal rule.[15] Rational buyers will therefore infer that silent sellers either possess a barren cow or a cow of unknown type. Using this information, buyers can calculate the conditional probability that a cow offered by a silent seller is barren. This probability is given by[16]

$$q^* = q/[q + (1 - \alpha)(1 - q)]. \tag{5.1}$$

Note that $q^* > q$ given $\alpha > 0$.

Now consider the outcome under the two excuse rules. First, under a rule of no excuse, silent sellers will only be able to charge a price of $q^*V^B + (1 - q^*)V^F$, which is less than V^e. As a result, uninformed sellers are hurt by asymmetric information since the expected value of their cow is actually V^e. Alternatively, informed owners of barren cows benefit since $q^*V^B + (1 - q^*)V^F > V^B$. This is an example of the "lemons" (or adverse selection) problem, where sellers of inferior-quality products attempt to benefit from buyer ignorance by masquerading as sellers of high-quality products (Akerlof, 1970).

Under a rule of excuse for mistake, owners who know their cows are barren will no longer have an advantage in concealing their type, and will therefore sell them to butchers for V^B. Uninformed owners will either sell to breeders for V^F with the condition that the cow will be returned if barren, or to butchers for V^B with the condition that they can demand them back if fertile. In either case, their expected return is V^e (ignoring transaction costs). This shows that uninformed owners prefer warranted sales to unwarranted sales, all else equal, since they can avoid the lemon problem. Thus, if warranties are costly to write, owners are better off under a rule of excuse for mistake compared to no excuse.

In terms of transaction costs, it turns out that if the prevailing excuse rule is applied to all contracts, then the two rules again result in the same number of expected transactions. To see this, note first that if $q = 1/2$, then $q^* > 1/2$. Thus, under a rule of no excuse, the number of transactions needed for the cow to reach its highest valuing user is minimized if silent sellers sell initially to butchers. (I assume that sellers pay the transaction costs and therefore wish to minimize them; Smith and Smith, 1990.) Thus, resale will only be necessary for uninformed owners of fertile cows. The expected number of transactions is therefore

$$\alpha(1 - q) + (1 - \alpha)q + \alpha q + (1 - \alpha)(1 - q)2.$$

Substituting $q = .5$ into this expression yields $1.5 - \alpha(.5)$. Thus, if $\alpha = 1$ all owners are informed and only one transaction is necessary (i.e., owners of barren cows cannot conceal their type), whereas if $\alpha = 0$, the situation is identical to the symmetric uncertainty case and 1.5 transactions are necessary on average. In general, $\alpha > 0$ lowers the average number of transactions compared to the symmetric uncertainty case.

Under excuse for mistake, both types of informed owners require only one transaction—owners of fertile cows because they willingly reveal their type, and owners of barren cows because they gain nothing from concealing their type. As for uninformed owners, they are indifferent about whom to sell to initially (given $q = 1/2$), and on average 1.5 transactions are necessary. Combining these cases yields an expected number of transactions equal to $\alpha + (1 - \alpha)1.5 = 1.5 - \alpha(.5)$, which is the same as above. This shows that, in terms of transaction costs, neither rule is preferred, as in the symmetric information case. What an excuse rule does, however, is prevent informed owners of barren cows from redistributing wealth to themselves and away from uninformed owners.[17] Thus, the effect of the excuse rule when information is casually acquired is purely distributional.

2.4.2. INFORMATION CAN BE PRODUCED BY THE PARTIES

In this section I modify the above model to allow one of the parties to produce information at a cost, assuming initially that both parties are uninformed. Rather than consider all possible cases, I will assume only the seller can produce information prior to exchange.

Suppose all buyers and sellers are initially uninformed about the cow's type, but sellers can learn the type before exchange at cost c. Also suppose that, if the seller does not learn the type, it is revealed anyway after trade. Thus, learning the information before trade can be socially valuable only by economizing on transaction costs—that is, by getting the cow to its highest valued use with fewer transactions. Specifically, suppose the cost per transaction is t. If the seller does not acquire information before trade, we saw earlier that, with symmetric uncertainty, the expected number of transactions needed to move the cow to its highest valuing user is 1.5 given $q = 1/2$. Thus, total transaction costs are $1.5t$. If, however, the seller spends c to learn the cow's type, only one transaction will be required, costing t. Thus, it is socially valuable to spend c if $c < .5t$ (Smith and Smith, 1990). (Note that $t = 0$ represents the case where information never has social value (Shavell, 1994).)

Now consider the seller's *private* incentives to spend c. Assume that the buyer is unaware of the seller's decision to test, so the latter can conceal unfavorable results, but can reveal favorable results at no cost. Also assume (without loss of generality) that the seller pays the transaction costs. Under a rule of no excuse, if the seller does not test the cow the price is V^e, and the expected transaction costs are $1.5t$ Thus, the seller's expected return is $V^e - 1.5t$.

If the seller does test, she will reveal the result if the cow is fertile and receive $V^F - t$ by selling to the breeder, but she will conceal the result if the cow is barren and receive $V^e - t$ by selling to the butcher.[18] Thus, the seller's net return from testing is

$$-c + q(V^e - t) + (1 - q)(V^F - t) = -c + qV^e + (1 - q)V^F - t.$$

She will therefore test if

$$-c + qV^e + (1 - q)V^F - t > V^e - 1.5t.$$

When $q = 1/2$, this condition becomes

$$c < .5t + .5(V^F - V^e) \qquad (5.2)$$

It follows from (5.2) that under a rule of no excuse, the seller will test *too often*, given that the private return exceeds the social return by the term $.5(V^F - V^e)$. Moreover, the seller may test even when information has no social value (i.e., when $t = 0$).

Note that the term $.5(V^F - V^e)$ in (5.2) reflects the seller's ability to conceal unfavorable results of the test but to reveal favorable ones. This ability requires that buyers not be able to infer an unfavorable result from the seller's silence, which in turn requires that buyers are either naive or ignorant of the possible existence of private information on the part of the seller. Scheppele (1988) refers to the latter situation as the seller's having a "deep secret." In contrast, a "shallow secret" is one whose existence is known by the uninformed party, although he does not know the *content* of the secret. Scheppele argues that rational individuals behind a veil of ignorance would choose a legal rule that compels disclosure of deep secrets but not shallow secrets. In the current example, such a rule is consistent with efficiency because the depth of the secret—the fact that the buyer cannot infer an unfavorable result from silence—leads to an inefficient incentive to test. As we have seen, however, such a rule might not be efficient if the deep secret concerned socially valuable information, since a disclosure requirement might impede incentives for parties to gather the information in the first place (Craswell and Schwartz, 1994, p. 171).

Now consider the seller's incentive to test under a rule of excuse for mistake. If the seller does not conduct the test, she can either sell the cow to the butcher for V^B and reclaim it if it is fertile, or sell it to the breeder for V^F and accept return if it is barren. When $q = 1/2$, she is indifferent as both yield a net expected return of $V^e - 1.5t$.

If the seller conducts the test, she will sell it to the breeder for V^F if it is fertile, and she will sell it to the butcher for V^B if it is barren. Thus, she no longer has the ability to conceal the cow's type in the event of an unfavorable result since barren cows sold as fertile will simply be returned. Thus, the seller's expected return from testing is now $V^e - t - c$. In this case, the seller's decision to test is equivalent to the social decision. Consequently, when information can be acquired at cost, the mistake doctrine is preferred on efficiency grounds, provided that it is costless to administer (Smith and Smith, 1990).

If litigation costs are positive, however, excuse for mistake will not necessarily dominate no excuse (Rasmusen and Ayres, 1993). To illustrate, suppose litigation costs of L are incurred to void a contract when a mistake is discovered (assume the seller pays them). Note that L is relevant only when the seller does not test, since if she tests, she will always reveal the cow's type.[19] The expected return from not testing is now $V^e - 1.5t - .5L$, where the final term is the expected litigation cost. The condition for testing thus becomes

$$c < .5t + .5L. \qquad (5.3)$$

The seller again will test too often compared to the zero litigation cost case because of the expected litigation costs. Moreover, a comparison of (5.2) and (5.3) shows that the seller will have a greater incentive to test under excuse for mistake if $L > V^F - V^e$. Thus, if litigation costs are high, a rule of no excuse may be the more efficient rule.

2.5. Mutual versus Unilateral Mistake

The foregoing analysis has not attempted to distinguish formally between excuse for mutual and excuse for unilateral mistake. Rather, it has assumed that excuse for mistake, when available, could be invoked if one or both of the parties were initially uncertain. Rasmusen and Ayres (1993), however, have tried to distinguish between the two doctrines in an effort to determine whether the distinction the law makes is sensible. The issues they examine are similar to those discussed earlier: promotion of efficient exchange, production of information, and risk allocation. They conclude that making discharge easier under mutual mistake is *not* generally consistent with efficiency.

3. Performance Excuses

A performance excuse represents an argument by the promisor that, despite the validity of the contract, he should nevertheless be discharged from performance as a result of some contingency. Traditional defenses of this sort include *frustration of purpose*, which describes a situation where the purpose of the contract has been destroyed, and *physical impossibility*, which is a situation in which performance has become physically impossible. More recently, courts have also excused performance based on *commercial impracticability*, or the claim that, owing to some unforeseen contingency, performing the contract would be economically burdensome for the promisor.

The first two of these excuses (frustration of purpose and impossibility) represent changes in circumstances that are generally unrelated to market conditions. For example, they are the result of "acts of God," like a fire or death of the promisor. In contrast, commercial impracticability concerns a change in market conditions. Goldberg (1988) has argued that this distinction is important because, if the parties could have bargained over acceptable performance excuses beforehand, they would have included nonmarket changes (acts of God), but they probably would not have included market changes. The reason is that, in the event of a nonmarket change, the cost to the promisee of finding a substitute may be either higher or lower—and in expected terms it will be zero—because the change will not be systematically correlated with the cost or price of performance. In contrast, in the event of a market change, the promisor most likely wants to be excused because the contract price is too low. Consequently, it will generally be costlier for the promisee to find a substitute. Thus, at the time the contract is formed, the expected cost to the promisee of an impossibility defense is high if market changes are included, but may be low if only acts of God are included.

Although this argument suggests reasons for allowing the promisor to *breach* a contract, note that it does not fully justify the impossibility defense because it offers no reason for setting damages equal to zero (Goldberg, 1988). To justify this provision, we will have to ask whether breach of contract with *zero damages* ever promotes efficiency of risk sharing, breach, or reliance. When we do this, it will turn out that a version of the commercial impracticability defense may in fact be desirable in certain circumstances.

3.1. Impossibility and Risk-sharing

As suggested in the previous chapter, the analysis of contract remedies from the perspective of risk sharing asks how the risks from an unforeseen contingency should be shared ex post between the parties. The problem for the court is to determine, after the fact, how the parties would have allocated the risk if they could have foreseen it, and then to replicate this outcome with a court-imposed remedy. Posner and Rosenfield (1977) have examined the impossibility defense from this perspective.[20]

They argue that the promisor should be excused from performance without paying damages if the promisee is the superior risk bearer, but the promisor should not be excused if he is the superior risk bearer. To determine the superior risk bearer, the court should ask which party was in a better position to have *prevented or reduced* the risk,[21] or, if it could not have been prevented, which party was in a better position to have *insured* against the risk.

To illustrate how the court might determine the superior risk bearer in a given case (for it must be a case-specific inquiry), let us consider one of Posner and Rosenfield's examples. Suppose a supplier contracts to deliver a certain quantity of an agricultural product on a given date, but an unexpected drought prevents delivery. In cases of this sort, courts have generally discharged the contract when the supplier is a *grower*, but not when the supplier is a *dealer*. Posner and Rosenfield argue that this distinction makes sense in terms of the optimal allocation of risk (even if courts do not justify the distinction in those terms). In the case of a grower, the buyer is the superior risk bearer, they argue, because the buyer can diversify his purchases geographically to insure against regional variations in weather, whereas the grower cannot diversify. In the case of a supplier-dealer, the same reasoning suggests that the supplier can diversify his sources of supply and thereby efficiently bear the risk. More generally, the optimal risk bearer is the party that is better able to assess the magnitude and probability of the risk, and/or the party that can more easily self-insure or obtain market insurance.

3.2. Risk-sharing, Breach, and Impossibility

The preceding section suggested that discharge owing to impossibility (or commercial impracticability) should be granted when the promisee (the buyer) is the superior risk bearer. This implicitly assumed that zero damages are efficient in that case, whereas positive damages are efficient in the case where the promisor (the seller) is the superior risk bearer. However, our analysis in the preceding chapter suggested that, in general, zero damages are not optimal from a risk-sharing perspective, and further, that they would never lead to the correct breach decision. In this section, I ask whether those conclusions remain true when risk sharing and breach are considered simultaneously. The analysis is based on the unified treatment of these criteria by White (1988).[22]

The model is similar to that in section 2 of the previous chapter. The value of performance to the buyer is V, the buyer's fixed (and sunk) investment in reliance is r, the price is P, a fraction a of which is prepaid, and the seller's normal production cost is C_l, where $V - r - C_l > 0$, making the contract profitable. There is some probability, however, that the seller will realize an exceptionally high cost, C_h, such that $C_h > P$, in which case it is unprofitable for him to perform. In this case, we have seen that it is efficient for the seller to breach if the cost of performance exceeds the buyer's valuation, or if $C_h > V$, given that r is sunk. We have also seen that the damage measure that induces efficient breach is expectation damages. Recall that expectation damages leave the buyer indifferent between performance and breach. Thus, in this case D solves $D - aP - r = V - P - r$, yielding $D = V - (1 - a)P$. To verify that this induces efficient breach, observe that the seller will breach if $P - C_h < aP - D$, or, substituting for D, if $V < C_h$.

Now combine this with efficient risk bearing. As in the previous chapter, we consider four cases, depending on the risk preferences of the two parties. First, if both parties are risk neutral, then only efficient breach matters, so expectation damages is optimal. Second, if the seller is risk neutral and the buyer is risk averse, optimal risk sharing implies that the seller should bear all the risk. That is, the buyer's income should be the same in both the breach and nonbreach state, but this also yields expectation damages. Thus, the optimal remedy for breach and risk-sharing coincide in this case.

In the third case, the seller is risk averse and the buyer is risk neutral. Optimal risk sharing thus dictates that the seller's income be the same in the breach and nonbreach states, or that $P - C_l = aP - D$. Thus, $D = C_l - (1 - a)P$. If we substitute this value of D into the seller's breach decision, we find that he will breach if $C_l < C_h$, which in general will lead to excessive breach given that $V > C_l$ by assumption. In the final case, both parties are risk averse. Thus, the damage amount that optimally shares risk will be between the previous two; that is

$$C_l - (1 - a)P < D < V - (1 - a)P. \qquad (5.4)$$

Again, this will lead to excessive breach. Thus, only the first two cases are consistent with both efficient breach and risk sharing.

In order for the impossibility defense, as defined here, to be consistent with efficient breach and risk sharing, $D = 0$ would have to be optimal in some cases. Note first that $D = 0$ can never be consistent with efficient breach because the latter requires $D = V - (1 - a)P$, which is strictly positive by assumption. As for efficient risk sharing, $D = 0$ is possible if the range in (5.4) contains zero. This requires that $C_1 - (1 - a)P$ be negative, which is possible for small enough a since $P > C_1$. Thus, if the pre-paid portion of the price is not too large and the seller is risk averse, then $D = 0$ can be optimal from a risk-sharing perspective. However, this represents a special case. Consequently, the Posner and Rosenfield (1977) argument that discharge is an efficient method for risk sharing is not generally true, even if the seller (promisor) is risk averse.

3.3. Breach, Reliance, and Impossibility

The preceding section suggested that the impossibility defense does not fit neatly into the general economic theory of contract breach, at least in terms of efficient risk sharing and breach. Although it was potentially consistent with risk sharing in certain cases, it was never consistent with efficient breach, which requires expectation damages. In this section, I will show that if we adopt a slightly different interpretation of impossibility, that interpretation can lead to efficient breach and reliance.[23]

The reason impossibility failed to achieve efficient breach in the previous section is that we defined it to be a zero damage remedy, which will always induce excessive breach. But impossibility is not really a zero damage remedy because it does not discharge the promisor's obligation to perform in *all* states; rather, it allows discharge only in those states where performance is physically impossible or commercially impracticable. In other states, the promisor is obliged to perform or to pay damages. This suggests that discharge owing to impossibility is contingent on the state of nature, rather than being a blanket defense.

To examine the impact on incentives of this alternative interpretation, let us consider in particular the commercial impracticability defense, which allows discharge if performance is economically burdensome to the promisor.[24] This can be done in the context of the model of production uncertainty from the previous chapter. In particular, let the seller's cost of performance, C, be a random variable with distribution function $F(C)$, and let $V(r)$ be the buyer's value of performance as a function of reliance, r, where $V' > 0$. In this setting, recall that breach is efficient when $C > V(r)$, given r, and that optimal reliance solves the equation[25]

$$F(V(r))V'(r) = 1. \tag{5.5}$$

We have seen that an expectation damage remedy will result in efficient breach given r, but that it will result in overreliance unless damages are limited to the buyer's expectation interest evaluate at r^*. As an alternative possible solution, consider a damage remedy that has the following form:

$$D = \begin{matrix} V(r) - P, & \text{if } C \le T \\ 0, & \text{if } C > T. \end{matrix} \qquad (5.6)$$

According to (5.6), if the promisor breaches, he pays expectation damages if his production costs are less than (or equal to) a threshold, T, but zero damages if his costs exceed a threshold. The seller's obligation to pay damages is thus contingent on his realized cost of performance: if that cost exceeds a particular level, he is excused from paying damages altogether. This rule thus resembles the commercial impracticability defense as reinterpreted above.

The question is, will (5.6) induce efficient breach and reliance? The answer is yes given a suitable choice of T. First, consider the breach decision. It follows from (5.6) that, in the range where $C \le T$, the seller will breach efficiently given the obligation to pay expectation damages over this range. Alternatively, in the range where $C > T$, the seller will breach when performance is unprofitable, or when $C > P$, which implies excessive breach given that $V(r) > P$. Now suppose that $P \le T < V(r)$, as shown in figure 5.1, panel (a). In that case, the seller will breach for any $C > T$ since $C > P$ over this range, and he will perform for $C \le T$ since $C < V(r)$ over this range.[26] Since $T < V(r)$ by construction, the seller will breach too often in this case.

Now suppose that $T = V(r)$ as shown in figure 5.1, panel (b). In this case, the seller will breach when $C > T$ (since $D = 0$ and $C > P$) and perform when $C \le T$ (since $D = V(r) - P$ and $C \le V(r)$). Thus, the breach decision is efficient. Finally, consider the case where $T > V(r)$, as shown in panel (c). In this case, the seller will breach when $C > T$ (since $D = 0$ and $C > P$), but he will also breach when C is between $V(r)$ and T. This is true because $D = V(r) - P$

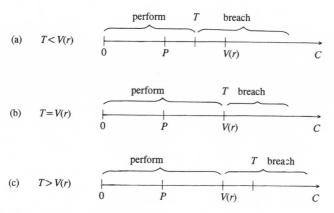

FIGURE 5.1 The promisor's breach decision under commercial impracticability when the cost of performance is uncertain.

and $C > V(r)$; that is, breach is efficient over this range. By the same argument, the seller performs when $C \leq V(r)$ because $D = V(r) - P$ and performance is efficient.

This argument shows that breach will occur efficiently, given r, provided that $T \geq V(r)$. Now consider the buyer's reliance decision. The preceding argument and (5.6) imply that the buyer's expected return from the contract is given by

$$
\begin{aligned}
F(V(r))[V(r) - P] &+ [F(T) - F(V(r))][V(r) - P] - r \\
&= F(T)[V(r) - P] - r,
\end{aligned}
\tag{5.7}
$$

where the term $F(T) - F(V(r))$ in the first line is nonnegative given $T \geq V(r)$. The buyer's problem is to choose r to maximize (5.7), which yields the first-order condition

$$
F(T)V'(r) + [V(r) - P]f(T)(\partial T / \partial r) - 1 = 0.
\tag{5.8}
$$

Comparing this condition to (5.5) shows that efficiency requires $T = V(r)$ and $\partial T / \partial r = 0$. These conditions are simultaneously satisfied if we set $T = V(r^*)$.

This result implies that the contract should be discharged in exactly the range of C where breach is efficient. This rule achieves efficient behavior by both the promisor and promisee using the same principle as the negligence rule in torts. Specifically, it allows one party (the promisor) to avoid paying damages based on a threshold criterion, and it forces the other party (the promisee) to bear her own damages in equilibrium. Another version of (5.6) that exploits this same principle would be to set $D = V(r) - P$ if $r \leq r^*$ and $D = 0$ if $r > r^*$. This sets the threshold according to efficient behavior by the promisee rather than the promisor (as was the case with (5.6)). This version, however, apparently has no counterpart in actual contract law.[27] Yet another version is the limited expectation-damages remedy discussed in the previous chapter (section 1.2.4).

The question of interest here is how well the damage rule in (5.6) explains the commercial impracticability doctrine. One problem is that, in an efficient equilibrium, the promisor would never pay damages for breach, a result that seems contrary to reality.[28] In addition, performance in cases where $C > V(r^*)$ does not appear to be truly impracticable in the sense intended, for example, by the Uniform Commercial Code. Thus, we must conclude that this theory does not provide a complete explanation for the doctrine (Sykes, 1990, p. 63).

A final observation concerns risk aversion. None of the models we have examined have been able to address simultaneously the three criteria of breach, reliance, and risk sharing. The model in this section, for example, is not consistent with optimal risk sharing because in breach states damages are zero, which we know is not generally optimal. It therefore appears that any doctrine attempting to address all three criteria can yield only a second-best solution (Sykes, 1990).

3.4. Summary: Optimal Precaution Against Breach

The economic analysis of mistake and impossibility in this chapter, and of limited liability in the previous chapter, are unified by a common thread—namely, the goal of inducing parties to take optimal precaution against breach.[29] This outcome requires that promisors internalize the social costs and benefits of performance in making their breach decisions, and that promisees consider the cost of breach in making their reliance choice or in deciding what information to reveal prior to contracting.

Although expectation damages provides good incentives for promisors regarding breach, we saw that unrestricted compensation for promisees can lead to moral hazard (overreliance) and adverse selection (nondisclosure) problems. We have also seen, however, that the doctrines of mistake, commercial impracticability, and limited liability, when coupled with expectation damages, were capable of resolving these problems by limiting compensation to promisees. Thus, although the various contract doctrines appear quite different and are applied in different factual situations, economic theory provides a framework for viewing them in a common light.

4. Contract Modification: The Preexisting Duty Rule

Up to now, we have assumed that circumstances that make performance of a contract unprofitable for the promisor, given the contract terms and breach remedy, will generally result in breach. In that event, the court decides the final assignment of liability. In some cases, however, the parties can avoid breach by agreeing to modify the original terms of the contract. For example, if a seller's cost of production turns out to be too high, he may be induced to perform rather than breach if the price is increased. In this section, I examine the law governing such modifications—specifically, when they are enforceable—and then ask whether the prevailing law is consistent with efficiency.

4.1. The Law of Contract Modification

Recall from section 1 that under traditional contract law, the presence of consideration is an essential element of an enforceable contract. In the case of contract modifications, courts have held that they are enforceable only if the modification is supported by additional consideration. That is, the party seeking the modified terms must also promise to give up something in return; satisfying the original promise is not sufficient to support the modification. This requirement of additional consideration is referred to as the *preexisting duty rule*.

Economists view the problem of contract modification in a different way. Rather than focusing on the presence or absence of fresh consideration, they ask whether the proposed modification is efficiency enhancing or merely an attempt by one party to extract a larger share of the surplus from the exchange.

In the former case, the modification should be enforced, but in the latter it should not be.

Posner has argued that, despite the preexisting duty rule, courts seem to have been sensitive to this distinction.[30] For example, in the case of *Goebel* v. *Linn*,[31] the court enforced a price increase that a purchaser of ice had agreed to pay to the supplier, despite the absence of additional consideration. The buyer had agreed to the price increase because he had no alternative source and had relied on the promised delivery. He was therefore susceptible to opportunism. However, the ice supplier required the higher price because a warm winter had resulted in a poor "ice crop." Thus, the modification was a good-faith attempt by the supplier to avoid breach and possibly bankruptcy.

The court ruled differently in *Alaska Packers' Assn.* v. *Domenico*.[32] In this case, a group of seamen were hired for a fishing voyage at a preset wage. Once at sea, however, the seamen refused to work unless their wage was raised. The employer gave in, having no alternative supply of workers, but later reneged on the agreement. In this case, the court did not enforce the modification, given that it was clearly opportunistic and not based on a genuine change in economic circumstances (the cost of fishing had not changed), in contrast to the previous case. Consistent with these two rulings, both the Uniform Commercial Code[33] and the Restatement (Second) of Contracts[34] allow enforcement of modifications if they are made in good faith and in the presence of unforeseen circumstances.

In the next section I will develop a simple model of modifications to examine in greater detail the conditions under which modifications will occur.[35] The key factors turn out to be whether promisees view breach as a good substitute for performance, and whether promisees can observe promisors' cost of performance. Based on these results, I will draw implications for the efficiency of enforcement of modifications.[36]

4.2. An Economic Model of Contract Modification

Consider a contract between risk neutral buyer B and seller S. Let V be the (fixed) value of performance to the buyer and let P be the initially agreed upon price, where $V > P$. As before, the seller's cost of performance, C, is unknown at the time the price is set, though both parties know its distribution $F(C)$. Although a fully contingent contract would account for all possible realizations of C, perhaps by specifying a price schedule, I assume that this is too costly.[37]

When C is realized, S and possibly B observe its value. At that time, S has three options: perform, breach, or seek modification. If S performs, the payoffs are $P - C$ and $V - P$ for S and B, respectively. If S breaches, the parties can either go to court—in which case they incur litigation costs of l_S and l_B, and S pays B damages of D—or they can settle out of court. The condition for settlement is that S pay B an amount m that makes both parties better off than going to trial would. Given the payoffs from trial, the condition for settlement is

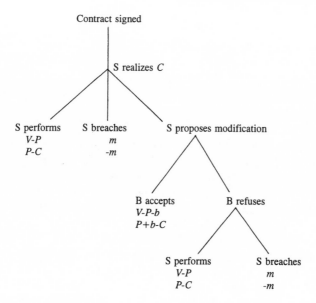

FIGURE 5.2 Sequence of decisions that may result in modified performance of a contract rather than breach.

$$D - l_B \leq m \leq D + l_S \tag{5.9}$$

This condition always holds given positive litigation costs. Thus, I assume that the parties always settle out of court. In other words, S "buys out" the contract. In this case, the payoffs are m and $-m$ for B and S, respectively.

The final option for S is to propose that B pay a price increase of b dollars as a condition for performance. If B rejects the proposal, S must either perform or buy out the contract. If B accepts, S performs, yielding a payoff of $V - P - b$ for B and $P + b - C$ for S.[38] If S refuses, the payoffs are as described above. The sequence of decisions and the payoffs are shown in figure 5.2, where at each endpoint B's payoff is listed above S's payoff.

Which of these outcomes—performance, buy out, or modification—occurs in equilibrium depends on several factors. One is whether B observes S's cost of performance prior to S's performance decision. I begin by considering the case where B observes C. In deriving the equilibrium, I assume that modifications are enforceable.

4.2.1. THE BUYER OBSERVES THE SELLER'S COST OF PERFORMANCE

As usual, the equilibrium is derived in reverse sequence of time. Thus, the final decision is whether S buys out the contract or performs, given B's refusal to modify. Given the payoffs in figure 5.2, S will perform if

$$P - C \geq -m, \text{or}$$
$$m \geq C - P \tag{5.10}$$

and buy out if the reverse is true. Since $m > 0$, a sufficient (but not necessary) condition for performance is $P - C \geq 0$. Thus, whenever the contract is profitable for S, he will perform.

At the previous stage, B decides whether to accept the modified price given that S has proposed it. Since B can observe C in the current scenario, B knows if (5.10) is satisfied or not. If it is satisfied, B knows that if she refuses modification, S will perform. Clearly, B will therefore refuse any price increase (i.e., $b \geq 0$) in this case. On the other hand, if (5.10) does not hold, B knows S will buy out the contract if B refuses modification. Thus, B will accept modification if and only if

$$V - P - b \geq m, \text{ or}$$
$$V - P \geq b + m. \tag{5.11}$$

Whether this condition holds depends on the particular values of m and b. Suppose that m is equal to its lower bound in (5.9), $D - l_B$, plus an amount ϵ that reflects B's share of the surplus from the settlement. Substituting $m = D - l_B + \epsilon$ into (5.11) and rearranging yields

$$b \leq [(V - P) - D] + l_B - \epsilon. \tag{5.12}$$

The right-hand side of (5.12) reflects the largest possible price increase that B would accept to avoid a buyout. It has three elements. The first is the expression in brackets, which represents the amount, if any, that damages *undercompensate* B compared to performance. Note, for example, that this term vanishes under expectation damages, though in certain circumstances even expectation damages may not be a perfect substitute for performance.[39]

The second term is the buyer's litigation costs of breach. Although these are not actually incurred in a buyout, they affect B's bargaining position adversely.[40] The final element, ϵ, is B's expected surplus from a buyout. The larger that is, the lower is the upper bound on b. In general, the upper bound on b reflects those factors that make buyout inferior to performance.

If the right-hand side of (5.12) is positive, modification is possible. The next question is whether S will propose modification. First, if (5.10) holds, we saw that S prefers performance over a buyout, and that B will refuse any price increase. Thus, S performs.

If, however, (5.10) does not hold, S prefers a buyout over performance. The condition for S to prefer modification over buyout is given by

$$P + b - C \geq -m, \text{ or}$$
$$b \geq C - P - m \tag{5.13}$$

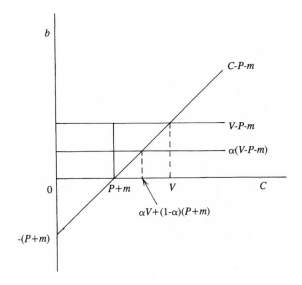

FIGURE 5.3 Ranges where contract modification occurs in equilibrium under certainty and uncertainty.

where the right-hand side is positive in this case. Note that (5.13) defines a lower bound on b, while (5.12) gives an upper bound. Combining them shows that modification is mutually acceptable if

$$V \geq C. \tag{5.14}$$

Figure 5.3 shows these bounds graphically.

Overall, these results show that modification occurs for C between $P + m$ and V. Modification will not occur for $C \leq P + m$ because B knows S will perform rather than breach over this range, nor will it occur for $C > V$ because the maximum b that B will accept leaves S worse off than a buyout. More important, (5.14) shows that, in principle at least, modification allows performance to occur up to the efficient point, whereas if modification were not allowed, too little performance would occur. This suggests that, for the case where B can observe S's cost of performance, a rule of enforcement of modifications is desirable. The reason modification can enhance efficiency is that court-imposed remedies are generally inadequate substitutes for performance from the promisee's perspective.

4.2.2. THE BUYER CANNOT OBSERVE THE SELLER'S COST OF PERFORMANCE

Objections to enforcing modifications are generally based on the potential for opportunism–that is, the attempt by promisors to obtain more favorable terms even when circumstances have not changed. The *Alaska Packers* case is an example. The possibility for opportunism did not arise in the preceding analysis because B could observe S's cost. Thus, she could simply refuse modifications when C was low, knowing that S would perform. If, however, B cannot observe C, opportunism is possible because B cannot determine when S's claim of high costs is merely a bluff.

To examine the possibility of opportunism, I assume that there are two types of sellers, those with high costs, C_h, and those with low costs, C_l, where α is the fraction of high-cost sellers. Further, I assume that

$$C_h > P + m > C_l. \tag{5.15}$$

Thus, according to (5.10), high-cost sellers prefer buyout over performance, and low-cost sellers prefer performance over buyout.[41] This is the relevant difference from a buyer's perspective, since buyers would only accept modification from sellers who would not otherwise perform.

Since B cannot observe C in this case, B can only calculate a conditional probability, denoted A, that the seller truly has high costs given that S proposes modification. Thus, define θ_i to be the probability that a type i seller proposes modification in equilibrium, in which case the conditional probability that the seller has high costs is

$$A = \alpha\theta_h/[\alpha\theta_h + (1 - \alpha)\theta_l]. \tag{5.16}$$

Also, let ϕ be the probability that B accepts a proposed modification.

Consider first the strategy of a high-cost seller. His two options are to buy out the contract for an amount m, or to propose a price increase of b. He will choose the latter if

$$\phi(P + b - C_h) - (1 - \phi)m \geq -m, \text{ or}$$
$$\phi(P + b + m - C_h) \geq 0. \tag{5.17}$$

Assume for now that buyers accept modification at least sometimes—that $\phi > 0$. It follows from (5.17) that a high-cost seller will propose modification if

$$b \geq C_h - P - m. \tag{5.18}$$

Note that the right-hand side is positive by (5.15). It thus represents a lower bound on b for a high-cost seller to propose modification rather than to buy out the contract.

The two options for a low-cost seller are to perform at the original price, or to claim to be a high-cost seller and propose a price increase of b. The seller will prefer the latter if

$$\phi(P + b - C_l) + (1 - \phi)(P - C_l) \geq P - C_l, \text{ or}$$
$$\phi b \geq 0 \tag{5.19}$$

Thus, given $\phi > 0$, a low cost seller will propose modification whenever $b \geq 0$—that is, whenever high-cost sellers are able to obtain a price increase. Thus, any equilibrium in which modification occurs must be a "pooling" equilibrium in which both types of sellers propose modification. This is the problem of opportunistic modification. The question is, will buyers ever accept modification knowing that in some cases the seller has low costs?

For simplicity, I will consider only pure strategy equilibria in which B always accepts modification for some $b > 0 (\phi = 1)$, and both types of sellers always propose it $(\theta_h = \theta_l = 1)$. Note first that if $\theta_h = \theta_l = 1$, then from (5.16) $A = \alpha$. In this case, the condition for B to accept modification is

$$
\begin{aligned}
&V - P - b \geq \alpha m + (1 - \alpha)(V - P), \text{ or} \\
&b \leq \alpha(V - P - m).
\end{aligned}
\tag{5.20}
$$

This condition defines an upper bound on b such that modification is acceptable to B. Combining it with the lower bound in (5.18) shows that an equilibrium exists if

$$
C_h - P - m \leq b \leq \alpha(V - P - m).
\tag{5.21}
$$

Note that the lower bound is identical to that in the certainty case (see (5.13)), given that both types of sellers act like high-cost sellers. The upper bound, in contrast, is lower compared to (5.11) given $\alpha < 1$ (see figure 5.3). This reflects the fact that buyers discount the maximum price increase that they will accept according to the possibility that some sellers have low costs and will therefore perform in the absence of modification.

The fact that buyers are willing to accept smaller price increases implies that performance will not generally occur up to the point where $V = C$. This is because buyers will sometimes refuse modification with a high-cost seller who would have performed (efficiently) at the higher price. Thus, the inability of buyers to observe sellers' costs reduces efficiency, in that performance will occur too infrequently compared to the first-best outcome. Nevertheless, enforcement of modification still improves efficiency compared to nonenforcement, despite the possibility of opportunism by low-cost sellers.

A conditional enforcement rule that enforces only modifications with high-cost sellers (as espoused by the UCC) may be preferable to a general enforcement rule if it succeeds in deterring low-cost sellers from obtaining modification (i.e., if it replaces the pooling equilibrium derived here with a "separating" equilibrium). However, this outcome is not guaranteed because it would be costly for buyers to overturn opportunistic modifications ex post, and even if they did so, the higher litigation costs for both parties might outweigh the resulting gains.

5. Summary

This chapter considered the question of what contracts should be enforceable. Since the economic theory of contracts is based on freedom of contract between rational parties, the presumption is that courts should generally enforce any contracts that have been mutually agree to. Thus, economic justifications for nonenforcement must be based on their ability to correct some sort of market imperfection.

In this chapter I applied this criterion to several doctrines concerning contract enforcement. In particular, I examined defenses claiming that the contract was not validly formed (formation defenses); claims that the contract, though valid, should not be enforced owing to unforeseen contingencies (performance excuses); and rules governing the enforcement of contract modifications. In many (but not all) cases it was possible to show that the traditional legal rules are consistent with efficient contracting.

SIX

THE ECONOMICS OF PROPERTY LAW

Property is perhaps the most fundamental area of the common law. It is also basic to economics in that property rights are essential for exchange. In this chapter and the next, I develop an economic analysis of property law. This chapter focuses on the legal protection of property rights, the transfer of property rights between private individuals (both voluntary and involuntary), and the law with regard to incompatible property rights (or externalities).

I begin the analysis with the fundamental distinction between property rules and liability rules, which forms the basis for much of the economic analysis of property. The key to the distinction is the interaction between *consent* as the basis for mutually beneficial exchange and the *transaction costs* associated with obtaining consent. Consensual exchange is governed by property rules, and nonconsensual exchange is governed by liability rules. Thus, property rules ensure that exchanges are Pareto-efficient (i.e., both parties are made at least as well off), but if transaction costs are high, they may preclude some efficient exchanges from being completed. In that case, liability rules can facilitate exchange by removing the requirement of consent and replacing it with a coerced exchange according to terms set by the court.

With this distinction in mind, I first examine the problem of controlling external costs associated with incompatible, or overlapping, property rights. I consider the efficiency of several methods, including money damages, taxes, subsidies, zoning, and covenants. I then turn to the legal rules governing land transfer between private individuals. I first consider the merits of different methods for protecting and transferring title to land, especially in relation to the possibility of past errors or fraud in the line of title. I then examine situations in which involuntary transfer of land, for example under the statutory doctrine of adverse possession, might be economically desirable.

1. Property Rules and Liability Rules

The discussion of the Coase theorem in chapter 1 concerned the efficiency of the *assignment* of property rights, or entitlements, in externality situations. The basic conclusions were that when bargaining between the parties is possible, the efficient assignment of entitlements will be achieved regardless of the initial assignment; whereas if bargaining is not possible, the initial assignment is important for efficiency. The assignment of entitlements is not the whole story, however. The rules for protecting that assignment are also important, since they dictate the circumstances under which subsequent transfers of entitlements can take place. The two basic rules for protecting entitlements are property rules and liability rules.[1]

The distinction between property rules and liability rules was first drawn by Calabresi and Melamed (1972).[2] To illustrate the distinction, consider party A who holds an entitlement protected by a property rule. Another party B can only acquire that entitlement by first obtaining A's consent, as when B purchases the entitlement. If instead A's entitlement is protected by a liability rule, B can acquire it without A's consent, provided B is willing to pay damages in an amount set by the court. The exchange is therefore nonconsensual.

Removing A's right to consent does two things. First, it prevents A from refusing exchanges that are not mutually beneficial. Although mutually beneficial exchanges can still be assured by setting compensation appropriately, in practice this is difficult because A's subjective value is unobservable. Courts therefore generally resort to awarding compensation equal to fair market value, which almost surely understates A's valuation. As a result, inefficient exchanges are possible. The second consequence of removing A's right to consent is that it prevents A from being able to bargain for a share of the surplus from the transaction. Although this does not reduce efficiency per se, it is unfair from A's perspective.

Liability rules may nevertheless improve efficiency because, if transaction costs between A and B are high, consensual exchanges that are mutually beneficial may be foregone. When this is true, a coerced exchange can enhance value by avoiding transaction costs. The optimal rule for protecting entitlements therefore balances the transaction costs associated with property rules against the potential for inefficient exchange under liability rules. When transaction costs are low, the balance tips in favor of property rules, and when transaction costs are high, it tips in favor of liability rules (Calabresi and Melamed, 1972).

The principles underlying this distinction between property and liability rules are well illustrated by the case of *Boomer* v. *Atlantic Cement Co.*[3] The defendant was a large cement company whose operation caused damages to nearby residents. The residents brought suit for an injunction to halt the operation of the company, but the court ruled instead that the company could continue operation provided that it pay damages to the residents. Thus, the court protected the residents' right to be free from damages with a liability rule rather than a property rule. This choice is consistent with the conclusions of Calabresi and Melamed because transaction costs between the residents and the cement company presumably were high owing to the large number of residents. Thus, the effect of an injunction (property-rule protection of the residents' right) may well have been shutdown of the plant, whether or not that was the efficient result.

1.1. Protection of Possessory Interests in Property

Ownership of personal and real property is ordinarily protected by a property rule;[4] that is, individuals cannot take land or personal property without the owner's consent.[5] This is generally viewed as efficient given that exchange of property between individuals ordinarily involves low transaction costs. Thus, giving the possessor the right of consent to any exchange does not represent an impediment to bargaining. And, as noted above, it protects the possessor's subjective valuation of the property in question, which is not guaranteed by a liability rule (especially if compensation is based on fair market value).

Although the preceding argument suggests that property rules are preferred to liability rules when transaction costs are low, the Coase theorem says that property rules and liability rules should be equally efficient. The claim that liability rules may lead to inefficient exchanges if compensation is set too low is based on the implicit assumption that the possessor of the property will never bargain with potential takers. But if transaction costs are low, such bargaining is always possible and will lead to the efficient result. Suppose, for example, that the possessor of an object values it at $100, but any other individual can take it from him by paying its market value, $80. Suppose the taker values the object at $90. He will therefore take it inefficiently. However, note that the possessor will pay the taker up to $20 to refrain from taking it, and the taker will accept any amount greater than $10 = 90 − 80. A bargain is therefore possible whereby the possessor (efficiently) retains possession.

The preceding argument that property rules and liability rules are equally efficient methods for protecting entitlements to objects when transaction costs are low does not explain the predominance of property rules in actual practice. Kaplow and Shavell (1996) argue, however, that this simple example misses a fundamental impediment to bargaining under a liability rule as compared to a property rule when compensation is set too low. The problem is that the possessor will face innumerable potential takers who value the object more than its market value but less than the possessor. Since the possessor will find it infeasible to bribe all of them in the manner described above, the object will be inefficiently taken. The source of this problem is twofold: first, the object is undervalued by the court; and second, there is unlimited "entry" of takers.[6] Property rules prevent this problem by allowing the possessor to refuse inefficient transfers rather than having to pay bribes to prevent them. This will deter entry of takers who value the property less than the owner.

1.2. External Costs: The Laws of Trespass and Nuisance

I now turn to the problem of protecting an individual's entitlement to be free from external costs.[7] In this section, I focus specifically on the laws of trespass and nuisance, which govern costs imposed on landowners. In the next section, I undertake a broader, more theoretical analysis of various approaches for controlling externalities in general.

One of the fundamental rights associated with ownership of land (or any piece of property) is the right to exclude others from its use. Unwanted intrusions onto one's land are governed either by the law of trespass or the law of nuisance. Under the law of trespass the landowner can generally obtain an injunction preventing future intrusions, regardless of their nature. In contrast, under the law of nuisance, the landowner can typically obtain relief (either an injunction or damages) only by showing that the harm is substantial and that the interference is unreasonable.[8]

Merrill (1985) has provided an economic theory that seeks to explain this difference in the treatment of unwanted intrusions under trespass and nuisance.[9] The key to the argument is the transaction cost between the parties to the dispute. Both the Coase theorem and the preceding discussion of property rules and liability rules suggest that when transaction costs are low, it is efficient for the parties to resolve incompatibilities on their own, via consensual exchange. This is facilitated by court enforcement of entitlements by property rules. However, when transaction costs are high, we have seen that involuntary exchange may be more conductive to efficiency. In this case, courts should take a more active role by coercing exchange at a prescribed price.

According to Merrill's argument, the difference between trespass and nuisance fits broadly into this dichotomy: when transaction costs are low, the law of trespass should govern, and when transaction costs are high, the law of nuisance should govern. This categorization conforms with the above theory in that trespass imposes injunctive relief for the plaintiff, *regardless* of the circumstance of the intrusion. Thus, it is like a property rule. If the intrusion is cost-justified (i.e., efficient), then, given, low transaction costs, the defendant and plaintiff presumably will strike a mutually acceptable bargain that allows the defendant to continue the activity. If, however, the intrusion is inefficient, the defendant will honor the injunction and cease the activity.

As for nuisance law, it conforms to the above theory in that the court adopts a balancing, or reasonableness, test before imposing a remedy. This reflects greater court intervention in resolving the dispute, owing to the fact that transaction costs may inhibit resolution by the parties on a voluntary (consensual) basis. Although this argument is complicated a bit by the fact that both damages and injunctions are available under nuisance law (thus, the analysis does not fit neatly into the property rule-liability rule framework), both remedies are available only after a balancing test by the court to determine the reasonableness (i.e., efficiency) of the nuisance-creating activity.[10]

TABLE 6.1   Thresholds Distinguishing Trespass and Nuisance

Trespass	Nuisance
Defendant's act occurred on plaintiff's land	Defendant's act occurred on defendant's land
Harm is 'direct'	Harm is 'indirect'
Invasion by 'tangible' matter	Invasion by 'intangible' matter
Interference with 'exclusive possession' of land	Interference with 'use and enjoyment' of land*

*If the interference with use and enjoyment becomes severe, it amounts to 'constructive' interference with exclusive possession and is governed by trespass (Merrill, 1985).

As a broad test of the theory, Merrill (1985) examined the various thresholds that the common law has set to distinguish the spheres of trespass and nuisance. If the theory is correct, these thresholds ought to distinguish roughly between low and high transaction cost intrusions. Table 6.1 lists several of these thresholds. Clearly the correlation is not exact, but these thresholds provide at least some support for the view that the law is attempting to distinguish between high and low transaction cost intrusions.

2. Controlling Externalities: Formal Analysis

This section develops a more complete and formal analysis of the efficiency of property rules, liability rules, taxes and/or subsidies, and other methods for controlling externalities. To be concrete, I will consider the familiar case of a factory that emits smoke, causing damage to a neighboring laundry. Let $D(x)$ be the dollar amount of damage the laundry suffers per unit of time, which is a function of the dollar spending on abatement by the factory, denoted x. (Assume for now that the laundry cannot take any steps to reduce its damage.) In this simple setting, the only efficiency question concerns the choice of abatement by the factory. The socially optimal amount of abatement minimizes the sum of the cost of abatement plus the damages suffered by the laundry, or $x + D(x)$. The first-order condition for optimal abatement is thus

$$1 = -D'(x). \tag{6.1}$$

Let x^* be the solution to (6.1), as illustrated in figure 6.1. (Note the similarity of this problem to the simple accident model of chapter 2, where abatement corresponds to care.)

2.1. Tax-Subsidy Approach

The traditional approach to resolving externalities of this sort is to use Pigouvian taxes or subsidies.[11] According to this approach, the government imposes a tax on, or pays a subsidy to, the polluter in such a way that the polluter internalizes the externality and chooses the socially optimal level of abatement. This is

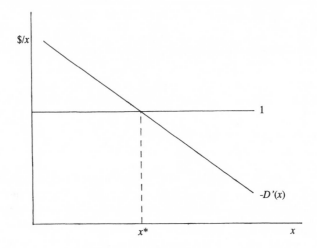

FIGURE 6.1 Efficient abatement of an externality.

accomplished by ensuring that the marginal tax is equal to the marginal external damages $(t' = D')$, or that the marginal subsidy is equal to the negative of the marginal external damages $(s' = -D')$, at the optimal abatement level. As long as this is true, the actual form of the tax or subsidy schedule is irrelevant for efficiency, although it will clearly matter for distribution of wealth. Also unimportant in the current version of the model is whether the laundry is compensated for its damages; again this is only a distributional issue (assuming no income effects). In more general versions of the problem, however, both of these issues become important for efficiency, as we shall see.

2.2. Liability Rules

The liability approach to controlling externalities requires the party suffering the damage (the laundry) to bring a nuisance suit in hopes of collecting damages or obtaining an injunction. I have already provided a general discussion of the choice between damages and injunctions (liability rules and property rules) based on transaction costs. Here I focus on the incentives they create for efficient abatement of externalities.

Since one function of damages is to compensate the victim, the polluter's liability is typically set equal to the victim's actual damages, $L(x) = D(x)$. Clearly, this form of liability will induce the factory to engage in optimal abatement for the same reason that strict liability induces injurers to take optimal care in accident settings. The analogy to torts also suggests that a negligence form of liability will induce optimal abatement by the factory. (Recall that nuisance law uses a type of negligence, or balancing test, before imposing liability or injunctive relief.) The difference between strict liability and negligence is that the victim does not receive compensation under negligence if the polluter engages in optimal abatement. In the current version of the model, this difference again is purely distributional, but it will matter for efficiency below.

Notice that the discussion of liability to this point has implicitly assumed that the victim (the laundry) has a right, or an "entitlement," to be free from pollution.[12] Suppose instead that the factory initially has the right to pollute. Perhaps the factory was preexisting and was therefore awarded the right to pollute under the common law doctrine of "coming to the nuisance" (Wittman, 1980). This change in the entitlement point, however, does not preclude the use of liability rules for achieving optimal abatement. Specifically, suppose that in this case, the laundry can compel abatement by the factory as long as it (the laundry) pays the factory's "damages," or its cost of abatement. Thus, $L = x$ for the laundry, and its problem is to choose x to minimize $L + D(x) = x + D(x)$, which results in the optimal choice of x.

Although the solution just suggested seems odd in comparison to the solution in which the polluter is liable, it serves to demonstrate the symmetry of the problem and the fact that the polluter and the pollutee simultaneously "cause" the harm (Coase, 1960). Moreover, it is not as unrealistic a solution as one might suppose, as illustrated by the case of *Spur Industries, Inc.* v. *Del E. Webb Development Co.*[13] This case concerned a developer who brought a nuisance suit against the owner of a feedlot in an effort to shut it down owing to its foul odor. The court granted the developer's request, but because the feed lot was preexisting (the developer had encroached on it), it required the developer to pay the owner's cost of relocating. If we view the feedlot's relocation as abatement of the externality, then this solution is identical to that just described. This case and the *Boomer* case are therefore both examples of externalities resolved by liability rules, but they differ in terms of the initial assignments of entitlements.

2.3. Property Rules

Recall that property rules differ from liability rules in that either party can block a movement away from the initial assignment of rights. That is, each party can seek and enforce an injunction against the other party. As noted above, if transaction costs are high, the efficient outcome will arise therefore only if the initial assignment is efficient. If the initial assignment is not efficient and transaction costs are low, the Coase theorem tells us that the parties will be able to improve their positions by bargaining.

To illustrate, suppose that the laundry initially has the right to be free from pollution. It can therefore obtain an injunction requiring the factory to abate the pollution completely. The factory, however, can seek to purchase rights to pollute from the laundry. At the margin, the maximum amount it will pay is $1 per unit of abatement that it saves. The laundry, on the other hand, will accept no less than its marginal damages, or $-D'(x)$ per unit of the reduction in x. A transfer of pollution rights will therefore be mutually beneficial as long as $-D'(x) < 1$, or for all x to the right of x^* in figure 6.1. If all gains from exchange are exhausted, the factory will purchase pollution rights to the point where $-D'(x) = 1$, which is the efficient point.

Now consider the case where the factory initially has the right to pollute. In this case, the factory is free to pollute (i.e., to set $x = 0$) unless the laundry purchases the right by paying the factory to undertake abatement. The maximum amount the laundry will pay for an increment in abatement is $-D'(x)$, its marginal damages, and the minimum amount the factory will accept to increase abatement by one unit is $1, its marginal abatement cost. Thus, the laundry will purchase abatement as long as $-D'(x) > 1$, which is true to the left of x^* in figure 6.1. Again, the efficient outcome is achieved if the parties exhaust all gains from bargaining.[14]

Thus, both property rules and liability rules potentially achieve the efficient outcome. The difference is that, under liability rules, bargaining between the parties is not necessary because the court sets the price of the exchange. As for the initial entitlement point, its impact is solely distributional under both types of rules and therefore does not affect marginal abatement incentives.

2.4. Bilateral-Care Externalities

In this section I consider briefly how the preceding analysis is affected if the victim of the externality also has the ability to abate the damages. Specifically, suppose that the damages suffered by the laundry are now $D(x,y)$, where x continues to be the factory's abatement expenditures and y is the laundry's abatement expenditures (White and Wittman, 1979). Assume that

$$D_x < 0, D_{xx} > 0, D_y < 0, D_{yy} > 0, D_{xy} > 0. \qquad (6.2)$$

The social problem in this case is to choose x and y to minimize $x + y + D(x,y)$. The first-order conditions are thus

$$1 = -D_x(x) \qquad (6.3)$$

and

$$1 = -D_y(y). \qquad (6.4)$$

Consider first the tax-subsidy approach. Let $t(x,y)$ be the tax (or subsidy) schedule faced by the factory. As in the unilateral-care case, as long as the marginal tax is such that $t_x = D_x$, the factory will choose the optimal level of abatement, given the level of abatement chosen by the laundry. At the same time, the laundry will also choose the optimal level of abatement, provided that either it does not receive compensation for its damages or the compensation is a lump sum (i.e., independent of its choice of y). The tax-subsidy approach induces both parties to choose optimal abatement because both are fully liable for the damages at the margin.

Now consider liability rules. In this case, we know from our analysis of tort law that strict liability will induce optimal abatement by the factory (given y), but it will not induce optimal abatement by the laundry, given that the laundry receives full compensation for its damages. However, a negligence rule will induce both parties to choose optimal abatement because the injurer avoids liability by choosing optimal abatement (provided that the due standard is set at x^*), thereby making the victim responsible for its own damages.[15]

Finally, consider property rules. As long as bargaining between the parties is costless, the conclusion from above is not changed by the possibility of victim care—namely, the parties will trade property rights until the efficient outcome is achieved.[16]

2.5. Long Run Efficiency

The analysis so far has concentrated on efficient abatement of the externality, assuming that the number of parties involved was fixed. We may characterize this as short-run efficiency. In the long run, however, entry and exit of polluters and victims is possible, a process that will also affect the severity of the externality. An examination of long-run efficiency in this context is therefore important because, as several authors have pointed out, not all of the rules that induce efficient abatement in the short run create the correct entry-exit incentives in the long run (Frech, 1979; White and Wittman, 1979). The reason is that entry-exit incentives depend on the distribution of wealth or profits, and, as noted, different rules create different distributions.[17]

To examine long-run efficiency in a formal manner, we need to amend the simple model to allow entry and exit of factories and laundries.[18] Thus, let n_f and n_l be the number of factories and laundries in operation, respectively, and let q_f and q_l be the output levels for each factory and laundry. Also, let $P^f(n_f q_f)$ and $P^l(n_l q_l)$ be the inverse demand curves for the two industries, which are downward sloping, and let $C^f(q_f)$ and $C^l(q_l)$ be the production costs for each of the two types of firms. $D(x)$ is now defined to be the external cost emitted per factory, so $n_f D(x)$ is the total external cost emitted and x is abatement per factory. The model is therefore one of unilateral care, and the externality is assumed to be independent of the output levels of the factories (for simplicity).

Assume that each laundry in operation incurs the full external cost—that is, the externality is a pure public "bad." Thus, the total external damage incurred by the laundries collectively is $n_l n_f D(x)$. The social problem is to choose the output levels of each type of firm, the number of each type of firm, and the level of abatement per factory, to maximize social welfare, which is given by[19]

$$W = \int_0^{n_f q_f} P^f(z)dz + \int_0^{n_l q_l} P^l(u)du - n_f C^f(q_f) - n_l C^l(q_l) - n_f n_l D(x) - n_f x. \quad (6.5)$$

Since we are interested in optimal abatement and entry rather than the output of each firm (given that damages are independent of output levels), I consider only the choices of x, n_f, and n_l. The first-order conditions for these variables, respectively, are:

$$-n_l D'(x) = 1 \tag{6.6}$$

$$P^f(n_f q_f) q_f - C^f(q_f) - n_l D(x) - x = 0 \tag{6.7}$$

$$P^l(n_l q_l) q_l - C^l(q_l) - n_f D(x) = 0. \tag{6.8}$$

Condition (6.6) determines optimal abatement per factory. Note that it is a standard Samuelson condition for a pure public good (i.e., the sum of the marginal benefits equals marginal costs). Conditions (6.7) and (6.8) are zero profit conditions that determine optimal entry. Both include damages, given that entry of either type of firm increases total external costs.

Now consider the determination of these variables in a competitive equilibrium under various cost-internalization rules. Consider first the tax-subsidy approach. As noted above, both taxes and subsidies induce optimal abatement by the factory as long as the marginal tax or subsidy equals marginal damages. In the case of a tax, this requires that $t'(x) = n_l D'(x)$. As for the entry decision, only a tax equal to the full damages will lead to the correct number of factories. Specifically, if $t(x) = n_l D(x)$, then the profit per factory is

$$\pi^f = P^f q_f - C^f(q_f) - n_l D(x) - x. \tag{6.9}$$

Comparing (6.9) and (6.7) shows that, if factories enter until profit is zero, the number of firms will be optimal. The number of laundries will also be optimal provided that they are not compensated for their damages out of the tax revenue. Specifically, in the absence of compensation, the profit per laundry is

$$\pi^l = P^l q_l - C^l(q_l) - n_f D(x). \tag{6.10}$$

which, compared to (6.8), shows that, if laundries enter until they earn zero profit, the number of laundries will be efficient.

In contrast to a tax, a subsidy will not lead to efficient entry. There will be too many factories because they will not face the full damages that their entry imposes—indeed, they receive a payment for entering. As for laundries, even though they do face the full damages of $n_f D(x)$ under the subsidy (again assuming they are not compensated), too few will enter because n_f in (6.10) is too large.

Now consider liability rules. Note first that under a strict liability rule, too many laundries will enter because they are fully compensated for their damages. Thus, they ignore the impact that their entry has on total damages. Although each factory faces full liability of $n_l D(x)$, this amount will be too high in equilibrium because of the excessive number of laundries. Thus, too few factories will enter the industry, and each will undertake too much abatement, although abatement is efficient given the number of laundries—see (6.6).

A negligence rule will induce factories to undertake optimal abatement (given that the due standard is set at x^*), but it will result in entry of too many factories because, by undertaking optimal abatement, they avoid liability (Polinsky, 1980b). On the other hand, laundries will bear the full amount of damages, $n_f D(x^*)$, but too few will enter because n_f is too large. In general, therefore, liability rules do not result in correct entry-exit decisions because they do not create bilateral responsibility for damages.

Finally, consider the situation under property rules. Recall that under property rules, the ultimate allocation of resources results from bargaining between the parties over rights to pollute. Bargaining begins from an initial entitlement point, or assignment of rights. Thus, suppose that laundries as a group initially have the right to be free from pollution. For example, suppose that shares of the right are equally distributed among the optimal number of laundries in the industry. In order for factories to enter and pollute, they have to purchase rights from the laundries. Frech (1979) shows that, if transaction costs are low, this scenario leads to efficient abatement by factories, and efficient entry of both factories and laundries. The same result holds if the factories initially have the right to pollute, and laundries have to purchase the right to be free from pollution.

Rather than demonstrate these results formally, I will provide an intuitive explanation of why property rules lead to efficient long-run decisions while liability rules do not.[20] Consider the situation under strict liability. In this case, any laundry entering the industry is fully compensated for its damages and therefore ignores the marginal contribution to total damages resulting from its entry. The right to compensation is therefore not exclusive, but is available to any potential entrant. Thus, entry occurs until the value of that right is driven to zero. This is not true under property rules because, once rights to pollution (or freedom from pollution) are allocated (either to polluters or victims), entrants can obtain them only by purchasing them from a holder. Entry is therefore not excessive because in equilibrium, the price of obtaining a right upon entry will reflect the social cost of entry.

Holderness (1989) has illustrated this difference between liability rules and property rules in the long run by distinguishing between *open* and *closed* classes of right holders. When a right is assigned to an open class, a share of the right can be freely obtained by entry into the class because, by definition, entry is unrestricted. This is the case under liability rules where, for example, mere entry into the laundry business confers on the entrant the right to compensation. (Liability rules need not create open classes, however, if entrants do not automatically receive compensation.)[21] Alternatively, if a right is assigned to a closed class, entry is not free; a share of the right can be obtained only by purchasing it. This resembles the situation under property rules. An example of a situation where a right is assigned to a closed class is when a regulation "runs with the land" because in that case the right can be obtained only by purchasing the land, the price of which will capitalize the value of the right.[22]

2.6. Zoning, Covenants, and Nuisance Law

The most common response to the presence of externalities in the land market is zoning. Nearly all U.S. cities have some form of zoning regulations,[23] which typically take the form of land-use restrictions within designated areas, as well as more detailed structural restrictions.[24] The economic theory of zoning, according to White (1975, p. 32) is based on the fact that "similar land uses have no (or only small) external effects on each other whereas dissimilar land uses may have large effects."[25]

The pervasiveness of zoning does not necessarily imply, however, that it is an efficient response to land market externalities in all cases. According to Ellickson (1973), for example, the high administrative and enforcement costs of zoning will often exceed the resulting reductions in "nuisance costs," thereby making the system inefficient.[26] The existence of inefficient regulations per se would not be a major concern, however, if the penalty for violation were an appropriate fine. In that case, landowners could simply choose to violate inefficient regulations by paying the fine, thereby leading to an efficient outcome. In this way zoning would function like a liability rule. However, the fact that zoning ordinances are more like property rules, in that they require compliance, forecloses this route to efficient land use.

Zoning represents a form of public regulation of externalities. There are also private forms of control, the most common of which are land-use covenants and nuisance law. Land-use covenants typically take the form of deed restrictions and are most commonly imposed by a developer restricting the types of activities that all subsequent deed holders can undertake. Thus, deed restrictions "run with the land." This aspect of covenants is important because it avoids the high transaction costs that would be incurred if new entrants into the neighborhood had to negotiate contracts anew with all existing owners. And, because the developer generally puts the covenants in place before he sells off the individual parcels, he has an incentive to structure them efficiently in pursuing his objective of maximizing the market value of the development as a whole (Hughes and Turnbull, 1996). Thus, in terms of efficiency, covenants represent a good alternative to zoning in controlling externalities, at least for land that is undeveloped and initially owned by a single individual (Ellickson, 1973, p. 717).

In contrast, covenants and other forms of private bargaining are not good methods for controlling externalities in established urban areas where land ownership is highly fragmented. Although immediate neighbors may be able to resolve minor disputes between themselves in an efficient manner through Coasian bargaining, high transaction costs are likely to prevent this remedy on the scale of the neighborhood as a whole (Ellickson, 1973, p. 718; White 1975, p. 32). In this case, centralized controls like zoning are generally superior to private bargaining (assuming that the regulations assign rights more efficiently than the status quo).[27]

As we have already seen, nuisance law represents another private mechanism for internalizing externalities. Ellickson (1973) has argued that nuisance law is particularly useful in the case of localized harms where costs are concentrated on a few individuals. However, it is not effective in the case of dispersed harms because of the free-rider problem. In that case, no one individual will suffer enough harm to make it worthwhile to initiate a lawsuit, even though the aggregate harm may exceed the cost of litigation (Landes and Posner, 1987, chap. 2). In this case, public regulation again may be a better alternative.

3. Land Transfer

Efficiency dictates that resources should move into the hands of the highest valuing user. Thus, from an economic perspective, an important function of property law is to facilitate such transfers.[28] This is principally done by protecting the rights of property owners (as established by previous consensual transfer) against competing claims. In this section, I examine the factors that determine the most efficient system for determining and enforcing title to land.

3.1. Voluntary Transfers of Land

3.1.1. POSSESSION VERSUS FILING SYSTEMS FOR ESTABLISHING TITLE

In a world of perfect information about all previous transfers of a piece of property, the law should simply enforce the rights of the current possessor, given the knowledge that all previous transfers were consensual. When there is uncertainty about whether a fraudulent (nonconsensual) transfer occurred in the past, however, the law confronts a tradeoff. Should it protect the rights of the current possessor (who acquired the property legitimately), or the last possessor prior to the break in the chain of consensual transfers? A rule that protects the possessor limits the information necessary for an exchange to occur—in particular, a buyer need not inquire into the entire history of transactions involving the property to establish his right to ownership—but it subjects current owners to the risk of losing their property in a nonconsensual transfer.

Baird and Jackson (1984) have argued that the Anglo-American system of property conveyance is sensitive to this tradeoff. They compare a system where title is established by mere possession to a system that relies on public records of property transactions that can be used to trace the history of a title—referred to as a filing system. On the one hand, a possession-based system makes it easy to identify, and transact with, the rightful owner, but it raises the likelihood of theft or other fraudulent conveyance. Filing systems, on the other hand, reduce the likelihood of nonconsensual transfer, but they are costly to administer (an examination of the title history is generally necessary), thereby increasing the transaction cost of a transfer.

The optimal system depends on the magnitude of the various costs and benefits for particular types of property. Land is the prototypical type of property for which a filing system is preferred. Land is stationary and not transferred often, both of which hold down the administrative costs of a filing system. Moreover, shared ownership at a point in time or over time is often desirable, making it costly to rely on possession alone as evidence of ownership. (The later discussion of the doctrine of adverse possession illustrates this point.) In contrast, personal property is less well suited to a filing system, especially goods that are easily mobile and homogeneous.[29] In this case, the best description of the property is the identity of the possessor. Henceforth, I will focus on land and filing systems for real estate.

3.1.2. FILING SYSTEMS AND TITLE INSURANCE

Two types of filing systems have been employed in the United States. The most common is the *recording system*, which maintains a record of the entire sequence of consensual transfers of a piece of property. This record serves as *evidence* to a prospective buyer that the current possessor has good title, but it does not *establish* title. In particular, if a flaw in the line of title is discovered (owing, for example, to a theft or recording error), the current owner is at risk of losing the property to the last rightful owner. As protection against this possibility, property owners typically purchase title insurance.

The other system that has been used in some states in the U.S., the Torrens system, *establishes* (registers) that the current possessor has title to the property against all future claims. This system therefore resembles one based on possession. It differs, however, in that, prior to registration, an effort is made to determine if a defect in the title exists; after registration, if a claimant appears, he or she can obtain compensation from a public fund created out of registration fees.

The primary difference between these two systems (leaving aside institutional details) is this: under the recording system (with title insurance), in the event of a legitimate claim the claimant receives the property and the current owner receives monetary compensation, whereas under the Torrens system, the claimant receives compensation and the current owner retains the property.[30] The question is whether this difference matters from an economic perspective. The remainder of this section addresses this question.[31]

A simple graphical analysis can be used to compare the impact of the two systems. I consider two parties, the *current owner* of the property and a *claimant*. The owner has utility $U_o(W_o, L_o)$ where W_o is the owner's initial wealth and L_o is his holding of land. I assume that (W_o, L_o) is optimal in that it maximizes the owner's utility subject to his budget line as shown by point A in figure 6.2. (Note that the slope of the budget line is the negative of the market price of land, p.)[32] The convexity of the owner's indifference curves indicates that he does not view land and wealth as perfect substitutes. For example, the minimum amount he would accept in wealth to surrender his entire holding of land is given by the segment DW_o in figure 6.2, which is clearly greater than its market value, BW_o.[33] Thus, if the owner were to lose his land and receive its market value, his utility would fall from U_o^1 to U_o^2, as shown in figure 6.2.

The difference between these outcomes represents the owner's subjective valuation of the land. Presumably, this value grows over time as the owner

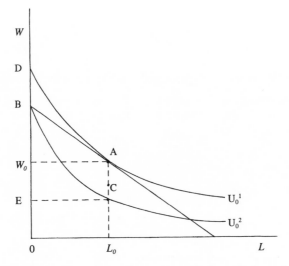

FIGURE 6.2 Utility of a landowner before (A) and after (B) loss of property given market-value compensation.

continues to occupy the land (i.e., the indifference curve becomes more convex). As Oliver Wendell Holmes observed, "man, like a tree in the cleft of a rock, gradually shapes roots to its surroundings, and when the roots have grown to a certain size, can't be displaced without cutting at his life."[34] Of course, protection of subjective value is one of the main economic functions of a system based on consensual transfer of property (i.e., one based on property rules).[35]

Now consider the claimant. The claimant also has utility defined over wealth and land, $U_c(W, L)$. Since she is not the current occupier of the land in question, her initial point is (W_c, O) as shown in figure 6.3, yielding utility U_c^1. In contrast to the occupant's indifference curves, the claimant's indifference curves are drawn as straight lines, reflecting the fact that she views land (specifically, the piece of land in question) and wealth as perfect substitutes. Although this is extreme, it captures the idea that the impact of occupation creates an attachment to the land beyond its mere equivalent in wealth. To the claimant, who has possibly never occupied the land (e.g., she may be an heir of a previous legitimate owner), acquisition of the land is simply a way to acquire wealth (in an amount equal to its market value).

The implication of this form of the claimant's preferences is that she is indifferent between acquiring the land, which would move her to point B in figure 6.3, and receiving compensation equal to its market value, which would put her at point A. Both options increase her utility by the same amount, namely, from U_c^1 to U_c^2.

The analysis to this point shows that a system that leaves the land in the hands of the current owner and awards monetary compensation (equal to its market value) to the claimant (point A in the two figures) is Pareto-superior to one that awards the land to the claimant and monetary compensation to the current possessor (point B). Specifically, the current owner is strictly better off

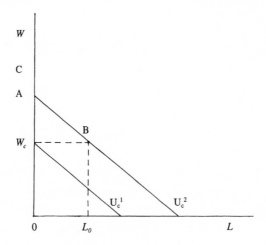

FIGURE 6.3 Utility of a claimant after acquiring land (B) or its market value (A).

retaining the land compared to receipt of its market value (A versus B), whereas the claimant is indifferent between the two options. Point B, however, is probably not the final outcome when the claimant receives the land. In particular, the displaced owner will likely buy back the land. To see why, note that beginning from point B in figure 6.2, the maximum amount the owner would pay to reacquire the land is given by segment BE. This amount clearly exceeds its market value, BW_o, which is the minimum amount the claimant would accept to surrender the land. Thus, a mutually beneficial exchange is possible whereby the original possessor reacquires the land from the claimant.

The particular outcome after the exchange depends on how the parties share the surplus; one possible outcome is given by point C in the two graphs. The relevant comparison between the two land-transfer systems is thus between points A and C: A is the outcome under the system that awards the land to the owner, and C is the outcome under the system that awards the land to the claimant.

The conclusions of this analysis are as follows. First, each party strictly prefers the system that awards the land to him or her. I have already shown that this is true for the original owner (he prefers A to C in figure 6.2). It is also true for the claimant, despite the fact that she values the land at its market value, because, if she is awarded the land, she is able to obtain a share of the owner's subjective valuation of the land (above the market value) when she sells it back to the owner (as reflected by the distance between C and A in figure 6.3). Second, under both systems, the land ends up in the hands of the party who values it most (the owner), provided transaction costs are low. This, of course, is simply an illustration of the Coase theorem (Coase, 1960).

In reality, transactions are not costless, in which case the most efficient allocation of rights should minimize the impact of transaction costs on resource allocation. This suggests that awarding the land to the original owner-possessor is preferred to awarding it to the claimant, because such a system requires fewer transactions for the land to end up with the highest valuing user (by hypothesis, the original owner).[36] The fact that the predominant system in the United States (the recording system) does not conform to this conclusion suggests that the goal of the system is to protect the interests of legitimate claimants over current (innocent) owners, even when this outcome conflicts with efficiency.

3.1.3. INCENTIVES FOR LAND INVESTMENT

The preceding discussion of systems for protecting title to land focused on maximizing the value of land through exchange. In this section, I examine how they affect the incentives of landowners to increase the value of land through investment in improvements, given the risk of a future claim against the property.

Let $V(x)$ be the value of a piece of land after x dollars have been invested in improvements, where $V' > 0$ and $V'' < 0$. In the absence of risk, the landowner will choose the level of investment to maximize $V(x) - x$, yielding the first-order condition

$$V'(x) - 1 = 0. \tag{6.11}$$

Let x^* be the resulting risk-free level of investment. Suppose, however, that a claim will arise with probability θ. In the presence of this risk, the landowner's level of investment will depend on the land title system in place. Consider two systems: under system A the landowner retains title to the land and improvements, and under system B the landowner loses title to the land and improvements but may receive indemnification. Clearly, system A will induce the landowner to make the optimal level of investment in the land because he faces no risk of losing it. System B, however, confronts the landowner with the risk of losing the land. Thus, in the absence of indemnification, he will choose x to maximize $(1 - \theta)V(x) - x$, which yields the first-order condition

$$(1 - \theta)V'(x) - 1 = 0. \tag{6.12}$$

The landowner therefore underinvests in the land given $\theta > 0$.

Suppose, however, that under system B the landowner purchases title insurance under which he is reimbursed for the full value of the property in the event of a claim.[37] In this case, the landowner chooses x to maximize

$$V(x) - x - p \tag{6.13}$$

where p is the insurance premium. Note that if the landowner views p as fixed at the time he chooses x, then he makes the optimal investment choice in this case.[38] Thus, investment incentives are equally efficient under system A and system B with full insurance.[39]

3.2. Adverse Possession

The final topic in this chapter concerns the acquisition of title to land by adverse possession. Under this doctrine, the occupier of a piece of land other than the true owner can acquire title if the owner does not raise an objection to the occupation within a statutorily set period of years.[40] Thus, adverse possession is in effect a statute of limitations on the owner's right to seek a remedy for trespass. As such, it is a form of involuntary transfer of land (though the owner's failure to raise an objection may be interpreted as a form of implied consent). In addition to occupying the land continuously for the statutorily required period of time, a would-be owner's possession must be open, notorious, exclusive, and hostile to the owner's interests, and also represent a claim of a right to the land.[41]

The usual economic justifications for this doctrine are that it lowers the transaction costs of clearing title to land, and that it prevents owners from leaving land idle for long periods of time (Cooter and Ulen, 1988, pp. 154–157). Although both of these arguments are consistent with the economic goal of facilitating the exchange of property, they conflict with the above argument that in cases of trespass, transaction costs are typically low. Thus, the parties can be expected to achieve efficiency through bargaining, an outcome best promoted by the court's enforcing (rather than transferring) property rights. Moreover, the fact that land is left "idle" by the current owner does not imply per se that it is being used suboptimally. These conclusions suggest that an alternative theory of adverse possession is called for. The remainder of this chapter provides such a theory.[42]

The typical adverse-possession case involves a boundary dispute between adjacent landowners. For example, suppose owner A wishes to build a structure on a portion of his land near his boundary with B, but the exact location of the boundary is uncertain. In particular, suppose there is a strip of land whose ownership is in doubt. Let m be the value of that land to A prior to development, and let n be the value to B, where $m > n$. Thus, if it were known prior to development that B owned the land, A would purchase it for a price $p \in [n, m]$, assuming low transaction costs.

Now suppose that the value of the land to A *after* development is $V > m$, where the excess of V over m reflects irreversibilities in the development process. As a result, if it were discovered after development that B owned the land, the maximum amount A would pay to acquire it would increase to V. The difference $V - m$ therefore represents an "appropriable quasi-rent" (Klein, Crawford, and Alchian, 1978). Because of this quasi-rent, it is desirable for the parties to determine ownership of the disputed strip of land before A develops in order to facilitate efficient land use and avoid wasteful rent-seeking expenditures after the fact.

Although determination of the boundary prior to development is preferable, it is inevitable that errors will occur, either because A is convinced that the land is his due to an error in a previous survey or because the current survey results in an error. Alternatively, A may encroach intentionally, a strategy that will figure prominently later. In the case of an error, the next best outcome is for B to correct the error in a timely fashion—that is, to "mitigate" A's error efficiently. However, this creates a problem owing to the fact that A's valuation of the land in question will presumably grow over time, both because he will possibly increase his investment in the property and because his subjective "attachment" to the property will increase in less tangible ways (as described by the Holmes quote earlier). Thus, B may not in general have an incentive to correct A's error in an efficient (timely) manner because by waiting B can extract a higher payment as A's valuation grows.

The theory of adverse possession I will offer views the doctrine as a solution to these problems associated with boundary errors. According to the theory, the doctrine is structured to create incentives for A to avoid boundary errors prior to investing in development (the first-best solution), but at the same time to maintain incentives for B to mitigate errors in a timely manner after A has developed (the second-best solution). (Note that this view of adverse possession resembles the analysis of tort rules in the context of sequential-care accidents as discussed in chapter 3.)

To examine this dual function of adverse possession, note that B's ability to appropriate quasi-rents from A derives from B's right to eject A from the land if B discovers that B owns it after A has developed. This is because B's land is protected by a property rule that allows B to exclude others from its use. Thus, one way to prevent B from extracting quasi-rents after A develops in error is to protect B's land instead by a liability rule in cases of boundary encroachment. In this case, if B discovers A's encroachment, A can acquire title to the land without B's consent simply by paying its market value.

Although this solution prevents rent seeking and delayed discovery of errors by B, it creates problems in terms of A's incentives. First, it eliminates A's incentive to discover errors before developing. Clearly, A would prefer a coerced exchange of the land at market value after the fact rather than having to bargain with B before the fact. Second, it creates an incentive for A to encroach *intentionally* on B's land in an effort to acquire it more cheaply than by bargaining with A. Thus, liability rule protection, like last clear chance in torts (see chapter 3), creates good incentives for the party moving second, but bad incentives for the party moving first.

As an alternative solution, consider a rule that protects B's land in the event of encroachment with a *time-limited* property rule. Under this solution, B retains the right to eject A from the land if a bargain is not reached, but only for a limited period of time, after which A acquires title and therefore cannot be ejected. Broadly speaking, this rule captures the essential structure of adverse possession.

A time-limited property rule has two advantages over an unlimited property rule. First, it gives B an incentive to correct errors in a timely manner; second, it limits bargaining costs between A and B. It is not as good as a liability rule in this regard because B can still extract quasi-rents before the property rule expires. However, this possibility serves the useful purpose of providing A with an incentive to avoid boundary errors in the first place. That incentive takes the form of a penalty on A for failing to discover errors—namely, the possible payment of (limited) quasi-rents to B.

Note that, because the magnitude of the quasi-rents increases over time, the expected amount of this penalty increases with the length of time the property rule is in place. Thus, a longer limit improves the incentives for A to discover errors in the first place, but a shorter period improves the incentives for B to correct errors in a timely fashion. The optimal limit thus balances these two effects.

The preceding results can be illustrated with a simple model. Consider first the incentive of B to discover a boundary error following development by A near B's boundary. Let s be the cost of a survey to ascertain the true boundary, and let r be B's prior assessment that A has encroached on B's land. Recall that the value of the development to A *after* construction is $V > m$. Thus, if B expects to extract a payment equal to the full value of the land to A in the event of an error, B will survey in hopes of discovering an error if

$$rV > s. \qquad (6.14)$$

In addition, since we assumed V is increasing over time, B has an incentive to delay reporting the error in an effort to increase V. A time limit on B's property-rule protection reduces the severity of this problem. Let a be the probability that B will conduct a survey (i.e., the probability that (6.14) holds).

Now consider A's decision to survey *before* developing, given a. Recall that p is the price A pays if he discovers that the land is B's and bargains with B to purchase it before developing. Also let q be A's prior assessment of the probability that the land is his. The expected value to A of surveying before developing is therefore

$$-s + qV + (1 - q)(V - p) = V - (1 - q)p - s. \qquad (6.15)$$

If instead A develops without first surveying, his expected value is

$$qV + (1 - q)(1 - a)V. \qquad (6.16)$$

Therefore A will survey if (6.15) exceeds (6.16), or if

$$(1 - q)(aV - p) > s. \qquad (6.17)$$

The tradeoff underlying the optimal time limit on B's property rule can be seen by examining (6.17) and (6.14). Note that as the time limit is reduced, (6.17) is less likely to hold, both because V's growth is limited and because a is smaller (i.e., by (6.14) B is less likely to survey the smaller is V). The time limit must therefore be long enough so that aV is large enough to give A an incentive to survey prior to developing (the first-best solution). However, the limit should not be too long in order to give B an incentive to discover and correct errors in a timely manner (the second-best solution). The optimal limit balances these two effects. Condition (6.17) also shows the problem with protecting B's land with a liability rule after an error is discovered. Specifically, if A could acquire the land for its market value p without having to bargain with B, then (6.17) would never hold.

I conclude this discussion by suggesting that the requirements for adverse possession listed earlier conform broadly with the foregoing theory. Consider first the requirement that possession be hostile and under a claim of right. Hostility in this context means that possession is contrary to the wishes of the owner. There has been some debate, however, about whether the possessor's *intent* matters. In particular, the so-called Maine rule says that mistaken possession is *not* sufficiently hostile to the owner's right—that is, intent is required—whereas the newer Connecticut rule holds that the possessor's state of mind is immaterial.[43] Note that under either rule, an intentional encroacher should prevail. Nevertheless, a recent study of adverse possession cases by Helmholz (1983) found that, when there is evidence that the encroacher intentionally took possession in an effort to acquire title, the court has generally ruled *against* awarding title (assuming all other requirements are met), whereas in the event of a good-faith error they have ruled in favor of awarding title.

Although these results conflict with the stated law concerning intent, they are consistent with the theory here. Recall in particular that the function of protecting B's land with a time-limited property rule was to penalize A for boundary "errors," the penalty being extraction of quasi-rents by B. The time limit puts an upper bound on this penalty as a way to prevent excessive rent extraction by B after the fact. In the case of intentional encroachment, providing B with an incentive to correct errors ex post is less important than deterring A ex ante. Thus, it is desirable to increase the penalty on A by extending the duration of B's property rule, which is exactly what the court is doing in denying title after the "ordinary" statutory period has elapsed.

Adverse possession also requires that possession be actual, open, notorious, and exclusive. These requirements clearly are designed to give the true owner an ample opportunity to discover the possessor's encroachment and correct the error in a timely manner. There is one instance, however, where actual possession is not necessary for possession to ripen into title. That is where the possessor has "color of title," or a document that appears to confer title but that is defective. In most states, color of title eases the acquisition of title by adverse possession, and in some states it is required. This is consistent with the theory, first, because color of title reduces the likelihood that encroachment is an intentional attempt to circumvent the market; and second, because it is more likely that the possessor will have invested in the land (i.e., V will be larger), making him more susceptible to quasi-rent extraction after the fact.

Finally, possession must be continuous for the statutory period. This is also consistent with the theory, in that periodic abandonment by the possessor is a sign that he has not invested significantly in the land (i.e., extraction of quasi-rents is not a serious problem) and that he did not occupy it in error. While abandonment breaks the continuity of possession, sale does not. Specifically, buyers are allowed to "tack" their period of occupancy to that of previous owners in order to satisfy the statutory period.[44] This also makes sense because, unlike abandonment, the act of sale does *not* necessarily signal an absence of quasi-rents, and, moreover, sale by the possessor is a clear sign to the true owner of the possessor's claim of title. Thus, it provides an opportunity to correct good-faith errors.

4. Summary

This chapter has been primarily concerned with how the law deals with the problem of incompatible property rights, or what economists call externalities. I began the analysis by drawing the distinction between property rules and liability rules since it is fundamental to the economic analysis of property. The idea behind the distinction is that, when transaction costs are low, voluntary exchange based on property rules should be the primary mechanism for transferring rights, even when incompatibilities exist. However, when transaction costs are high, incompatibilities can lead to inefficiency, so coerced exchange based on liability rules may be desirable. It is interesting to note how this distinction tracks the boundary between contracts (voluntary transfer of rights under property rules) and torts (involuntary transfer of rights under liability rules).

Given this theoretical view of property rights, I evaluated the efficiency of several actual methods for dealing with overlapping property rights, including nuisance law, trespass, Pigouvian taxes and subsidies, zoning, and land use covenants. I also examined legal rules governing the transfer of land between private individuals, both through voluntary and involuntary means. In the next chapter, I will extend the analysis of property to examine the relationship between private individuals and the government.

SEVEN

GOVERNMENT TAKING
AND REGULATION OF
PRIVATE PROPERTY

This chapter examines government acquisition and regulation of private property. Unlike private individuals, who must bargain with owners when they wish to acquire property, the government can acquire private property for public use without the owner's consent, provided that it pays just compensation. Thus, private property owners have only liability-rule protection of their property vis-à-vis the government. The first part of this chapter is an economic analysis of government takings of this sort. It examines the economic justification for the government's power of eminent domain, the meaning of just compensation, and the implications of eminent domain for the land-development decisions of property owners.

In contrast to physical acquisitions or intrusions, government regulation of private property generally does not require compensation. Instead, it is viewed as a legitimate exercise of the government's police power. There is a longstanding question, however, about whether or when a regulation ever becomes so burdensome to a property owner as to require compensation under the takings clause. Regulations that cross this threshold are referred to as regulatory takings. In the second part of this chapter I develop an economic framework for determining where this threshold should be. I then employ the framework to discuss several related topics, such as whether investment-backed expectations are necessary for compensation to be paid, whether capitalization of the threat of regulation into land prices renders the compensation question irrelevant, and what the impact of compensation is on the timing of development.

1. The Economics of Eminent Domain

The Fifth Amendment to the U.S. Constitution guarantees, in part, that the government shall not take private property for public use without paying "just compensation".[1] This seemingly straightforward protection of private property from arbitrary government seizure has generated a large literature attempting to interpret and justify its various components. In this section, I will provide an economic perspective on eminent domain. I will first give an economic justification for the existence of this power, and then discuss the question of just compensation—how courts measure it compared to how it should be measured, and why the two measures differ. Finally, I will examine the implications of eminent domain for land-use incentives.

1.1. The Justification for Eminent Domain

Eminent domain gives the government the power to acquire property from private individuals through nonconsensual transfers. Thus, a private individual's property is protected by a liability rule, rather than a property rule, vis-à-vis the government. A common justification for this power is that it prevents individuals from refusing to sell their property to the government at a "reasonable" price. This argument is faulty, however, because the subjective value an individual attaches to his or her property is worthy of protection in economic exchange—indeed, an important reason for protecting property by a property rule is to allow individuals to refuse transactions that do not make them better off.[2] Recall that the analysis in the previous chapter emphasized this feature of systems governing land transfers between private individuals.

Since subjective value is important, and property rules protect subjective value, there must be another justification for eminent domain. The answer is that, when the government is assembling a large amount of land to build a public project like a highway, individual owners whose land is necessary for the project acquire monopoly power in their dealing with the government. That is, they can hold out for prices in excess of their true (subjective) valuation of the land given that it would be costly, once the project is begun, for the government to seek alternative locations. (The problem is thus similar to the encroaching developer in the discussion of adverse possession in the previous chapter.)[3] Although the government theoretically could solve this problem by acquiring all the necessary land prior to construction, it would be difficult to conceal the project as the pattern of acquisitions was revealed. Moreover, because the project is publicly funded, it usually is public knowledge well in advance because of the need to appropriate funds. Private developers assembling a large number of properties clearly face the same problem. One argument for why they do not have eminent-domain power is that it would be easier for them to acquire the property while disguising their ultimate intent—for example, through the use of "dummy" buyers. Another is that the government, in contrast to private developers, uses its eminent-domain power almost exclusively to provide public goods rather than for private gain (the public-use requirement) (Ulen, 1992).[4]

The real justification for eminent domain, then, is the need to prevent hold-outs, which is a form of transaction cost. This justification is therefore a special case of the earlier argument that property rules are desirable when transaction costs are low and liability rules are desirable when transaction costs are high.

1.2. Just Compensation

Courts generally define just compensation to be *fair market value*. As we saw in the previous chapter, however, this amount almost certainly undercompensates landowners, possibly by a large amount. This is because landowners do not generally view land and wealth as perfect substitutes, whereas market value compensates them as if they did.[5] Fair market value is not only unfair to landowners, it also potentially leads to an excessive transfer of private property to public use because the government does not have to pay the true opportunity cost of the resources it acquires. Thus, while the holdout problem precludes the efficient assembly of property through market exchange, eminent domain with market-value compensation potentially leads to too much assembly (Munch, 1976). I consider the role of compensation in restraining government behavior in more detail later.

Of course, the takings clause does not *define* just compensation to be fair market value, so it is not a necessary feature of eminent domain that it result in undercompensation. However, the problem with setting compensation equal to the owner's true valuation is that this amount is unobservable, and owners would clearly have an incentive to overstate it.[6] Thus, taking measurement costs into account, fair market value may be the best proxy for just compensation.

1.3. Eminent Domain and Land-Use Incentives

The feature of eminent domain that has drawn the most attention from economists, especially recently, is its impact on land-use incentives. In particular, how does the possible threat of condemnation affect a landowner's incentive to invest in developing his or her land? The first formal analysis of this question was by Blume, Rubinfeld, and Shapiro (1984). The principal result that they derived (or at least the one that has received the most attention) was that a rule of no compensation for takings results in efficient investment decisions by landowners. In the following sections I first demonstrate the no compensation result using a simplified version of the Blume, Rubinfeld, and Shapiro (BRS) model,[7] and in subsequent sections I present some arguments against no compensation.

1.3.1. THE NO-COMPENSATION RESULT

Consider the following simple model of land development in the presence of a taking threat. Let $v(x)$ be the value of a plot of land to an individual landowner, where x is the amount he invests in developing it (in dollars), $v' > 0$, $v'' < 0$. Further, suppose that there are a total of n identical landowners, and the government randomly takes $m < n$ plots in order to produce a public good valued at B per person, which I treat as exogenous for now. The probability that a given plot of land will *not* be taken is thus given by $p = (n - m)/n$, and the probability that a plot will be taken is given by $1 - p = m/n$. Let $C(x)$ be the compensation paid to each of the m landowners whose land is taken, where $C \geq 0$ and $C' \geq 0$.

Assume that this compensation, which totals $mC(x)$, is financed by a tax T imposed on each of the owners whose land is not taken.[8]

Given that the taking decision in this simple model is treated as exogenous, the only efficiency issue is the amount of investment that landowners make in their land. I assume that the choice of x must be made by each landowner prior to the taking decision. Given this assumption, the social problem is to choose x to maximize the expected return to landowners, including the value of the public good. That is, x solves

$$\text{maximize } (n - m)v(x) + nB - nx \tag{7.1}$$

(note that neither T nor $C(x)$ appears in the social problem as they are simply transfers). The resulting first-order condition is

$$(n - m)v'(x) - n = 0$$

or, dividing through by n and substituting $p = (n - m)/n$,

$$pv'(x) - 1 = 0 \tag{7.2}$$

That is, the optimal x equates the expected marginal value of investment in each plot to the marginal cost. Denote the solution to (7.2) x^*.

Now consider the private problem facing the landowner. He chooses x to maximize the expected private value of his plot, taking as given the probability of a taking, $1 - p$, the compensation rule $C(x)$, the value of the public good B, and the tax T. Thus he chooses x to

$$\text{maximize } p[v(x) - T] + (1 - p)C(x) + B - x. \tag{7.3}$$

The first-order condition arising from (7.3) is

$$pv'(x) + (1 - p)C'(x) - 1 = 0. \tag{7.4}$$

Comparing this to (7.2) shows that efficiency requires $C'(x) = 0$. That is, compensation must be a lump sum, or independent of the amount that the landowner invests in the land. Intuitively, compensation that is positively related to x creates a moral hazard by providing the landowner insurance against the possibility of a taking. Note that a special case of lump sum compensation is $C(x) = 0$, or no compensation.

1.3.2. ARGUMENTS AGAINST THE NO-COMPENSATION RESULT

Although no compensation was shown to be a special case of an efficient compensation rule, it has received the most attention. In this section I will therefore provide several arguments that have been made against it. We shall see, however, that even positive compensation rules retain the lump sum character that we derived in the previous section.

The first and most common objection to no compensation is that it allows the government to acquire resources at no cost. This is not a problem if the government is unswervingly devoted to acquiring resources only when it is efficient to do so. Fischel and Shapiro (1988, 1989) refer to such a government as "Pigouvian." However, modern public-choice theory suggests that this is unlikely to be the case. A more realistic view treats the government like any other economic agent who responds to economic incentives. If compensation is zero in this case,

> The resources under the control of the central authority will be perceived to be costless. The opportunity costs will be ignored, and land use regulation without compensation will lead to overproduction of environmental amenities . . . . (Johnson, 1977, p. 65).

Such a government is said to have "fiscal illusion" (Blume, Rubinfeld, and Shapiro, 1984). In the current setting, this implies that the government will make its taking decision by comparing the benefit of the public good to the amount of compensation it must pay the owners of the land it takes.

In this version of the model, the taking decision must therefore be endogenous. To capture this formally, let the per-person value of the public good, B, be a function of the amount of private land the government takes. That is, $B = B(m)$, where $B' > 0$ and $B'' < 0$. This model differs from the previous version, in that m is now a choice variable of the government. I continue to assume, however, that the particular m plots that will be taken are chosen randomly from among the total of n plots. Thus, at the point that landowners must choose x, they continue to view the probability of a taking as $1 - p = m/n$, given the anticipated choice of m.

As above, I first consider the social problem. In the current version of the model there are two choices, which are made sequentially. First, the n landowners choose x, and then the government makes its taking decision. The efficient outcome is found, as usual, by proceeding in reverse sequence. Thus, given that in equilibrium all landowners have chosen the same x, the optimal choice of m by the government solves

$$\text{maximize } nB(m) - mv(x). \tag{7.5}$$

The first term is the aggregate benefits from the public good and the second is the lost private value from the m plots of land that are used to produce B. The first-order condition from (7.5) is

$$nB'(m) - v(x) = 0 \tag{7.6}$$

which is the standard Samuelson optimality condition for a public good. Given this condition, the optimal choice of x solves[9]

$$\text{maximize } (n - m)v(x) + nB(m) - nx, \tag{7.7}$$

which yields the first-order condition

$$(n - m)v'(x) - n = 0.$$

Again, dividing through by n and substituting $p = (n - m)/n$ yields

$$pv'(x) - 1 = 0, \tag{7.8}$$

which is identical to (7.2). The solution to this problem is therefore x^*.

Now consider the actual problems facing the government and the landowner. Note first that a government with fiscal illusion will not solve the problem in (7.5), but will instead maximize the value of the public good net of the amount of compensation it must pay. That is, it will choose m to

$$\text{maximize } nB(m) - mC(x). \tag{7.9}$$

In solving this problem, the government will take the landowners' investment, x, and the compensation rule as given. The resulting first-order condition is

$$nB'(m) - C(x) = 0. \tag{7.10}$$

Comparing this to (7.6) shows that setting $C(x) = v(x)$ will induce the government to act efficiently. That is, the government will make the correct taking decision if and only if it has to pay the full value of the land to the owner.[10]

As for landowners, assume that each individual chooses x taking as given the investment decisions of all the other landowners. Further, each landowner views the government's taking decision (both m and p), and the amount of the tax he must pay, T, as being independent of his choice of x. Finally, the landowner knows the compensation rule $C(x) = v(x)$. Given these assumptions, each landowner chooses x to solve

$$\begin{aligned}
&\text{maximize } p[v(x) - T] + (1 - p)v(x) + B(m) - x \\
&= \text{maximize } v(x) - pT + B(m) - x.
\end{aligned} \tag{7.11}$$

The resulting first-order condition is

$$v'(x) - 1 = 0, \tag{7.12}$$

which clearly results in $x > x^*$. Again, this is due to the moral hazard associated with full compensation.

As was true of unlimited expectation damages for promisees in contract cases, full compensation for takings results in inefficient investment because it allows landowners to ignore the social value of a regulation. On the other hand, full compensation is necessary to prevent overregulation by the government. In the presence of this tradeoff, Fischel and Shapiro (1989) examined a compensation rule of the form $C(x) = sv(x)$, and showed that the optimal solution requires $0 < s^* < 1$, or partial compensation, though the outcome in this case is second-best. In contrast, Hermalin (1995) showed that the first-best outcome, as described by (7.6) and (7.8), is attainable under a pair of compensation rules. Under the first, the government pays the landowner compensation equal to the social value of the taking; under the second, the landowner has the option to buy back the land for the same payment.[11] As noted earlier, actual compensation rules tie payment to the fair market value of the land to the owner rather than its value in public use, and owners do not ordinarily have a buy-back option. Thus, Hermalin's rules are purely normative in that they do not explain the actual practice of courts.

Our discussion of breach of contract remedies in chapter 4 suggests yet another solution to this tradeoff—namely, limit compensation to the full value of the land to the owner, evaluated at the efficient level of investment. That is, set $C = v(x^*)$.[12] Note first that this rule continues to induce efficient behavior by the government. In addition, it will induce all landowners to choose x^* in equilibrium. To see this, note that under this rule, the problem in (7.11) becomes

$$\text{maximize } p[v(x) - T] + (1 - p)v(x^*) + B(m) - x. \tag{7.13}$$

Because compensation in this case is a lump sum, the first-order condition is

$$pv'(x) - 1 = 0, \tag{7.14}$$

which is identical to (7.8). Thus, all landowners choose $x = x^*$.

Even when the government does not have fiscal illusion, there is an argument for paying compensation for takings.[13] In the preceding model, I assumed that landowners took the probability of a taking as being independent of their investment decision. Equation (7.6), however, implies that m is in fact decreasing in x.[14] It follows that $\partial p/\partial x > 0$, given $p = (n - m)/n$ (where, recall, n is fixed). Assume that landowners anticipate this. That is, assume they anticipate that, by increasing their investment in land, they can reduce the chance that their land will be taken (i.e., reduce $1 - p$). At the same time, however, assume that they continue to view B and T as fixed. Suppose, for example, that, although they believe they can affect the probability that *their* land will be taken, they do not believe they can affect the overall amount that will be taken or the amount of the tax used to finance compensation. Finally, let C be the lump-sum amount of compensation paid in the event of a taking.

The landowner's maximization problem in this case is to

$$\text{maximize } p[v(x) - T] + (1 - p)C + B - x, \tag{7.15}$$

which yields the first-order condition

$$pv'(x) - 1 + (\partial p/\partial x)[v(x) - T - C] = 0. \tag{7.16}$$

Since $\partial p/\partial x > 0$, efficiency requires that $v(x) - T - C = 0$ at the optimum, or

$$C = v(x^*) - T. \tag{7.17}$$

Thus, even in the absence of fiscal illusion, compensation must be equal to the full value of the land at the optimal level of investment, net of the compensation tax.

The intuition for this result is as follows. If compensation were zero, the term in square brackets in (7.16) would be positive, implying that $pv'(x) < 1$ and that $x > x^*$. That is, when the landowner expects zero compensation (or, generally, undercompensation), he will *overinvest* in order to reduce the probability of a taking. On the other hand, if $C > v(x^*) - T$, the term in brackets is negative and the landowner will choose $x < x^*$. In this case, he expects overcompensation and will *underinvest* in order to increase the probability of a taking. Only full compensation eliminates these incentives to over- or underinvest.

The question is whether it makes sense to assume that landowners view p as a function of x. The answer is probably no for physical acquisitions of land, which rarely occur (indeed, p is probably near zero for most landowners). However, government regulations preventing certain land uses such as zoning and environmental restrictions are widespread and generally apply to all plots in a given area. In that case, p is not necessarily small, and it may be possible for landowners to affect its magnitude by their land-use decisions. In this case, the preceding argument probably makes sense.[15]

We have so far shown that a compensation rule that pays landowners the full value of their land at the efficient level of investment results in both efficient investment in land and efficient takings decisions when the government has fiscal illusion. One problem with this rule is that it requires courts to be able to calculate the efficient level of investment, x^*, a task that may prove difficult in practice. We have seen, however, that this problem has not prevented courts from adopting rules in other areas of the law that require similar calculations. For example, negligence rules require calculation of due standards of care in accident settings. Moreover, existing community standards for land use can often provide a good proxy for efficient development levels (Fischel, 1985).

Two additional arguments against the no-compensation result have been made in the literature. The first was by Michelman (1967) in perhaps the most influential article on takings to date. Michelman used a utilitarian standard for deciding, first, when a government should enact a taking and, second, when it should pay compensation. The standard is based on three factors: efficiency gains, demoralization costs, and settlement costs. Efficiency gains simply represent the social benefits minus the costs of a public project, or, in the notation of the above model, $nB - mv$. A *necessary* condition for enactment of the project under Michelman's standard is therefore $nB - mv > 0$.

In addition to efficiency gains, Michelman introduced two types of costs. The first is the demoralization cost associated with nonpayment of compensation. Demoralization costs represent

> the total of (1) the dollar value necessary to offset disutilities which accrue to losers and their sympathizers specifically from the realization that no compensation is offered, and (2) the present capitalized dollar value of lost future production (reflecting either impaired incentives or social unrest) caused by demoralization of uncompensated losers, their sympathizers, and other observers disturbed by the thought that they themselves may be subjected to similar treatment on some other occasion. (Michelman, 1967, p. 1214).

The second type of cost is the settlement cost (or what we would call transaction cost) associated with payment of compensation. Settlement costs represent "the dollar value of time, effort, and resources which would be required to reach compensation settlements adequate to avoid demoralization costs" (Michelman, 1967, p. 1214).

If S denotes settlement costs and D denotes demoralization costs, then Michelman's standard for compensation is that it should be paid if $S < D$, and not paid if $S > D$. Further, the public project should be enacted if and only if $nB - mv > \min(S, D)$. Note that this standard is intermediate between the Pareto criterion, which always requires *actual* compensation (i.e., $nB - mv > S$), and the Kaldor-Hicks criterion, which only requires *potential* compensation (i.e., $nB > mv$). Thus, Michelman's standard is more permissive than Pareto (e.g., if $S > D$ and $nB - mv > D$, the project should be enacted without compensation), but less permissive than Kaldor-Hicks (e.g., even if $nB - mv > 0$, the project should not be enacted if $nB - mv < \min(S, D)$) (Fischel and Shapiro, 1988, p. 280).

The final argument against the no-compensation result is based on the idea that compensation acts as a form of public insurance for landowners against the risk of government expropriation of their property (Blume and Rubinfeld, 1987; Rose-Ackerman, 1992). The need for public rather than private insurance is that moral hazard and adverse-selection problems prevent formation of a private insurance market for takings risk. Because of the administrative costs and incentive effects of compensation, however, it should be paid only when landowners are very risk averse and losses are large.

2. Regulation and Takings

Courts have generally granted the government broad powers to regulate private property in the interest of protecting public welfare. However, some government regulations can become so restrictive as to cause a substantial reduction in the value of private property. When this happens, courts have occasionally found the regulation to be a taking and ordered the government to pay compensation. The problem is to determine where the threshold that separates noncompensable regulations (police-power actions) from compensable ones (regulatory takings) should be set.

Courts and legal scholars have fashioned several tests to locate this threshold. I will begin by reviewing some of these tests. I will then develop a simple economic model of land-use regulation that suggests a threshold test based on the tradeoff between efficient land use decisions and efficient regulator behavior.

2.1. Tests for Regulatory Takings

I will first consider several tests courts have actually used to distinguish between compensable and noncompensable regulations. The first is the *noxious-use doctrine*, which holds that a regulation is not compensable if it prevents activities that are "injurious to the health, morals, or safety of the community."[16] According to this doctrine, the decisive factor regarding compensation is the *intent* of the regulation (namely, prevention of a social cost). Justice Oliver Wendell Holmes introduced a new factor in the famous case of *Pennsylvania Coal Co.* v. *Mahon.*[17] Holmes argued that, regardless of the intent of the regulation, if it "goes too far" in reducing the value of the property to the owner it becomes a taking and compensation is due. This *diminution of value test* therefore focuses on the *impact* of the regulation on the private value of the property as the decisive factor for compensation. In *Penn Central Transportation Co.* v. *City of New York,*[18] the Supreme Court proposed a three-pronged test for compensation that included the previous two factors and added a third: the presence of investment-backed expectations on the part of the landowner. In particular, compensation is more likely, all else equal, if the regulation interferes with development plans that are investment-backed. In 1992 the Supreme Court added a new test, related to the noxious-use doctrine, that denies compensation for regulations aimed at preventing activities that would have been prohibited under the prevailing common law of nuisance. This nuisance exception was invoked by the Court in *Lucas* v. *South Carolina Coastal Council,*[19] and is also a feature of Richard Epstein's view of takings law (Epstein, 1985).

Several additional tests have been proposed in the academic literature on takings. For example, Sax (1964, 1971) argued that the government should pay compensation when it regulates property in the process of behaving like an enterprise (e.g., in providing goods and services), but it should not pay compensation when it arbitrates private disputes over external costs. This argument is similar to the so-called harm-benefit rule, which says that the government should pay compensation for regulations that provide benefits (e.g., public goods), but it should not pay compensation for regulations that prevent harms.

The problem with the harm-benefit rule, however, is that one can always define prevention of a harm as a benefit. To resolve this problem, Fischel (1985) proposed a version of the harm-benefit rule that defines the threshold between harms and benefits to be the prevailing community standards of land use. Specifically, under Fischel's rule, if a government regulation compels "supra-normal" behavior by landowners, compensation is due, but if it prevents "below normal" behavior, compensation is not due. Such a rule is efficient in the sense that it economizes on the transaction costs of paying compensation. Specifically, it sets the zero-compensation point at the normal-behavior standard, which most people will choose to satisfy voluntarily (i.e., without government intervention). Thus, only a few transactions are needed to prevent below-normal behavior and to reward above-normal behavior. Wittman (1984) uses a similar transaction-cost argument to distinguish between compensable and noncompensable regulations. It is interesting to note that Fischel's normal-behavior threshold resembles the one implicit in the nuisance exception in that activities that are below normal will generally coincide with those that are prevented under nuisance law.

2.2. A Model of Compensation for Regulations

In this section I will develop a simple model of government regulation of land use that can be used to answer the question of when compensation should be paid for regulations.[20] In particular, I will use the model to derive a threshold rule separating compensable and noncompensable regulations based on a trade-off between efficient land-use decisions and efficient regulator behavior. The economic issues are thus the same as those examined in section 1.3—namely, moral hazard and fiscal illusion.

Consider a landowner who has two possible uses of his land: use A, which I will call development, and use B, which I will call recreational use. Suppose that use A requires an initial, nonsalvageable investment, r, which can be thought of as the costs of preparing for development (e.g., the costs of planning, obtaining permits, etc.). After development is complete, land use A yields a private value of V_A, making the net value $V_A - r > 0$. Use B, alternatively, requires no initial investment and yields a private value of V_B. I assume that $V_A > V_B$, but I do not necessarily assume that $V_A - r > V_B$.

The social purpose of regulation in this model is to prevent a possible external cost associated with development. For example, this cost could be beach erosion that may be caused by development of beachfront land. Suppose, therefore, that if the landowner signals his intent to develop his land by spending r, the regulator may act to prevent development, depending on the realized value of the external cost (among other things). The sequence of events is important and is depicted in figure 7.1. It shows that the landowner moves first and signals his intended land use (A or B). If he chooses B, there is no further threat of regulation and the game ends. However, if he signals his intent to pursue land use A (by spending r), the regulator decides whether or not to permit development. If he does, the developer proceeds with land use A, but if he does not, the developer is only allowed to pursue land use B, with the resulting loss of his investment r.

2.2.1. SOCIALLY OPTIMAL REGULATION AND LAND USE

Consider efficient regulatory behavior. Since the regulator is assumed to act only if the landowner has signaled his intent to pursue land use A, the social cost of a regulation is the lost value to the landowner, $V_A - V_B \equiv \Delta V$, whereas the social

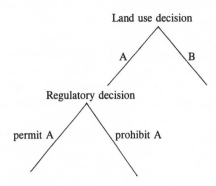

FIGURE 7.1 Sequence of moves by a landowner and a regulator when certain land uses (A) potentially generate external costs.

benefit of the regulation is the avoidance of the external cost, denoted E. Thus, once the value of E is realized, the condition for efficient regulation is

$$E \geq \Delta V. \tag{7.18}$$

The land-use decision is made prior to the realization of E. At that time, only the probability of a regulation is known, which depends on the distribution of E and condition (7.18). For simplicity, I assume that E can take on only two values, $E_H > 0$, which occurs with probability $1 - p$, and zero, which occurs with probability p. Further, I assume that E_H satisfies (7.18). That is, when E_H is realized, it is efficient for the regulator to prohibit land-use A. (Of course, when $E = 0$ regulation is not efficient.) Consequently, if the developer pursues land use A and the regulator is expected to act efficiently, the probability of a regulation is $1 - p$ and the probability of no regulation is p.

Given this specification, at the land-use decision stage the expected social value of spending r in anticipation of developing is given by $pV_A + (1 - p)V_B - r$,[21] and the expected value of not spending r is V_B. Thus, it is socially efficient to spend r if

$$pV_A + (1 - p)V_B - r \geq V_B$$

or if

$$p\Delta V \geq r. \tag{7.19}$$

This condition says that it is efficient to spend r if the expected value of pursuing use A exceeds the cost. (Note that it is the discrete analog to condition (7.2).)

2.2.2. ACTUAL REGULATION AND LAND USE

I next consider actual regulatory and land-use decisions. I assume that the regulator has fiscal illusion in that he makes his regulatory decision by comparing the benefit of the regulation, E, to the amount of compensation he must pay to the landowner, C.[22] Thus, if $C = \Delta V$, he will regulate efficiently, but if $C = 0$ (or, more generally, if $C < \Delta V$), he will overregulate because he views the regulation as being costless. In terms of the ex ante probability of regulation, I will capture the problem of fiscal illusion by defining $1 - q(C)$ as the probability of a regulation, written as a function of the amount of compensation C, where $1 - q(\Delta V) = 1 - p$ and $1 - q(0) > 1 - p$. That is, if compensation is full, the probability of regulation is equal to the efficient probability, but if compensation is zero, the probability of regulation exceeds the efficient probability.

Now consider the landowner. Let s be the landowner's prior assessment of the probability that full compensation will be paid if she pursues land-use A and a regulation is imposed, and let $1\text{-}s$ be her assessment of the probability that zero compensation will be paid in that event. Thus, if the landowner spends r with the intention of pursuing land-use A, her expected return is

$$s[q(\Delta V)V_A + (1 - q(\Delta V))(V_B + \Delta V)] + (1 - s)[q(0)V_A + (1 - q(0))V_B] - r. \tag{7.20}$$

Substituting $\Delta V = V_A - V_B$ into this expression and comparing it to the return from recreational use, V_B, yields the condition for the landowner to pursue use A:

$$[s + (1 - s)q(0)]\Delta V \geq r. \tag{7.21}$$

Comparing this to the condition for efficient land use in (7.19) shows the problem one faces in designing an efficient compensation rule. For example, suppose $s = 1$, or that compensation is always full. In that case, (7.21) becomes $\Delta V \geq r$, which results in excessive investment in development. This is a result of the moral-hazard problem associated with full compensation. Alternatively, suppose $s = 0$, or that compensation is always zero. In that case, (7.21) becomes $q(0)\Delta V \geq r$, which results in too little investment in development given that $q(0) < p$. Thus, the threat of overregulation when compensation is zero causes the landowner to underinvest.

2.2.3. EFFICIENT COMPENSATION RULES

The preceding suggests that there is a fundamental conflict between the desire to induce efficient behavior by the landowner and the desire to reduce efficient regulation.[23] In an effort to resolve this conflict, I consider a conditional compensation rule of the form

$$C = \begin{array}{ll} \Delta V, & \text{if } \Delta V \geq T \\ 0, & \text{if } \Delta V < T \end{array} \tag{7.22}$$

for some threshold T. That is, compensation is full if ΔV exceeds a threshold, but it is zero otherwise. It is possible to show that there are two values of T for which this rule simultaneously induces efficient behavior by the landowner and the regulator.

The first form of (7.22) that is efficient sets $T = \Delta V^*$, where ΔV^* solves the equation $p\Delta V^* = r$. That is, ΔV^* is the value of ΔV for which land use A and land use B are equally desirable from a social perspective (given efficient regulation). According to this version of (7.22), if a regulation occurs, compensation should be full if the landowner efficiently chose land use A (i.e., if she spent r when $\Delta V \geq \Delta V^*$), but it should be zero if she inefficiently chose land use A (i.e., if she spent r when $\Delta V < \Delta V^*$). This rule is referred to as an *ex ante rule* because it defines the threshold in (7.22) based on the land-use decision, which is made prior to the realization of E.

Figure 7.2 shows graphically why setting $T = \Delta V^*$ in (7.22) induces the landowner to behave efficiently.[24] In the graph, ΔV^* is defined by the intersection of $p\Delta V$ and r according to (7.19); to the left of ΔV^*, land-use B is efficient, and to the right of ΔV^* land-use A is efficient. The darkened segments show the private return to the landowner under the efficient ex ante rule. Specifically, when $\Delta V \geq \Delta V^*$ (A is efficient), compensation is full and (7.21) reduces to $\Delta V \geq r$. Since $\Delta V > r$ over this range, the landowner correctly chooses land-use A. On the other hand, when $\Delta V < \Delta V^*$ (B is efficient), compensation is zero and (7.21) becomes $q(0)\Delta V \geq r$. Since $q(0) < p$, $q(0)\Delta V < r$ over this range and the landowner correctly chooses land-use B.

As for the regulator, he behaves efficiently as well under this rule because any time the landowner chooses land-use A, compensation is full (assuming landowners act efficiently in equilibrium). In principle, therefore, $C = 0$ is relevant only when the regulator does not have the opportunity to act anyway. Thus, he will regulate only when it is efficient to do so.

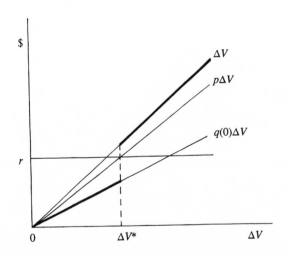

FIGURE 7.2 Efficient threshold for the ex ante rule.

Note the rule in (7.22) induces efficiency by both parties for the same reason that the negligence rule works in bilateral-care accident cases. Specifically, it specifies a threshold for one of the parties (the landowner under the ex ante rule) such that, by acting efficiently, that party can avoid liability (or, in the current setting, receive full compensation). As a result, the other party (the regulator) bears full liability in equilibrium (i.e., must pay compensation) and therefore also acts efficiently.

The second form of (7.22) that induces efficient behavior by both parties sets $T = E$, the realized value of the external cost. This version is thus referred to as the *ex post rule*. Note that the ex post rule differs from the ex ante rule in that it sets the threshold based on efficient behavior by the regulator rather than the landowner. That is, compensation is full when $\Delta V \geq E$, or when it is inefficient to impose the regulation ex post; whereas compensation is zero when $\Delta V < E$, or when it is efficient to impose the regulation ex post. This definition of the threshold induces the regulator to act efficiently because by doing so he can avoid paying compensation. Moreover, since compensation is zero for efficient regulations, landowners will make the correct land-use decisions as well.[25]

2.2.4. IMPLICATIONS OF THE EFFICIENT RULES

The efficiency of the ex ante and ex post versions of (7.22) has several implications for the analysis of regulatory takings. First, note that the general form of (7.22) resembles Holmes's diminution of value rule, in that it conditions compensation on the extent of the landowner's loss, ΔV, in the event of a regulation. However, the two versions of (7.22) imply different standards for when a regulation "goes too far." In particular, the ex ante rule implies that a regulation goes too far when it prevents a land use that was efficiently chosen by the landowner in an ex ante sense. Alternatively, the ex post rule says a regulation goes too far when it is inefficiently imposed.[26]

Second, notice that the ex post rule resembles the noxious-use doctrine in that it provides a standard for defining a noxious use. Specifically, if we define noxious uses to be those uses that are efficiently regulated ex post, then nonpayment of compensation for such regulations is efficient according to the ex post version of (7.22). By similar reasoning, the ex post rule is consistent with both the nuisance exception (if nuisances are defined according to be those activities that are efficiently regulated)[27] and Fischel's normal behavior standard (if below normal behavior corresponds to behavior that is efficiently regulated).

Third, the fact that both the diminution of value rule and the noxious-use doctrine are consistent with the above rules (and therefore with efficiency) suggests that Holmes's decision in *Pennsylvania Coal* may not have been a significant break with previous law, as has sometimes been argued.[28] It further suggests that Brandeis's dissent in *Pennsylvania Coal*, which was based on the noxious-use doctrine, may not have been based on a disagreement with Holmes about the *law*, so much as about the *facts* of the case. For example, if we suppose that both Holmes and Brandeis were employing the ex post version of (7.22), then the disagreement reduces to the fact that Holmes believed $\Delta V \geq E$ (i.e., the regulation was inefficiently imposed), whereas Brandeis believed $\Delta V < E$ (i.e., the regulation was efficiently imposed). As a result, they reached opposing conclusions regarding compensation even though they agreed on the law (in this interpretation).

This same argument might explain the decision not to compensate the coal companies in *Keystone Bituminous Coal Assn.* v. *DeBenedictus*,[29] despite the fact that the question being decided was nearly identical to that in *Pennsylvania Coal*. Again, the different decisions in the two cases need not imply that the judges were applying different theories of compensation. Rather, it might simply mean that the facts of the cases differed; that is, $\Delta V < E$ in *Keystone* (implying no compensation was efficient), whereas $\Delta V \geq E$ in *Pennsylvania Coal* (implying compensation was efficient).

Fourth, the ex ante version of (7.22) is similar to the common law doctrine of *coming to the nuisance*, which says that, in a situation of incompatible land uses, the property right should be awarded to the party that was there first. Thus, if that party is ordered to cease operation, it is owed compensation. The case of *Spur Industries* v. *Del Webb* discussed in the previous chapter provides an example of how the ex ante rule relates to this doctrine.[30] Recall that in this case, the court ordered a feedlot to shut down because of the external cost it imposed on a residential development. However, the developer was required to compensate the owner of the feedlot for his cost of relocation because its existence predated the development and because there was no indication at the time the feedlot was established that development would impinge upon it. In other words, the feedlot was efficiently established in an ex ante sense (i.e., $\Delta V \geq \Delta V^*$), so compensation was due when it was regulated.[31]

Finally, since we have seen that two versions of (7.22) are efficient, factors other than efficiency can be used to choose between them. Two such factors are fairness and transaction costs. Fairness generally argues for payment of compensation in equilibrium, which favors the ex ante rule. In contrast, transaction-cost considerations argue against compensation, which favors the ex post rule.

2.3. Investment-Backed Expectations and Compensation

As noted earlier, in *Penn Central Transportation Co.* v. *City of New York*, the Supreme Court suggested that, along with the nature of the regulation and its impact on the landowner's expected return, a relevant consideration in judging whether a regulation is a taking is the extent to which it interferes with a landowner's "investment-backed expectations." This suggests that compensation is more likely to be paid, all else equal, if the landowner had made reliance expenditures in anticipation of developing, as compared to merely claiming that he intended to develop. We can examine a simplified version of this requirement for compensation by amending the simple land use model in section 2.2 as follows.[32]

Suppose that the compensation rule is specified such that if a regulation is imposed, $C_r \geq 0$ is the amount paid if the landowner had spent r, and $C_0 \geq 0$ is the amount paid if he had not. (Note that I implicitly set $C_0 = 0$ in the original model.) For simplicity, suppose that the probability of a regulation is equal to the efficient probability, $1\text{-}p$, regardless of the compensation rule (i.e., I will ignore fiscal illusion) and whether or not the landowner invested r.[33] Finally, assume that if the landowner does not spend r, he does not intend to develop in the future.

Given these assumptions, the landowner's expected return from spending r is

$$pV_A + (1 - p)(V_B + C_r) - r \tag{7.23}$$

and his expected return from not spending r is

$$pV_B + (1 - p)(V_B + C_0) = V_B + (1 - p)C_0. \tag{7.24}$$

The landowner will therefore spend r if and only if (7.23) is greater than (7.24), or if and only if

$$p\Delta V + (1 - p)(C_r - C_0) \geq r. \tag{7.25}$$

Comparing this condition to (7.19) shows that a sufficient condition for efficient land use is to set $C_0 = C_r$. That is, landowners who spent r should *not* receive greater compensation than those who did not. It follows from (7.25) that if $C_r > C_0$, landowners will have an incentive to overinvest in order to qualify for the higher compensation in the event of a regulation. Thus, an investment-backed expectation rule appears inconsistent with efficient land use.

One way to retain the investment-backed expectation rule without distorting incentives is to combine it with a reasonableness requirement. That is, set $C_r > C_0$ if and only if r was spent efficiently. Note that this rule reduces to the efficient ex ante rule if we set $C_r = \Delta V$ and $C_0 = 0$.

2.4. Capitalization and Compensation

A frequent argument made against paying compensation for regulations is that when landowners purchased land that is subject to the threat of a regulation, they paid a price that discounted (or capitalized) the possibility of that regulation. Consequently, the argument goes, they have already received implicit compensation. This argument owes much to Michelman's article (Michelman, 1967), but courts understood it as far back as 1823 when, in the case of *Callender* v. *Marsh*, the court said:

> Those who purchase house lots . . . are supposed to calculate the chance of [regulations] . . . and as their purchase is always voluntary, they may indemnify themselves in the price of the lot which they buy.[34]

Several authors have suggested, however, that this argument is flawed.[35] The reason is that, even if the purchaser had full knowledge of the threat of a regulation when he bought the land, and therefore paid a discounted price, the threat had to arise at some previous point in time, and the owner at that point suffered a capital loss.

To see this, let R be the purchase price that a developer paid for the parcel of land in this model.[36] If we assume that the landowner extracted the entire expected value of the land in the purchase price, then

$$
\begin{aligned}
R &= pV_A + (1 - p)(V_B + C) - r \\
&= V_A - (1 - p)(\Delta V - C) - r.
\end{aligned} \tag{7.26}
$$

Now suppose that $C = 0$. Then (7.26) shows that $\partial R/\partial(1 - p) = -\Delta V < 0$, or the regulatory threat causes the price to fall in proportion to the impact of the regulation on the value of the land. This is the basis for the capitalization argument. By the same reasoning, the anticipation of any compensation is capitalized, in proportion to the probability of a regulation—that is, $\partial R/\partial C = 1 - p > 0$.

The loss to a landowner whose ownership predated the threat of a regulation can be seen by noting that when $p = 1$ (i.e., when there is no threat of a regulation), $R = V_A - r$. Thus, at the point that *notice* of a regulation is first given (i.e., when p falls below one), the value of the land drops by the difference between $V_A - r$ and (7.26), or by $(1 - p)(\Delta V - C)$. Thus, the only way that the original landowner is fully protected against this capital loss is if compensation is full (i.e., $C = \Delta V$), for in this case, R is independent of p. If policymakers wish to insure landowners against this type of loss without sacrificing efficiency, then the ex ante rule is superior to the ex post rule given that, in an efficient equilibrium, full compensation is paid under the former but not under the latter.

2.5. The Timing of Development: Vested Rights and Reversibility

A developer will occasionally begin investing in a project only to find that a change in the zoning regulations prevents its completion. Although local governments need to have some freedom to revise their zoning laws in response to changing circumstances, landowners also need some protection of their sunk investments when a zoning change occurs. The courts have provided a basis for such protection in the form of *vested rights*.[37] A vested right allows the landowner to proceed with the project despite the zoning change under certain conditions.

In order for a landowner to acquire a vested right, he generally must have made a substantial investment in the property in reliance on a valid building permit. How much investment is necessary to be deemed substantial is not clear; generally courts engage in a balancing test that weighs the costs and benefits of the zoning change. In addition to making substantial investments, the landowner must have acted in good faith—for example, he must not have rushed the development process in an effort to beat an impending zoning change. More generally, the good-faith test asks "whether a landowner's conduct was consistent with how a reasonable property owner would have acted in the same circumstances" (Mandelker, 1993, p. 239).

These tests for awarding a vested right can be interpreted in the context of this model as asking whether the landowner proceeded with development in an efficient manner. Thus, they are consistent with the efficient ex ante rule in the sense that they award a vested right if $\Delta V \geq \Delta V^*$ (i.e., if development was efficient), but they do not award a vested right if $\Delta V < \Delta V^*$ (i.e., if development was not efficient).

Note that the threat to withhold a vested right if the landowner developed prematurely is effective only if the development is *reversible*—that is, only if the development process can be halted and the resulting external cost avoided or eliminated if the landowner developed inefficiently. This will not always be possible. An example where it is not is when the owner of timber land harvests his trees prematurely in order to avoid the imposition of regulations aimed at preserving the habitat of an endangered species. In this case, it may be necessary to promise compensation for the threatened regulation in order to offset the incentive for preemptive development. The magnitude of compensation cannot be too large, however, for then landowners may have an incentive to *delay* development inefficiently. One way to ensure efficient incentives is to condition the payment of compensation on the efficiency of the landowner's decision—that is, on whether his decision to wait was efficient. Notice that such a rule is simply a dynamic version of the ex ante rule.[38]

3. Summary

In this chapter I examined the relationship between private landowners and the government. I first considered eminent domain, or the government's power to take private property for public use provided that it pays just compensation. Eminent domain is an example of protecting property rights with a liability rule, in that it allows the government to acquire the property without the owner's consent. The economic justification for this power thus relies on the high transaction costs involved in a government's assembly of land for public goods. I also examined the question of what amount of compensation should be paid for takings based on considerations of fairness and the efficiency of decision making by landowners and the government.

The takings question extends beyond physical acquisitions of land by the government to regulation of land uses aimed at preventing externalities. The key issue in this context is to determine when a regulation becomes so onerous on the landowner as to constitute a taking for which compensation is due. The second part of this chapter examined how courts and scholars have historically answered this question and suggested how economic theory can provide a unifying view.

EIGHT

THE ECONOMICS OF LITIGATION
AND SETTLEMENT

This chapter and the next examine the decision by the parties to a legal dispute as to whether to settle out of court or go to trial. For the purposes of the analysis, the specific nature of the dispute is not relevant; all that matters is that one party—the plaintiff—is seeking some amount of money from the other party—the defendant—as compensation for damages the latter imposed on the former.[1] Economists are interested in the resolution of legal disputes for at least three reasons. First, the manner in which they are resolved has an important effect on the cost of operating the legal system. Second, economic theory is useful in explaining and predicting how rational litigants will resolve disputes and can therefore offer suggestions for lowering the cost of litigation. Finally, the manner in which parties resolve disputes has implications for the structure of legal rules, which in turn affects investments in the future by individuals to avoid disputes in the first place.

The fact is that the vast majority of civil cases are settled or dropped before they go to trial. For example, the data on civil litigation in table 8.1 shows that only 5 percent or less of all civil cases commenced in U.S. district courts between 1987 and 1993 eventually went to trial. The most recent available state court data, from 1988, similarly indicate that the trial rate for civil cases disposed of in state courts was quite low, at 9.2 percent.[2] These results turn out to be quite consistent with what economic theory predicts, given rational behavior of litigants, low costs of bargaining compared to trials, and symmetric (though not necessarily perfect) information. Indeed, if we assume, as seems plausible, that trials cost more than settlements in terms of transaction costs, then it becomes difficult to explain why *any* disputes go to trial. Thus, the primary question to be answered in this chapter is, why do trials ever occur? In the following sections I review several models that have been used in the literature to answer this question. I go on to use the results of these models to examine several related issues, including the impact of various cost-allocation rules and the practice of pretrial discovery on the trial rate and cost of litigation. I also address the question of whether the common tends to evolve in the direction of efficiency without the conscious help of judges or litigants.

156

TABLE 8.1   Trial Rates for Civil Cases in U.S. District Courts, 1987–1993 (in 1000s except for percentages)

	1987	1988	1989	1990	1991	1992	1993
Total cases commenced	239.0	239.6	233.5	217.9	207.7	226.9	228.6
Trials	11.9	11.6	11.2	9.2	8.4	8.0	7.9
Trial rate (%)	5.0	4.9	4.8	4.3	4.0	3.4	3.5

Source: Statistical Abstract of the U.S., 1994.

1. The Differing Perceptions Model

The first and simplest explanation for trials is based on the fact that litigants may have different perceptions about the outcome of a trial.[3] These differences may be due to private information the parties have about the strength of their cases, uncertainties about the relevant law, or both. It is easy to show in this context that, if both parties are optimistic about their chances of winning at trial, they may be unable to reach a mutually beneficial settlement, thus resulting in a trial. The intuitive reason for this is that pretrial bargaining takes place against the background of a trial, with each party trying to do better than what they expect at trial. Thus, if both parties expect to do well at trial, they may be unable to find a settlement that both prefer to trial. The next section illustrates this result with a simple bargaining model.[4]

1.1. The Basic Model

Suppose a plaintiff (p) has filed a lawsuit against a defendant (d) in order to receive compensation for damages. Prior to trial, the parties engage in pretrial bargaining in hopes of arriving at a settlement that would result in the defendant making a payment $S \geq 0$ to the plaintiff. If they fail to reach a settlement, a trial ensues.

Suppose the parties may differ in their perceptions of the outcome of a trial. Specifically, let P_p be the plaintiff's perception of her probability of winning at trial, and let J_p be her perception of the judgment she will receive (in dollars) if she wins.[5] Similarly, let P_d and J_d be the defendant's perceptions of these variables (i.e., the plaintiff's probability of winning and expected judgment). Let the costs of a trial for the two parties be C_p and C_d, and let the costs of settlement be R_p and R_d. I assume that $C_j > R_j$, $j = p, d$, to capture the higher costs of trial compared to settlement. Although pretrial bargaining can be costly, trials must be costlier because the cost of going to trial includes as one component the cost of the failed pretrial bargaining (i.e., R_j is a component of C_j).

I assume that both parties are risk-neutral maximizers of expected wealth. (Note that, if anything, this assumption biases the model away from settlements since risk aversion may be a big reason for avoiding trial.) The expected value of a trial for the plaintiff is thus $P_p J_p - C_p$, and the value of settling for an amount

S is $S - R_p$. The plaintiff will therefore be willing to settle if $S - R_p \geq P_p J_p - C_p$, or if

$$S \geq P_p J_p - (C_p - R_p). \tag{8.1}$$

The defendant similarly calculates the expected cost of a trial to be $P_d J_d + C_d$ and the cost of a settlement to be $S + R_d$. Thus, the defendant will settle if $S + R_d \leq P_d J_d + C_d$, or if

$$S \leq P_d J_d + (C_d - R_d). \tag{8.2}$$

Combining conditions (8.1) and (8.2) shows that a "settlement range" exists if the following condition holds:

$$P_p J_p - P_d J_d \leq (C_p - R_p) + (C_d - R_d). \tag{8.3}$$

where the right-hand side is positive given the higher costs of trials compared to settlements.

Several implications follow from condition (8.3). First, if $P_p = P_d$ and $J_p = J_d$, then (8.3) always holds. Thus, if the parties agree on the expected outcome of a trial, a settlement range always exists given the higher cost of trials compared to settlements. In fact, when the parties agree, the right-hand side of (8.3) represents the joint surplus from settling rather than going to trial, and the choice of S determines the division of the surplus. Of course, a settlement is not guaranteed whenever (8.3) holds because the parties may not be able to agree on how to divide the surplus[6] (i.e., condition (8.3) is necessary but not sufficient for a settlement).

Condition (8.3) also provides an economic explanation for the practice of pre-trial discovery, which allows the parties to obtain information about their opponent's case prior to trial. If this process is truly informative, then it will tend to increase the settlement rate by reducing differences in perceptions about the outcome of a trial (i.e., the left-hand side of (8.3) will decrease). It does not necessarily follow, however, that discovery saves litigation costs because it is costly to make and comply with discovery requests, and because the parties may also attempt to use it strategically to impose excessive costs on their opponents in hopes of inducing them to accept less favorable terms (or to drop the suit). I will examine these and other aspects of discovery in section 4.

1.2. The Selection of Disputes for Litigation

Suppose that the parties agree on the stakes of the case, J, and disagree only about the probability that the plaintiff will win at trial. In that case, (8.3) can be rearranged to show that a sufficient condition for trial is

$$P_p - P_d > [(C_p + C_d) - (R_p + R_d)]/J \tag{8.3'}$$

where the right-hand side is positive. According to (8.3'), a case is more likely to go to trial, all else equal, the greater is the difference in the parties' perceptions about the likelihood of a plaintiff victory (i.e., the more optimistic the two sides are). As a result, Priest and Klein (1984) have argued that the set of cases that go to trial is not a random sample of all cases filed.[7] This is referred to as the *selective litigation hypothesis*. Priest and Klein have further argued that a trial is more likely the closer a dispute is to being a toss-up since, on average, such cases will result in a larger disagreement between the parties (i.e., a larger $P_p - P_d$). This hypothesis is referred to as the *50 percent rule* because it implies that the plaintiff's win rate for cases that go to trial will be approximately 50 percent, assuming symmetric stakes for the parties.

Eisenberg (1990) conducted an empirical test of the selection hypothesis and the 50 percent rule using both Priest and Klein's data (collected from Cook County, Illinois) and federal data on various areas of civil litigation. In general, he rejected the 50 percent rule but not the selection hypothesis. In another study, Waldfogel (1995) found strong support for the selection effect in a sample of federal civil cases filed in New York between 1984 and 1987, both across case types and across judges. He further showed that among tort, contract, and intellectual property cases, plaintiffs had higher stakes than defendants in contract and intellectual property cases, but defendants had higher stakes in tort cases. Finally, he found that tort cases caused the greatest uncertainty among litigants, suggesting more uncertainty about the legal standard in this area compared to contracts and intellectual property.

Using experimental methods, Thomas (1995) similarly found evidence in support of the selection hypothesis but not the 50 percent rule. In contrast, Stanley and Coursey (1990), also using experimental methods, could not reject the hypothesis that settlements are an *unbiased* sample from the population of all disputes.

1.3. Selective Litigation and Legal Change

Condition (8.3') also has implications for the nature of legal change. Specifically, it implies that a trial is more likely the larger is J, all else equal. Thus, disputes involving higher stakes are more likely to go to trial. This observation has led to the suggestion that the common law will tend to evolve in the direction of efficiency without the help of judges.[8] The basis for this argument is that less efficient laws will tend to result in disputes involving higher costs for victims (i.e., higher J's) all else equal. Thus, disputes over inefficient laws will go to trial with greater frequency than disputes over efficient laws. As a result, judges will have more opportunity to evaluate inefficient laws compared to efficient ones, given that judges cannot select the cases they hear (with the exception of the Supreme Court). And, as long as judges do not systematically decide *against* efficiency, the number of inefficient laws will decrease relative to the number of efficient laws.

Although the logic of this argument is correct, it has been criticized on various grounds. First, if the costs of inefficient laws are dispersed, then they may not be litigated more frequently than efficient laws because individual victims will not internalize the full benefits of overturning the law and therefore may not have a sufficient incentive to challenge it. Similarly, if the costs of efficient laws are concentrated, they may be litigated more frequently than inefficient laws. Finally, if precedent is important in a particular area of the law, it may result in inefficient laws being *reinforced* rather than overturned as a result of more frequent litigation (Landes and Posner, 1979, pp. 261–262).

A more realistic version of the above litigation model allows the level of litigation expenditures of the parties to be endogenous (that is, under the control of the parties rather than being fixed). For example, it is reasonable to assume that the more a party spends on litigation, all else equal, the greater will be his or her chances of winning at trial. To capture this, we can write the probability of plaintiff victory as $P(C_p, C_d)$, where $\partial P / \partial C_p > 0$ and $\partial P / \partial C_d < 0$. (Note that in this formulation, litigation expenditures are a form of rent seeking in that they do not change the size of the judgment but only affect its expected distribution.) When litigation expenditures are endogenous, it is easy to show that, the higher are the stakes of the case, J, the more both parties will spend on litigation (Goodman, 1978; Katz, 1988). This effect will tend to magnify the "favored" party's chances of winning. Thus, if the favored party is systematically an advocate of efficient rules, on one hand, this will enhance the tendency of the law to become more efficient. On the other hand, if precedent is important, this effect may further strengthen existing inefficient rules.

1.4. Empirical Implications for the Evolution of the Law

Priest (1987) and Cooter (1987a) empirically tested the above model of legal change based on the hypothesis that, when the law is changing, litigants will be more uncertain about the outcome of a trial (i.e., $P_p J_p - P_d J_d$ will be larger), and hence, the settlement rate should be lower. The empirical results broadly confirmed this hypothesis by revealing a significant positive relationship between legal change and litigant disagreement.

The data could not tell, however, whether legal change precedes (causes) disagreement, or whether disagreement precedes legal change. As Cooter (1987a) noted, the first possibility implies that litigant behavior reacts to changes in legal doctrine, suggesting that the law is idea-driven. In contrast, the second implies that legal doctrine responds to disagreement among litigants that, under certain circumstances noted above, will propel the law toward efficiency. Cooter says that in this case the law is market driven. The fact that neither was favored by the evidence is consistent with the notion that both forces likely play a role in the process of legal change according to a feedback relationship. In particular, legal change leads to litigant uncertainty and increased litigation, but at the same time, the higher litigation rate provides fuel for further legal change.

1.5. Legal Error and Differences in Litigant Perceptions

Previously I suggested that different perceptions about the outcome of a trial could be due to private information or uncertainty about the law. Another explanation could be legal error of the sort examined in chapter 3 (section 2.2).[9] In particular, suppose the dispute concerns whether the defendant violated a legal standard (e.g., due care), and the court makes both type I errors (false acquittals) and type II errors (false convictions). As above, let q_1 and q_2 be the probabilities of these errors (which are fixed), and assume that $1 - q_1 > q_2$.

Legal error will result in different perceptions about the outcome of a trial by the litigants if the plaintiff is uncertain about whether the defendant truly violated the legal standard. For example, if α is the plaintiff's assessment of the probability that the defendant violated the standard, then the plaintiff expects to win at trial with probability

$$P_p = \alpha(1 - q_1) + (1 - \alpha)q_2. \tag{8.4}$$

Since the defendant knows whether he violated the legal standard, his belief about the plaintiff's probability of victory depends on his type. Specifically

$$P_d = \begin{array}{ll} 1 - q_1, & \text{if guilty} \\ q_2, & \text{if innocent.} \end{array} \tag{8.5}$$

Combining (8.4) and (8.5) shows that

$$P_p - P_d = \begin{array}{ll} -(1 - \alpha)(1 - q_1 - q_2) < 0, & \text{if guilty} \\ \alpha(1 - q_1 - q_2) > 0, & \text{if innocent.} \end{array} \tag{8.6}$$

It follows that condition (8.3) will always hold for guilty defendants (given constant $\tilde{J}$), but it may not hold for innocent defendants. Thus, if differences in perceptions are due only to legal error, then trials will be more likely when defendants did not violate the standard. This suggests, in contrast to the 50 percent rule, that the conviction rate at trial should be relatively low.[10]

Note, however, that if a settlement always occurs when condition (8.3) holds, then the defendant's decision to settle or go to trial would convey information to the plaintiff (and the court) about his type. In particular, if the defendant refused to settle, it would imply that $P_p - P_d > 0$, and the plaintiff could infer the defendant's innocence. Thus, the plaintiff would rationally revise her prior beliefs and set $\alpha = 0$, in which case $P_p = q_2 = P_d$. As a result, (8.3) would now hold and the parties would settle. This argument suggests that legal error cannot be the sole explanation for trials in the current model.[11] Either differences in perceptions also arise for other reasons noted above, or trials sometimes occur even when (8.3) holds.

1.6. Judicial Decision making and the Evolution of the Law

To this point, the discussion of the evolution of the law toward efficiency has for the most part relied on invisible hand–type arguments to explain how self-interested behavior by litigants determines the path of the law. These models either ignore the behavior of judges or treat them in an ad hoc manner. There has, however, been recent interest in examining the behavior of judges in a more rigorous manner. This literature has taken two approaches. One approach examines the efficiency properties of the practice of decision by precedent (*stare decisis*), without explicitly asking why judges adopt it, and the other examines the behavior of judges as self-interested utility maximizers. I will briefly discuss each in turn.

When a judge decides a case according to precedent, she simply applies the ruling from a previous, similar case.[12] In contrast, judicial discretion involves deciding a case anew according to case-specific factors. Thus, the economic analysis of decision by precedent is essentially a version of the rules versus discretion choice described in chapter 1. It follows that decision by precedent is preferred when rules are preferred or, in this context, when: (1) decision costs by the court are high; (2) the costs of legal change are high (e.g., significant reliance expenditures have been made in reliance on the existing rule); (3) the environment is relatively stable; and (4) there is a high probability that the court, in exercising discretion, would overturn laws that are efficient (Heiner, 1986).

Despite the benefits of decision by precedent under these conditions, one might suppose, as noted above, that it would tend to inhibit the law's movement toward efficiency. It should be recalled, however, that inefficient *laws* do not necessarily imply inefficient *behavior*, given that parties can bargain around the law. Indeed, one of the advantages of a rule-based legal system is that it facilitates such bargaining, assuming low transaction costs. Thus, decision by precedent can be an important element of an efficient legal system by enforcing a stable background against which private individuals can bargain.[13]

The second approach to modeling judicial behavior is to view judges as acting, like any other economic agent, to maximize their utility.[14] One problem with this approach is that it is not clear exactly what should be in a judge's utility function. Several authors have suggested that reputation is a relevant factor, as measured, for example, by the number of times a judge's decisions are cited and/or reversed.[15] Aversion to reversal may explain why self-interested judges choose to adhere to precedent, whereas the desire to establish a reputation or to impose one's preferences on the law may explain why other judges (or the same judges in other cases) choose to depart from precedent.

Although judicial incomes are not tied directly to performance, they too can have an impact on judicial decision making. For example, a reduction in judicial salaries can lead to self-selection of judges who place a high nonpecuniary value on the act of judging (Greenberg and Haley, 1986). As a result, on one hand, the number of judges who have a taste for making new law, as opposed to applying existing law, may increase. On the other hand, lower salaries may attract more judges who value leisure and therefore adhere to precedent as an effort-minimizing mode of decision making (Posner 1995, p. 141). Given these offsetting effects, the impact of judicial salaries on legal change is ambiguous.

Although the existing models of judicial decision making have had some success in explaining various aspects of judicial behavior (e.g., the decision of whether or not to follow precedent), the motivation of judges and its connection to the evolution of the law is an open question. In particular, the connection (if any) between judicial self-interest and the evolution of the common law toward efficiency remains unclear.[16]

1.7. Lawyers and Legal Change

Up to now, we have focused on the role of litigants and judges in bringing about legal change. A group that is generally ignored in this process is lawyers. While the conventional view is that lawyers are simply advocates for litigants, and therefore do not pursue an agenda of their own, this abstracts from agency problems in the attorney-client relationship, which stem from the fact that lawyers, as repeat players in the legal process, will have different interests from litigants, who are generally one-time players.[17] Indeed, Rubin and Bailey (1994) have argued that the structure of the law, especially in certain areas, can best be understood as reflecting the interests of lawyers rather than judges or litigants.[18] Their argument is based on the theory of rent seeking, which suggests that concentrated interest groups are able to influence the outcome of legal decisions in a way that favors their particular interests.

Traditionally, rent seeking has been applied to legislative decision making under the presumption that the common law is less susceptible than statute law to interest-group influence.[19] Rubin and Bailey argue, however, that lawyers as a group meet the criteria of a well-organized interest group with a concentrated interest. Moreover, lawyers clearly have the ability to change the law, both as judges (through their precedents) and as legislators. In support of their argument, Rubin and Bailey present evidence that legal change in products liability law has tracked the interest of trial lawyers, and that the real incomes of tort lawyers have risen in response to those changes.[20]

One way that lawyers as a group can promote their self-interest is to increase the demand for their services by making the law more complex. White (1992) has used the differing perceptions model of litigation presented above to show the optimal level of complexity preferred by lawyers. In her model, the particular objective of lawyers is to maximize their gross income, which is given by $C_p + C_d$ for cases that go to trial, and $R_p + R_d$ for cases that settle. Since we assume that trial costs exceed settlement costs, this immediately implies that plaintiffs' lawyers and defendants' lawyers alike prefer to go to trial rather than to settle. Thus, they prefer a level of legal complexity that ensures that condition (8.3') holds.

To determine the optimal level of complexity, let c be an index of complexity, where larger c implies more complex laws. In general, we expect that litigation costs (both trial and settlement costs) will be increasing in c, since lawyers will need to spend more time examining facts and precedents. Thus, the right-hand side of $(8.3')$ will be increasing in c (assuming that trial costs increase faster than settlement costs for all levels of complexity). With regard to the left-hand side of $(8.3')$, the question is how increases in complexity affect litigants' perceptions— that is, how will increases in c affect $P_p - P_d$? If complexity increases the certainty of the outcome of trials by increasing the *accuracy* of judicial decisions, then $P_p - P_d$ will fall with c. On the other hand, if increases in c cause greater legal *uncertainty*, then $P_p - P_d$ will increase with c. In general, therefore, it is not clear how $P_p - P_d$ will vary with c. What matters, however, is the range of c over which $(8.3')$ holds. According to the interest-group theory, the objective of lawyers is to set c at the highest value such that $(8.3')$ holds in order to maximize litigation expenditures subject to the condition that all disputes go to trial.[21] Figure 8.1 illustrates the optimal level of complexity, c^*, assuming that $P_p - P_d$ first rises and then falls with c. In the graph, trials occur to the left of c^* and settlements to the right. Thus, c^* is the highest level of complexity in the "trial set."

In terms of the efficiency of the law, the interest-group theory of lawyers and legal change clearly casts doubt on the view that the common law will tend toward efficiency. For example, there is no reason to expect that the level of legal complexity that best serves the interests of lawyers will coincide with the optimal level of complexity for society as a whole.

2. The Asymmetric Information Model

A second class of models of litigation and settlement have attributed the existence of trials to asymmetric information. That is, one or both of the parties have private information about the strength of their case or their cost of going to

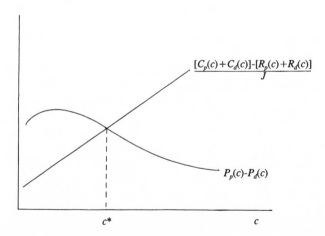

FIGURE 8.1 The level of legal complexity most preferred by lawyers.

trial.[22] (In a sense, this approach is a special case of the differing perceptions model.) The primary contribution of the recent models is the increased rigor of the analysis (through the application of game theory), which yields more specific empirical implications. In this section, I will develop a simple version of this type of model and use it to generate some comparative static results. I will then use the results to examine several issues related to the settlement process—for example, fee-shifting arrangements and discovery rules.[23]

2.1. The Basic Model

The typical asymmetric information model assumes that one party possesses private information about some parameter that affects his or her willingness to go to trial. Here, I will assume that the plaintiff has private information about the strength of her case.[24] Specifically, let P be the plaintiff's probability of victory. Suppose each plaintiff knows her own P, but defendants only know the distribution of P's in the population of plaintiffs, where $P \in [0, 1]$. Let $F(P)$ be the distribution function of P. I assume that the judgment in the event of plaintiff victory, J, is known and constant. As above, the costs of trial for the parties are C_p and C_d, and, for simplicity, I assume no settlement costs.[25]

The structure of the game is as follows. First, the plaintiff files a lawsuit at zero cost.[26] Then, the defendant makes a single, take-it-or-leave-it settlement offer, S.[27] If the plaintiff accepts, the parties settle; if she refuses, plaintiffs with $PJ - C_p \geq 0$ go to trial and plaintiffs with $PJ - C_p < 0$ drop their suit.[28] The game is solved in reverse sequence by first examining the plaintiff's decision to accept or reject S, and then deriving the defendant's optimal offer of S.[29]

The plaintiff's accept-reject decision is identical to that just described. Specifically, she will accept S if $S \geq PJ - C_p$ and reject S if $S < PJ - C_p$. In terms of the population of plaintiffs, those for whom $P \leq (S + C_p)/J$ will settle and those for whom $P > (S + C_p)/J$ will go to trial. Intuitively, only plaintiffs with relatively strong cases (high Ps) will go to trial. Since the defendant cannot observe individual P's, he can only calculate the probability that a given plaintiff will accept S. This is given by $F[(S + C_p)/J]$. The probability of a trial is therefore $1 - F[(S + C_p)/J]$.

Given the probabilities of trial and settlement, the defendant chooses S to minimize his expected costs, which are

$$TC = F[(S + C_p)/J]S + \{1 - F[(S + C_p)/J]\}\{E[PJ + C_d | P > (S + C_p)/J]\}$$

$$= F[(S + C_p)/J]S + \int_{\frac{S+C_p}{J}}^{1} (PJ + C_d)dF(P)$$

$$(8.7)$$

where $PJ + C_d$ is the defendant's expected cost in the event of a trial with a plaintiff of type P. The optimal settlement offer, S^*, solves the first-order condition

$$F[(S + C_p)/\tilde{J}] - f[(S + C_p)/\tilde{J}][(C_p + C_d)/\tilde{J}] = 0 \qquad (8.8)$$

where $f(\cdot)$ is the density function of $F(\cdot)$.[30]

Differentiating (8.8) yields the following comparative statics with respect to the optimal settlement amount:

$$\partial S^*/\partial C_d > 0, \quad \partial S^*/\partial C_p >< 0, \quad \partial S^*/\partial \tilde{J} >< 0. \qquad (8.9)$$

Intuitively, a higher cost of trial for the defendant (C_d) means that he will pay a higher amount to avoid a trial. In contrast, a higher cost of trial for the plaintiff (C_p) has an ambiguous effect. On the one hand, higher C_p lowers S^* because the plaintiff will accept less to avoid a trial, but on the other, it raises the maximum value of P for which settlement occurs $(S + C_p)/\tilde{J}$, implying an increase in the average quality of cases that settle. This tends to make the settlement amount larger. An increase in $\tilde{J}$ similarly has an ambiguous effect: it makes plaintiffs more willing to go to trial, which tends to raise S^*, but at the same time it lowers the average quality of cases that settle (i.e., $(S + C_p)/\tilde{J}$ falls), which tends to lower S^*.

The impacts of the exogenous variables on the probability of a settlement can be found by differentiating $F[(S + C_p)/\tilde{J}]$ (the probability of a settlement) and making use of the results from (8.9) to get

$$\partial F/\partial C_d > 0, \quad \partial F/\partial C_p > 0, \quad \partial F/\partial \tilde{J} < 0. \qquad (8.10)$$

Intuitively, a settlement is more likely the higher are the costs of a trial for either party and the lower are the stakes of the case. Note that these results are consistent with those from the differing perceptions model.

3. The Impact of Different Cost-Allocation Rules

We can use the preceding models of litigation to examine the impact on the settlement rate of various rules for sharing the costs of litigation. First, I will compare the American rule, under which both parties pay their own litigation costs (the rule we have employed up to now), and the so-called English rule, under which the loser pays the winner's litigation costs. Next, I will examine the impact of contingent fee arrangements between tort plaintiffs and their attorneys on the settlement decision. Finally, I will examine Rule 68 of the Federal Rules of Civil Procedure, which requires a plaintiff who refuses a defendant's settlement offer to pay the defendant's postoffer legal costs if the judgment at trial is less than the rejected offer.

3.1. The American Rule versus the English Rule

3.1.1. THEORETICAL ANALYSIS

In the context of the differing perceptions model,[31] the English rule implies that the expected value of a trial for the plaintiff is $P_p J - (1 - P_p)(C_p + C_d)$, reflecting the fact that if she wins, she incurs no litigation costs, but if she loses, she must pay both her own and the defendant's costs. The condition for the plaintiff to accept a settlement in this case (assuming zero settlement costs for simplicity) is therefore $S \geq P_p J - (1 - P_p)(C_p + C_d)$. The expected cost of a trial for the defendant under the English rule is $P_d(J + C_p + C_d)$, and the condition under which he will settle is $S \leq P_d(J + C_p + C_d)$.

Combining these conditions yields the condition for a settlement range to exist under the English rule:

$$(P_p - P_d)(J + C_p + C_d) \leq C_p + C_d. \tag{8.11}$$

The corresponding condition under the American rule is given by (8.3), or, after setting $R_p = R_d = 0$ and $J_p = J_d = J$, by $(P_p - P_d)J \leq C_p + C_d$.[32] Since the left-hand side of this condition is smaller than the left-hand side of (8.11), and the right-hand sides are equal, it follows that a settlement is *less* likely under the English rule. The reason is that the English rule increases the stakes of the case from J to $J + C_p + C_d$, which, as we have seen, increases the likelihood of a trial (given $P_p > P_d$). Since the comparative static results of the asymmetric information model in (8.10) also imply that a trial is more likely the higher are the stakes of the case, it also leads to the conclusion that the English rule will result in a lower probability of settlement, given that a case has been filed.

These results suggest that the English rule may result in *higher* litigation costs than the American rule. Advocates of the English rule argue, however, that its primary virtue is its greater ability to deter frivolous suits from being filed in the first place because of the greater cost of losing at trial.[33] We can examine this argument by adding a cost of filing suit, w. Consider first the case where a suit is expected to settle under both rules. If the amount of the settlement is the *same* under the two cost rules (e.g., if the amount of the settlement depends only on J), then the plaintiff will file if $S \geq w$ under both rules, and the number of suits filed will be the same under both.

In reality, however, the settlement amount will likely differ under the two rules. Suppose, for example, that, when a settlement range exists, the settlement amount divides the surplus from settling evenly (Cooter and Rubinfeld, 1989). The surplus is found by taking the difference between the maximum offer of the defendant and the minimum amount the plaintiff will accept. Under the American rule, this is given by

$$(P_d J + C_d) - (P_p J - C_p) = (C_p + C_d) - (P_p - P_d)J$$

which reduces to $C_p + C_d$ when the parties have symmetric expectations. In this case, the equilibrium settlement amount under the American rule, given equal division of the surplus, is equal to the plaintiff's expected value of a trial plus one half of the surplus, or

$$S_A = P_p J - C_p + (1/2)(C_p + C_d). \tag{8.12}$$

Under the English rule, the surplus from settling is given by

$$[P_d(J + C_p + C_d)] - [P_p J - (1 - P_p)(C_p + C_d)]$$
$$= [P_d + (1 - P_p)](C_p + C_d) - (P_p - P_d)J,$$

which also reduces to $C_p + C_d$ under symmetric expectations. Thus, the equilibrium settlement amount under the English rule is given by

$$S_E = P_p J - (1 - P_p)(C_p + C_d) + (1/2)(C_p + C_d). \tag{8.13}$$

In general, therefore, fewer suits will be filed under the English rule if $S_E < S_A$, or, using (8.12) and (8.13), if

$$P_p < C_d/(C_p + C_d). \tag{8.14}$$

Thus, the less optimistic the plaintiff is about prevailing at trial, the more likely it is that the English rule will lead to a lower settlement amount, and hence to fewer lawsuits (Shavell, 1982a). Note that this result provides support for the above claim that the English rule is better at deterring weak (i.e., low P_p) suits.

Now consider the case in which the plaintiff expects to go to trial instead of settling. The expected value of the suit under the American rule in this case is $P_p J - C_p$, and the plaintiff will file if this amount exceeds w. Similarly, under the English rule, the plaintiff will file if $P_p J - (1 - P_p)(C_p + C_d)$ exceeds w. Thus, more suits will be filed under the English rule if

$$P_p J - (1 - P_p)(C_p + C_d) > P_p J - C_p,$$

which yields the same condition as in (8.14). This is not surprising since the outcome of a settlement reflects the parties' expectations of the outcome of a trial.

The foregoing has assumed fixed litigation expenditures per trial. When litigation expenditures are endogenous rather than fixed, per-trial expenditures will likely be higher under the English rule compared to the American rule for two reasons. First, the stakes of the case are higher, which we argued above increases expenditures; second, because each party expects the other to bear his or her costs with some probability, the marginal costs of additional expenditures are lower.[34] The impact of this greater expenditure under the English rule is to increase the costs of going to trial relative to settling, thereby increasing the settlement range. This can be seen by rearranging (8.11) to get

$$(P_p - P_d)\mathcal{J} \leq [1 - (P_p - P_d)](C_p + C_d).$$

Thus, as $C_p + C_d$ rises, a settlement range is more likely to exist, all else equal.[35] This effect therefore works in the opposite direction of the above result that trials are more likely under the English rule in the fixed expenditure model.

If litigants are risk averse, they will generally prefer the American rule over the English rule because the latter increases the range of wealth—that is, both the gain from winning and the loss from losing are larger.[36] This effect will also tend to make settlement more likely under the English rule as compared to the American rule because trials are riskier (Coursey and Stanley (1988); Donohue (1991b).

As a final point, Donohue (1991b) has argued that if litigants can bargain over the allocation of legal costs, then, according to the Coase theorem, the settlement rate should be *independent* of the prevailing cost allocation rule. Despite the potential gains from such bargaining, however, the required cost shifting between litigants does not seem to occur in practice. This may be due to transaction costs, legal or institutional constraints, or the fact that litigants simply do not recognize the potential gains.[37]

3.1.2. EMPIRICAL EVIDENCE

The preceding analysis has produced the following empirical predictions: (1) if litigants are risk-neutral, there will be more trials under the English rule, holding litigation costs fixed; (2) if litigants are risk averse, there will be a tendency for fewer trials under the English rule; (3) litigation expenditures per trial will be higher under the English rule, thus mitigating the tendency for more trials in the risk-neutral case; and (4) the English rule will lead to more lawsuits being filed by optimistic plaintiffs.

Snyder and Hughes (1990) have tested some of these hypotheses using a sample of medical malpractice claims in Florida.[38] Generally, their results support the above predictions for the case of risk-neutral litigants. Specifically, they found that the English rule narrows the settlement range, thereby increasing the likelihood of trial between optimistic parties, and that litigation expenditures per case were higher under the English rule. In addition, they found that more claims were dropped under the English rule, a result that is also consistent with the theory because of the greater risk of pursuing a weak claim to trial.[39] In a later study using the same data, they found that the English rule led to a higher plaintiff win rate at trial, a higher average settlement amount, and a higher average award at trial (Hughes and Snyder, 1995). These results are consistent with the prediction that the English rule encourages the filing of higher quality claims by plaintiffs (i.e., claims by more optimistic plaintiffs).

Coursey and Stanley (1988) used experimental methods to examine the impact of different cost-allocation rules on settlement. Their results for the

English rule support the predictions for the case of risk-averse litigants.[40] Specifically, they found that settlements were more likely under the English rule.[41]

3.2 Contingent Fees and Settlement

Most tort plaintiffs in the United States file suit under a contingent-fee arrangement whereby they pay their lawyer a fixed percentage (usually a third) of any monetary award they receive, whether at trial or by settlement, and nothing if they lose.[42] In this section, I examine the impact of a contingent fee on the settlement decision.

Let β be the fraction of any recovery that the plaintiff retains.[43] Thus, the plaintiff's expected return at trial is $P_p \beta J$, and her return from accepting a settlement offer of S is βS. She will therefore be willing to settle if $S \geq P_p J$.[44] The condition for the defendant to be willing to settle is the same as above, namely $S \leq P_d J + C_d$. Combining this with the plaintiff's condition to settle yields the condition for existence of a settlement range under a contingent fee:

$$(P_p - P_d)J \leq C_d. \tag{8.15}$$

Compared to (8.3) with $R_p = R_d = 0$ and $J_p = J_d = J$, this condition shows that a settlement is less likely with a contingent fee. The reason is that the plaintiff perceives the marginal cost of going to trial as being zero and is therefore more willing to litigate rather than settle (Miller, 1987; Donohue, 1991a).

3.3. Rule 68

Rule 68 of the Federal Rules of Civil Procedure requires that a plaintiff who refuses a defendant's settlement offer pay the defendant's postoffer legal costs if the plaintiff receives a judgment at trial less than the rejected offer.[45] (No sanction is imposed if the plaintiff loses the trial.) The intent of this cost-shifting rule is to promote settlements, but several authors have shown that this may not always be the result.[46] In addition, the fact that the rule only allows shifting of costs to the plaintiff makes it pro-defendant in terms of its distributional effects. In this section I examine the impact of Rule 68 in the context of the differing perceptions model.[47] I assume that the background rule for cost allocation is the American rule. As in the previous section, I assume that settlement costs are zero and both parties have symmetric beliefs about the expected judgment at trial in the event of plaintiff victory.

In order to model the impact of Rule 68, we need to specify the probability that the judgment at trial will be less than any given settlement offer, S. To do this, suppose that the actual judgment is a random variable j with distribution function $G(j)$ and expected value J (which, recall, both parties agree on). Thus, $G(S)$ is the probability that $j < S$, in which case the plaintiff will bear both his own litigation costs, C_p, and also the defendant's costs, C_d. The fact that $G'(S) > 0$ implies that the larger is the defendant's settlement offer, the larger is the probability that a Rule 68 sanction will be imposed if the plaintiff goes to trial.

Given the possibility of a Rule 68 sanction, the expected value of going to trial for the plaintiff is

$$P_p\mathcal{J} - C_p - P_pG(S)C_d \tag{8.16}$$

where the final term is the expected sanction as a function of the settlement offer. Equation (8.16) represents the lowest settlement offer that the plaintiff will accept. Similarly, the expected cost of a trial for the defendant is

$$P_d\mathcal{J} + C_d - P_dG(S)C_d \tag{8.17}$$

where the final term is the expected reimbursement of costs under Rule 68. Equation (8.17) represents the highest settlement offer that the defendant would make.

The first thing to note about (8.16) and (8.17) is that both are reduced relative the American rule. That is, a trial is less valuable for the plaintiff, and less costly for the defendant, all else equal. This reflects the asymmetric nature of Rule 68 in that costs can be shifted only to the plaintiff. (Note that this is in contrast to the English rule.)

Equations (8.16) and (8.17) also imply that the necessary condition for a settlement under Rule 68 is given by

$$(P_p - P_d)\mathcal{J} \le (C_p + C_d) + (P_p - P_d)G(S)C_d. \tag{8.18}$$

This differs from the settlement condition under the American rule by the final term (compare condition (8.3) with $R_p = R_d = 0$ and $\mathcal{J}_p = \mathcal{J}_d = \mathcal{J}$). If $P_p > P_d$, this final term is positive, implying that settlement is more likely under Rule 68. Intuitively, the expected sanction increases the cost of a trial more for the plaintiff than it reduces the cost for the defendant when $P_p > P_d$. Thus, the settlement range expands. Alternatively, if $P_p < P_d$, the second term is negative. This does not imply that a settlement is *less* likely, however, because as long as the right-hand side is positive overall (which presumably is true), a settlement is always possible given that the left-hand side is negative.[48] The impact of Rule 68 in this case is simply to shrink the settlement range (without eliminating it), and as we noted, this can sometimes actually facilitate a settlement by easing bargaining over the surplus.

The preceding has examined the likely effect of Rule 68 on the settlement rate. As we noted earlier, however, it will also affect the average amount of settlements, and thereby the value of lawsuits. To see this effect, I will assume as earlier that the equilibrium settlement splits the surplus from settling whenever a settlement range exists (i.e., whenever (8.18) holds).[49] For simplicity, I consider the case $P_p = P_d$, which ensures that a range exists. In this case, it is easy to see that the surplus from settling, given by the difference between (8.17) and (8.16),

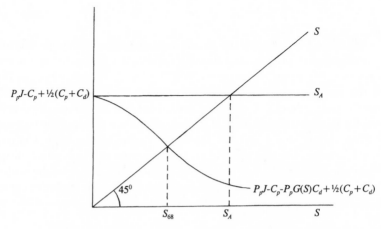

FIGURE 8.2 Equilibrium settlement amounts under the American rule (S_A) and Rule 68 (S_{68}).

is $C_p + C_d$, which is the same surplus as under the American and English rules when perceptions are symmetric.

In this case, the equilibrium settlement amount under Rule 68 is implicitly defined by the equation

$$S_{68} = P_p J - C_p - P_p G(S_{68}) C_d + (1/2)(C_p + C_d). \tag{8.19}$$

Figure 8.2 shows how the resulting settlement compares to the settlement under the American rule, given in (8.12). In the graph, the right-hand side of (8.19) is shown as decreasing in S (given that $G'(S) > 0$) with a vertical intercept that coincides with S_A (given that $G(0) = 0$). The equilibrium value for S_{68} implied by (8.19) therefore occurs at the point where the downward sloping curve intersects with the 45^0 line. Clearly, the equilibrium settlement is lower under Rule 68 than it is under the American rule (Miller, 1986, p. 105). This is a direct consequence of the pro-defendant nature of the rule. The result is that lawsuits are less valuable for plaintiffs, who will therefore have less incentive to file suits, all else equal. This in turn could have a detrimental effect on incentives for defendants to take precautions to avoid disputes in the first place (Spier, 1994, p. 202). Thus, even if Rule 68 promotes settlement, it is not clear that its overall impact is desirable.

Coursey and Stanley (1988) evaluated the impact of Rule 68 experimentally. They found, consistent with the above predictions, that Rule 68 increased the settlement rate compared to the American rule. They also found, as predicted, that the distributional effects of Rule 68 favored the defendant.

4. Discovery

The rules of discovery give parties to a lawsuit the right to request information from the other party prior to trial through the use of interrogatories, the request of documents, deposition of witnesses, and the like.[50] Presumably, this process allows the parties to obtain private information about the strength of their opponent's case, thereby facilitating settlement. In addition, discovery can increase the fairness and accuracy of dispute resolution, result in the termination of meritless claims, and lower the transaction costs of litigation (Cooter and Rubinfeld, 1994, p. 436). In this section I examine the extent to which discovery accomplishes these goals. I first look at the impact of discovery on the settlement decision, and then turn to its effect on transaction costs. In the latter context, I also consider the problem of discovery abuse.

4.1. Discovery and Settlement

I suggested in the context of the simple differing perceptions model that discovery will tend to promote settlement by causing the parties' perceptions of the outcome of a trial to converge. I now examine that claim in more detail.[51]

Recall that the condition for a settlement range to exist is

$$P_p J_p - P_d J_d \leq (C_p - R_p) + (C_d - R_d). \tag{8.3}$$

The exchange of information prior to trial makes this condition more likely to the extent that it causes $P_p J_p - P_d J_d$ to decrease. In other words, discovery promotes settlement when it makes the parties more *pessimistic* about the outcome of a trial.[52] Conversely, therefore, discovery can make trials more likely if it increases the parties' optimism. Although this seems less likely to occur, it is not impossible.

Discovery also affects the expected value of settling. If the parties settle and divide the resulting surplus evenly, the settlement amount is given by[53]

$$S = (P_p J_p + P_d J_d)/2 + (C_d - C_p)/2 + (R_p - R_d)/2. \tag{8.20}$$

It follows from (8.20) that, in the absence of compulsory information exchange, the parties will voluntarily reveal information that strengthens their positions and conceal information that weakens their positions.[54] In particular, the plaintiff will reveal information that increases $P_d J_d$, and the defendant will reveal information that decreases $P_p J_p$. Alternatively, the plaintiff will withhold information that decreases $P_d J_d$ and the defendant will withhold information that increases $P_p J_p$. In short, each party will reveal information that makes the other party more pessimistic, and withhold information that makes the other party more optimistic. Based on this argument, mandatory disclosure may actually increase the likelihood of trials by increasing optimism.

A final implication of (8.20) is that, if the parties have equal trial and settlement costs,

$$S = (P_p \mathcal{J}_p + P_d \mathcal{J}_d)/2$$

Thus, insofar as discovery aligns the expectations of the parties about trial with each other and with the true merits of the case (given by $P^* \mathcal{J}^*$), it increases the extent to which the settlement represents a fair, or "accurate," resolution of the dispute (i.e., if $P_p \mathcal{J}_p = P_d \mathcal{J}_d = P^* \mathcal{J}^*$, then $S = P^* \mathcal{J}^*$) (Cooter and Rubinfeld, 1994).

4.2. Discovery and Litigation Costs

In this section, I examine the impact of discovery on the cost of resolving disputes. I conduct the analysis in the context of the asymmetric information model, as this allows explicit consideration of the effects of discovery on the entire population of disputes, the settlement rate, and total litigation costs.

Recall from section 2 that in the asymmetric information model, the plaintiff had private information about her probability of winning at trial, P. For simplicity, I will assume that the discovery process allows the defendant to learn the value of P with certainty. However, both parties incur a cost of discovery: the plaintiff incurs a cost, k_p, of complying with the discovery request; and the defendant incurs a cost, k_d, of deposing witnesses or examining the requested material.

Note first that if discovery takes place, the parties will settle with certainty. This is so because, after discovery, they will have identical expectations about the outcome of a trial $(P\mathcal{J})$, in which case we have seen that a settlement range always exists.[55] Under the assumption of a take-it-or-leave-it settlement offer by the defendant,[56] the parties will settle for an amount $S = P\mathcal{J} - C_p$ following discovery.

The plaintiff, of course, has the option to drop her suit rather than comply with the defendant's discovery request. Since compliance is costly, she will do so if $S < k_p$, or if $P\mathcal{J} - C_p < k_p$. Thus, given the set of plaintiffs that have filed a suit, those who comply will have $P \geq (C_p + k_p)/\mathcal{J}$, and those who drop will have $P < (C_p + k_p)/\mathcal{J}$ (see figure 8.3).

Of course, potential plaintiffs will anticipate the outcome of the discovery process, and this will affect their decision of whether or not to file a suit in the first place (given a cost of filing). In particular, if plaintiffs (correctly) anticipate that defendants will use discovery, their expected value of filing suit is $P\mathcal{J} - C_p - k_p$. Thus, given a filing cost of w, the set of filers and non-filers will be as follows:

$$\begin{aligned}
&\text{file if} && P \geq (C_p + k_p + w)/\mathcal{J} \\
&\text{do not file if} && P < (C_p + k_p + w)/\mathcal{J}.
\end{aligned} \tag{8.21}$$

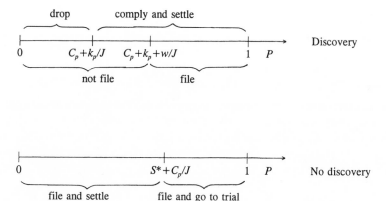

FIGURE 8.3 Partitioning of those plaintiffs who file suit under discovery (top panel) and no discovery (bottom panel).

This partitioning is shown in figure 8.3 (top panel). Note that the set of plaintiffs who drop their suit rather than comply is a strict subset of nonfilers (given $w > 0$). Thus, in equilibrium, only plaintiffs who intend to comply with the discovery request ever file.

So far I have characterized the response of plaintiffs to the use of discovery by defendants. I next examine the conditions under which defendants benefit (i.e., enjoy lower costs) as a result of discovery. To do this, I first calculate the defendant's expected costs with discovery, given the partitioning of plaintiffs in (8.21), and then compare it to the defendant's expected costs without discovery, given by (8.7), evaluated at the optimal settlement amount.[57] Recall that discovery allows the defendant to settle with all plaintiffs who have filed suit for an amount equal to their "reservation price," $PJ - C_p$, for all P. In addition, the defendant incurs discovery costs of k_d per plaintiff. Thus, the defendant's overall expected cost when he uses discovery is

$$TC_D = \{1 - F[(C_p + k_p + w)/J]\}E[PJ - C_p + k_d | P \ge (C_p + k_p + w)/J]$$

$$= \int_{\frac{C_p + k_p + w}{J}}^{1} (PJ - C_p + k_p)dF(P)$$

$$(8.22)$$

The next step is to calculate the difference between the defendant's expected costs without discovery given by (8.7) (denoted TC_N) and (8.22). To do this, it will be useful to partition the set of plaintiffs who file and settle under discovery into two groups: $P \in [(C_p + k_p + w)/J, (S^* + C_p)/J]$ and $P \in [(S^* + C_p)/J, 1]$, where S^* is the optimal settlement amount in the absence of discovery. Note that this partitioning assumes that $S^* + C_p > C_p + k_p + w$, or that $S^* > k_p + w$. As figure 8.3 shows, this assumption implies that the set of plaintiffs that would go to trial in the absence of discovery (lower panel) is a subset of those that would file and settle with discovery (upper panel). In other words, there is an overlap of the sets of plaintiffs that settle under both regimes. I will provide a reason for this assumption.

Given this partitioning, subtracting (8.22) from (8.7) yields the following expression:

$$TC_N - TC_D = \int_0^{\frac{C_p + k_p + w}{J}} S^* dF(P)$$

$$+ \int_{\frac{C_p + k_p + w}{J}}^{\frac{S^* + C_p}{J}} [S^* - (PJ - C_p + k_d)] dF(P) \qquad (8.23)$$

$$+ \int_{\frac{S^* + C_p}{J}}^1 [(PJ + C_d) - (PJ - C_p + k_d)] dF(P)$$

Consider the three terms of (8.23) separately. The first term is positive, reflecting the fact that, without discovery, plaintiffs over the range $P \in [0, (C_p + k_p + w)/J]$ file and settle for an amount S^* (given $S^* > w$), but under discovery these plaintiffs are deterred from filing. Next consider the third term. Note that the term in square brackets reduces to $C_p + C_d - k_d$, which I assume is positive. This terms reflects the fact that plaintiffs over the range $P \in [(S^* + C_p)/J, 1]$ go to trial in the absence of discovery but settle with discovery. The term is positive based on the assumption that the transaction costs of discovery for the defendant are less than his overall cost of going to trial.

The first and third terms therefore represent two benefits of discovery for the defendant: first, it deters weak plaintiffs from filing; and second, it allows the defendant to settle with strong plaintiffs rather than go to trial. The second term, however, is ambiguous in sign, reflecting the fact that, over the range $P \in [(C_p + k_p + w)/J, (S^* + C_p)/J]$, plaintiffs settle with and without discovery. Without discovery, all plaintiffs settle for S^*, but with discovery, they settle for their reservation price, $PJ - C_p$. In addition, the defendant incurs an extra cost of k_d for each plaintiff under discovery. Thus, if discovery is very costly for the defendant, this term will be negative, making the overall comparison ambiguous in sign. Note finally that if this range did not exist—that is, if $S^* < k_p + w$—discovery would unambiguously lower the defendant's costs. While this may be true, it seems more plausible that there exists a substantial range of plaintiffs that would settle whether or not the defendant makes use of discovery.

Suppose that (8.23) is positive, implying that the defendant will use discovery when it is available. The next question is whether discovery is *socially desirable* or not. To answer this question, we need to calculate expected social costs with and without discovery, given the equilibrium in each case. Without discovery, all plaintiffs on $P \in [0, 1]$ file suit, resulting in filing costs of w per plaintiff. In addition, plaintiffs on the interval $P \in [(S^* + C_p)/J, 1]$ go to trial, resulting in additional litigation costs of $C_p + C_d$ per trial. (Recall that we are assuming no costs per settlement.) Thus, total expected litigation costs without discovery are

$$SC_N = w + \{1 - F[(S^* + C_p)/\mathcal{J}]\}(C_p + C_d). \tag{8.24}$$

With discovery, only cases on $P \in [(C_p + k_p + w)/\mathcal{J}, 1]$ file, and all of these settle after discovery. Thus, expected litigation costs are

$$SC_D = \{1 - F[(C_p + k_p + w)/\mathcal{J}]\}(w + k_p + k_d). \tag{8.25}$$

Using the same partitioning as in (8.23), we can calculate the difference between these costs as:

$$
\begin{aligned}
SC_N - SC_D = &F[C_p + k_p + w)/\mathcal{J}]w \\
&- \{F[(S^* + C_p)/\mathcal{J}] - F[(C_p + k_p + w)/\mathcal{J}]\}(k_p + k_d) \\
&+ \{1 - F[(S^* + C_p)/\mathcal{J}]\}[(C_p + C_d) - (k_p + k_d)]
\end{aligned}
\tag{8.26}
$$

As above, the first and third terms are positive. The first reflects the fact that discovery deters some weak plaintiffs from filing suit, thereby saving filing costs, and the third captures the lower transaction costs of discovery compared to trial for strong plaintiffs. In contrast, the second term is negative, reflecting the higher transaction costs under discovery for plaintiffs that would have settled in any case.

In general, therefore, the impact of discovery on litigation costs is ambiguous (see figure 8.4). While it increases the settlement rate and deters some weak cases from being filed, it also raises the cost of settling cases. Thus, if the set of cases that would settle both with and without discovery is large, the net effect of discovery could be to raise costs.

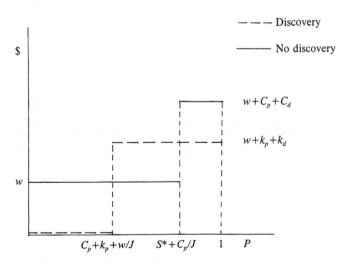

FIGURE 8.4 Total costs of litigation under discovery (dashed line) and no discovery (solid line).

4.3. Discovery Abuse

The preceding model has not captured the costs arising from "abuse" of discovery, meaning the use of discovery requests by defendants not to acquire information, but merely to impose costs on plaintiffs in hopes of inducing them to drop their suits or settle for a lower amount. For example, suppose that at a given point in the pretrial period the plaintiff's litigation cost of pursuing her case further rather than settling is given by $C_p(x)$, where x is the number of future discovery requests by the defendant, $C_p' > 0$. The plaintiff's reservation price at this point thus equals $PJ - C_p(x)$, which is decreasing in x. Notice, therefore, that, even if the defendant already knows PJ as a result of previous discovery requests, it may pay him to threaten to make further requests (i.e., to increase x) in an effort to lower the minimum amount the plaintiff will accept, even though x is uninformative (and therefore wasteful).

For example, let the defendant's cost of making further discovery requests be $C_d(x)$, where $C_d' > 0$. The defendant will therefore benefit from further discovery requests if $C_d'(0) < C_p'(0)$—that is, if the marginal gain from reducing the plaintiff's reservation price exceeds the marginal cost of an additional request. Some critics of discovery believe that this sort of abuse (choosing $x > 0$ even after PJ is known) is a significant problem requiring reform of the discovery process. As a remedy, Cooter and Rubinfeld (1994) propose a cost-shifting rule whereby the reasonable cost of complying with discovery requests would be shifted to the requesting party. Such a rule would deter frivolous requests because the requesting party could no longer strengthen his or her position by this strategy.

As a final observation, note that the analysis in this and the previous section has focused on the cost of discovery *after* the dispute has arisen. This ex post view ignores the possible impact of discovery on the incentives of parties to invest in precaution to avoid disputes in the first place. Based on this ex ante view, some requests otherwise seen as abusive (cost increasing) might turn out to lower overall social costs (Hay, 1994).

5. Application: The Decision of Repeat Defendants to Employ In-House Counsel or an Outside Attorney

I conclude this chapter by using the asymmetric information model from section 2 to examine the decision by a repeat defendant (e.g., an insurance company or manufacturer of a dangerous product) as to whether to employ a full-time, in-house staff of attorneys or to hire outside attorneys as claims arise.[58] In the context of products liability, the expanding scope of producer liability has led an increasing number of firms to adopt the former option. There are several potential benefits of this strategy. First, it allows defendants to integrate considerations of liability into their production and marketing strategy; second, it better aligns the interests of the defendant and attorney;[59] and third, it allows attorneys to specialize in a particular area of the law related to the defendant's activities.

In addition to these benefits, I will argue here that there is a strategic benefit to employing in-house counsel that arises from the fact that the defendant's *variable* costs of going to trial are thereby lowered, given that the attorney's salary is a *fixed* cost. As a result, only nonattorney costs of trial are variable. In contrast, if the defendant hires an outside attorney on an hourly basis, both attorney and nonattorney costs of trial are variable. Consequently, defendants hiring outside attorneys will be more willing to settle and will pay larger settlement amounts, all else equal.

I demonstrate these conclusions formally by amending the basic model in section 2.1 as follows. Let the defendant's *variable* cost of going to trial be $C_d = A_d + N_d$, where A_d are attorney costs and N_d are nonattorney costs, and let his *fixed* costs (if any) be F_d. In all other respects, the model is the same. Thus, if the defendant has both fixed and variable costs, his expected litigation costs are

$$TC = F[(S + C_p)/J]S + \int_{\frac{S+C_p}{J}}^{1} (PJ + A_d + N_d)dF(P) + F_d \qquad (8.27)$$

As above, the cost-minimizing settlement amount solves

$$F[(S + C_p)/J] - f[(S + C_p)/J][(C_p + A_d + N_d)/J] = 0. \qquad (8.28)$$

Note that the optimal settlement amount, S^*, does not depend on the fixed attorney cost F_d, but it does depend on the variable attorney cost A_d. In particular, since A_d is a portion of C_d, it follows from the comparative static results in (8.9) that $\partial S^*/\partial A_d > 0$. Thus, a defendant hiring an outside attorney as claims arise will pay a higher settlement amount than a defendant with a full-time, salaried attorney, all else equal. Also, since the probability of settlement is increasing in C_d by (8.10), the defendant with an outside attorney will be more likely to settle. Intuitively, since the defendant with an in-house attorney has lower costs of going to trial, he will be more willing to do so, thereby improving his bargaining position relative to the plaintiff. As a result, he will be able to settle for a lower amount.

The preceding argument does not necessarily imply, however, that in-house attorneys will lower the defendant's overall expected costs. The above benefits need to be weighed against the fixed costs that have to be paid even when no suits arise. To compare the costs of the two strategies, write (8.27) as

$$TC = VC(A_d) + F_d \qquad (8.27')$$

where $VC(A_d)$ are variable costs as a function of A_d. It follows from the Envelope theorem that, at the optimal settlement amount,

$$\partial TC/\partial A_d = \partial VC/\partial A_d = 1 - F[(S^* + C_p)/J] > 0. \qquad (8.29)$$

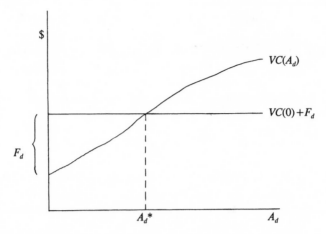

FIGURE 8.5 The cost of hiring an in-house attorney (horizontal line) compared to the cost of hiring an outside attorney (upward sloping line).

Thus, variable costs are increasing in A_d. Total expected costs with in-house counsel, $VC(0) + F_d$, and with an outside attorney, $VC(A_d)$, are graphed in figure 8.5 as a function of A_d. To the left of A_d^*, an outside attorney is cheaper, and to the right of A_d^* an in-house attorney is cheaper. Thus, an in-house attorney is more desirable the larger are variable attorney costs, A_d, and the smaller are fixed attorney costs, F_d.

6. Summary

This chapter focused on the cost of using the legal system to resolve disputes. The simplest economic models of dispute resolution showed that rational bargainers will always want to settle before going to trial. Since some cases, albeit a small number, actually go to trial, the problem was to develop more sophisticated models that explain the existence of trials. I examined two basic approaches that have been developed in the literature: the differing perceptions model, which says that trials occur when both parties are optimistic about their case, and the asymmetric information model, which says that trials occur when the defendant cannot observe the strength of the plaintiff's case.

I then used these models to examine several issues. First, I considered how the selection of disputes for trial affects the nature of legal change. In this context, I examined the question of whether the law evolves toward efficiency without the conscious help of judges, and then considered how self-interested judges and lawyers might influence the course of legal change. Finally, I examined the impact of various policies aimed at promoting settlement and lowering litigation costs, including the English rule for allocation legal costs, Rule 68 of the Federal Rules of Civil Procedure, and the practice of pretrial discovery.

NINE

THE ECONOMICS OF FRIVOLOUS
LITIGATION

It is a common perception that there are too many lawsuits filed in the United States. The available data on litigation rates provide some support for this perception. For example, figure 9.1 depicts the rapid growth in the number of civil cases filed in U.S. district courts beginning in the early 1970s, even after controlling for population growth.[1] A rising number of lawsuits, however, does not, by itself, indicate an increasing number of nonmeritorious, or "frivolous," suits;[2] perhaps some meritorious suits had previously been deterred. Since we saw in the last chapter that most suits end up either settling or being dropped before going to trial,[3] it is virtually impossible to offer data on the fraction of suits that are in fact frivolous. Thus, the question can be addressed only theoretically. In this chapter, I therefore survey various economic models of frivolous litigation that have been offered both to support the conjecture that some fraction of suits is frivolous, and to suggest remedies for this problem.

The literature on frivolous lawsuits generally defines them to be those cases that would not succeed if they went to trial. Thus, either the plaintiff sustained no actual damages ($J = 0$), or if she did, the prevailing law does not entitle her to recover them against the defendant ($P = 0$). In either case, the suit is without merit (i.e., $PJ = 0$). According to a broader definition, it is possible that the case has some merit—that is, $PJ > 0$—but the plaintiff's cost of pursuing the case to trial exceeds its expected value, $PJ - C_p < 0$. Although calling the latter type of case frivolous is more questionable, it turns out that the key feature of frivolous suits in the economic models presented below is that $PJ - C_p < 0$, whether PJ is positive or zero.[4] The reason is that $PJ - C_p < 0$ implies that the plaintiff would never rationally go to trial if the defendant refuses to settle. Given rational expectations, this raises the question of why plaintiffs ever file frivolous suits, and when they do, why defendants ever agree to settle them.

I will for the most part adopt this broader definition of frivolous suits in this chapter and propose several possible answers as to why frivolous suits can nevertheless succeed. I will also examine various procedural methods for reducing the incidence of frivolous litigation, including cost-shifting rules and court-imposed sanctions. I will conclude by asking whether contingent fees promote frivolous

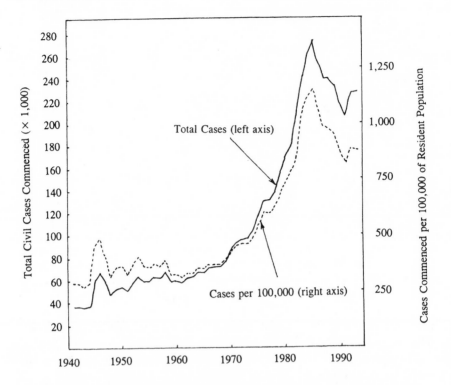

FIGURE 9.1 Total number of civil cases filed in the United States (solid line), and number filed per 100,000 of resident population (dashed line). *Source: Statistical Abstract of the U.S.*, various years; and *Historical Statistics of the U.S. from Colonial Times to 1970*, Part 1.

suits, as is commonly thought, and whether repeat defendants can succeed in deterring frivolous suits by developing "reputations for toughness."

1. The Differing Perceptions Model

I will first offer an explanation for frivolous suits based on the differing perceptions model.[5] We saw in the previous chapter that when the parties split the surplus from settling evenly, the settlement amount under the American rule for allocating costs is[6]

$$
\begin{aligned}
S_A &= P_p J - C_p + (1/2)(C_p + C_d) \\
&= P_p J + (1/2)(C_d - C_p).
\end{aligned}
\tag{9.1}
$$

According to the second line, the defendant pays the plaintiff the expected judgment at trial, plus an adjustment factor that is positive if the defendant has higher trial costs and negative if the plaintiff has higher trial costs. This adjustment factor is the key to the success of frivolous suits in the current model since, if $P_p\mathcal{J} = 0$, $S_A = (1/2)(C_d - C_p)$. Thus, frivolous suits settle for a positive amount if the defendant saves more by avoiding a trial than does the plaintiff. If the reverse is true, or if the parties have equal costs, frivolous suits will fail.[7]

Under the English rule for allocating costs, the settlement amount, given equal sharing of the surplus, is[8]

$$
\begin{aligned}
S_E &= P_p\mathcal{J} - (1 - P_p)(C_p + C_d) + (1/2)(C_p + C_d) \\
&= P_p\mathcal{J} + (P_p - 1/2)(C_p + C_d).
\end{aligned}
\tag{9.2}
$$

If $P_p\mathcal{J} = 0$, this reduces to $S_E = (P_p - 1/2)(C_p + C_d)$, which is positive if $P_p > 1/2$ (or, more generally, if P_p is greater than the plaintiff's share of the surplus from settling). Thus, if $P_p = 0$, frivolous suits never succeed under the English rule (Snyder and Hughes, 1990). However, if $\mathcal{J} = 0$ but $P_p > 0$, frivolous suits can succeed if P_p is large enough. This can happen, for example, if either the defendant or the court cannot observe the plaintiff's true injuries (both possibilities are examined in subsequent sections). In this case, the English rule can lead to more frivolous suits than the American rule if $P_p > C_d/(C_p + C_d)$.

One criticism of the preceding model is that, if the defendant offered $S = 0$ instead of the amount in (9.1), and the court does not make errors in evaluating the merits of the case, then the plaintiff would drop the suit rather than go to trial whenever $P_p\mathcal{J} = 0$. That is, the plaintiff's threat to go to trial is not credible.[9] Subsequent sections remedy this problem by presenting models in which the defendant perceives that there is a cost of refusing to settle the case.

2. The Legal Error Model

The model in this section assumes that the court makes errors in determining the defendant's liability. Recall from chapter 3 that if the court makes errors in determining whether the defendant satisfied the due standard under a negligence rule, plaintiffs can prevail at trial against "innocent" defendants. Suits of this sort therefore meet our definition of frivolous suits in the sense that, if there were no possibility of legal error, $P_p = 0$.[10]

In the presence of legal error, frivolous suits can succeed as a result of type II errors (false assignments of liability), which occur with probability q_2. Since we assume the plaintiff knows that the defendant satisfied the due standard, the plaintiff's expected value of going to trial (under the American rule) is $q_2\mathcal{J} - C_p > 0$ and the defendant's expected cost is $q_2\mathcal{J} + C_d$. This situation is thus identical to the standard differing perceptions model, with q_2 replacing P_p and P_d as the probability of plaintiff victory. If both parties assess the same probability of a type II error,[11] a settlement range always exists, and the surplus from settling is $C_p + C_d$. Equal division of the surplus therefore yields

$$
S_A = q_2\mathcal{J} + (1/2)(C_d - C_p)
\tag{9.3}
$$

under the American rule, and

$$S_E = q_2 \mathcal{J} + (q_2 - 1/2)(C_p + C_d) \qquad (9.4)$$

under the English rule. Thus, frivolous suits can succeed under both rules provided that S_A and S_E exceed the filing cost, w. As above, comparison of (9.3) and (9.4) shows that the English rule leads to more frivolous litigation if $q_2 > C_d/(C_p + C_d)$.

A final note about frivolous suits arising from legal error concerns their impact on deterrence of defendants. Suppose that courts make both type I and type II errors. Since type I errors are false "acquittals" (false findings of no liability), they will cause some legitimate suits to fail, resulting in underdeterrence of defendants. In particular, a defendant who causes damages of $\mathcal{J}$ will expect to incur liability of only $(1 - q_1)\mathcal{J} < \mathcal{J}$. The possibility of frivolous suits arising from type II errors has the potential to mitigate this underdeterrence problem. For example, if potential defendants face both types of errors, then their expected liability increases to $[q_2 + (1 - q_1)]\mathcal{J}$, which is greater (less) than $\mathcal{J}$ as $q_2 > (<)q_1$.

Even if type II errors help to maintain optimal deterrence, however, that does not mean that legal errors are irrelevant, given that one important function of civil litigation, besides deterrence, is to compensate victims (its "corrective justice" function). Legal errors erode this function, regardless of deterrence, because some uninjured victims are compensated while some injured victims are uncompensated.

3. The Timing of Litigation Costs

Rosenberg and Shavell (1985) developed a model in which frivolous suits succeed as a result of the *timing* of litigation costs. Specifically, their model assumes that, once a plaintiff files a suit, the defendant must incur costs of "defending himself" before the plaintiff has to make any additional expenditures. If the defendant does not defend himself—for example by failing to hire a lawyer and gather evidence—he will lose by a default or summary judgment. Thus, if the cost of defense is sufficiently high, the defendant will prefer to settle regardless of the merits of the plaintiff's case.

To see this formally, suppose both parties assess the same probability that the plaintiff will prevail at trial, P, and both know that the suit is frivolous, that is, that $P\mathcal{J} - C_p < 0$. Thus, the parties know that the plaintiff would not proceed to trial if the defendant offered no settlement. However, suppose that the defendant has to defend himself at cost d once the suit is filed, or he will lose by default and incur liability of $\mathcal{J}$. As a result, the plaintiff can make a settlement demand of $S = \min(d, \mathcal{J})$, which is the maximum amount the defendant will pay rather than face a summary judgment. Frivolous suits will therefore succeed in this setting if S is large enough to cover the plaintiff's filing cost; that is, if $\min(d, \mathcal{J}) > w$.

The result is different under the English rule. In this case, if the defendant chooses to defend himself at cost d, the plaintiff will drop the suit rather than go to trial, in which case the defendant, being the winning party, will recover his costs. Since it is costless for the defendant to defend himself in this case, he will never settle a suit that the plaintiff would not take to trial. Thus, frivolous suits will fail. This result reflects the importance of the credibility of the plaintiff's threat to impose costs on the defendant, either at or before trial, in order to obtain a settlement for a frivolous suit.

Although the Rosenberg and Shavell model may explain frivolous suits that settle for small amounts (remember that d is *not* the defendant's cost of a trial but the cost of an initial response to the suit), it does not explain large settlements. To explain these, I return to the asymmetric information model.

4. The Asymmetric Information Model

The final explanation of frivolous suits rests on the asymmetric information model introduced in chapter 8. Recall that the basic assumption of that model was that the plaintiff had private information about the merits of her case. This can lead to frivolous suits because the defendant cannot distinguish legitimate from frivolous claims, and therefore may prefer to settle all claims in order to avoid the costs of going to trial with legitimate claimants. The analysis of the asymmetric information model in section 2.1 of the previous chapter already demonstrated a simple version of this argument. Specifically, plaintiffs who settled were those for whom $PJ - C_p < S^*$, where S^* was the defendant's optimal settlement offer, and nothing prevented this group from including plaintiffs with $PJ - C_p < 0$.[12]

A more complete model of frivolous suits under asymmetric information developed by Katz (1990) relaxes two assumptions of this simple model. The first is that suits are costless to file, and the second is that there is a fixed number of frivolous suits. By allowing the number of frivolous suits filed to be endogenous, the current model will permit a fuller examination of the factors that allow such suits to succeed.

In the remainder of this chapter, I briefly lay out this more general model of frivolous suits. I then use it to examine (1) the impact of cost-allocation rules on the amount of frivolous litigation, (2) the impact of procedural rules that attempt to sanction frivolous suits, (3) whether contingent fees for personal injury cases promote frivolous litigation relative to hourly fees, and (4) whether "repeat defendants" can succeed in discouraging frivolous suits by developing a reputation for not settling cases.

4.1. The Basic Model

Suppose there are two types of potential plaintiffs: those who are truly injured and those who are not. Assume plaintiffs know their own type, but defendants do not. For example, if the suit is in torts, perhaps the defendant cannot observe the plaintiff's true injuries or whether the plaintiff was contributorily negligent. However, defendants do know the fraction of injured plaintiffs in the population, which I denote α. For uninjured plaintiffs, the expected value of a trial is $-C_p < 0$ given $PJ = 0$, and for injured plaintiffs the expected value is $PJ - C_p > 0$. Thus, only injured plaintiffs will go to trial if not offered a settlement. Further, I assume $PJ - C_p$ is greater than the filing cost w, so that it is profitable for injured plaintiffs to file a claim. Finally, the cost of a trial for the defendant is C_d, and, for now, settlement costs are zero.

4.1.1. DERIVATION OF THE EQUILIBRIUM

The equilibrium of this settlement game is found by proceeding in reverse sequence of time.[13] Thus, I first examine the plaintiff's decision of whether or not to accept the defendant's settlement offer of $S \geq 0$.[14] Since a frivolous plaintiff will never go to trial, she will accept any positive offer and drop the case if $S = 0$ is offered. A legitimate defendant, on the other hand, will accept any $S \geq PJ - C_p$ and go to trial otherwise.[15]

Given this behavior of plaintiffs, the defendant must choose what settlement offer to make. Clearly, he will never offer more than $PJ - C_p$, the minimum amount a legitimate plaintiff will accept, and since frivolous plaintiffs will accept $S = 0$, he will never offer an amount between zero and $PJ - C_p$. Thus, his two options are zero and $PJ - C_p$. The latter offer will result in a settlement with all plaintiffs, including frivolous ones, and the former will result in a trial with legitimate plaintiffs only.[16] In order to choose between these two outcomes, he needs to know the fraction of frivolous suits among the suits that have been filed. If we define θ as the probability that an uninjured plaintiff chooses to file suit, then the conditional probability that a plaintiff is legitimate, given that she has filed, is given by[17]

$$\alpha' = \alpha/[\alpha + (1 - \alpha)\theta]. \tag{9.5}$$

Note that $\alpha' = \alpha$ when $\theta = 1$, $\alpha' = 1$, when $\theta = 0$, and generally, $\alpha' \geq \alpha$ for $\theta \leq 1$. Intuitively, if all uninjured plaintiffs file suit, then the act of filing conveys no information to the defendant. At the other extreme, if no uninjured plaintiffs file suit, the act of filing signals with certainty that the suit is legitimate.

Given (9.5), the defendant will prefer to settle with all plaintiffs (i.e., offer $S = PJ - C_p$) if $PJ - C_p < \alpha'(PJ + C_d)$, and to go to trial with legitimate plaintiffs (i.e., offer $S = 0$) if the reverse inequality holds, where $PJ + C_d$ is the defendant's expected cost of a trial with an injured plaintiff. The point of indifference between the two strategies occurs at the following threshold for α':

$$t = (PJ - C_p)/(PJ + C_d). \tag{9.6}$$

Thus, if $\alpha' > t$, the defendant prefers to settle, if $\alpha' < t$, he prefers to go to trial, and if $\alpha' = t$, he is indifferent.

The defendant's optimal strategy can be described by variable σ, which represents the probability that he settles (i.e., offers $S = PJ - C_p$). It turns out that if $\alpha > t$—that is, if the fraction of injured plaintiffs exceeds the threshold in (9.6)—then it is optimal for the defendant to settle with all plaintiffs (i.e., set $\sigma^* = 1$). To see why, note that $\alpha' \geq \alpha$ (by definition), which implies that $\alpha' > t$ when $\alpha > t$. Thus, when the fraction of injured plaintiffs is high enough, settling with all plaintiffs is cheaper than going to trial with only injured plaintiffs. Since uninjured plaintiffs anticipate this outcome, they all file suit. Thus, in equilibrium, $\sigma^* = \theta^* = 1$. Note that this equilibrium resembles the outcome of the model in section 2.1 of the previous chapter, where the number of frivolous suits was fixed and all succeeded in obtaining a settlement (Bebchuk, 1988). In general, this outcome is more likely (1) the larger is the fraction of injured plaintiffs (α); (2) the higher are the costs of trial (C_p and C_d); and (3) the lower are the expected stakes of the case (PJ).[18] These effects are similar to those that make settlement more likely in the model from section 2.1 in chapter 8.

The equilibrium of the current model differs from the model in the previous chapter when $\alpha < t$. In this case, the only equilibrium involves mixed strategies. To see why, suppose initially that the defendant chooses to settle all cases ($\sigma = 1$) and all uninjured plaintiffs file suit ($\theta = 1$). It follows from (9.5) that $\alpha' = \alpha < t$, in which case the defendant prefers to go to trial rather than settle. Thus, suppose he sets $\sigma = 0$. Since frivolous suits are now unprofitable, $\theta = 0$, in which case $\alpha' = 1 > t$, and the defendant prefers to settle. This oscillating solution can be eliminated only by a mixed-strategy equilibrium in which the defendant is indifferent between settling and going to trial, and uninjured plaintiffs are indifferent between filing and not filing.

The defendant is indifferent when $\alpha' = t$, which, from (9.5) and (9.6) implies that

$$\theta^* = [\alpha(C_p + C_d)]/[(1 - \alpha)(PJ - C_p)]. \tag{9.7}$$

Thus θ^* indicates the fraction of uninjured plaintiffs that file suit in the mixed strategy equilibrium and t represents the equilibrium fraction of legitimate suits in the set of cases actually filed. In order for uninjured plaintiffs to be indifferent between filing and not filing, the expected value of filing, $\sigma(PJ - C_p) - w$, must equal zero. This yields the critical value of σ

$$\sigma^* = w/(PJ - C_p), \tag{9.8}$$

which represents the probability with which the defendant will settle in equilibrium.

Katz (1990) refers to this mixed-strategy equilibrium as a *free-entry* equilibrium, because frivolous suits "enter" until the expected return from doing so is zero. This contrasts with the previous pure-strategy equilibrium in which all potential frivolous suits were filed and settled with certainty, thereby yielding a strictly positive expected return (or "rent"). The free-entry equilibrium is more likely the smaller the number of truly injured plaintiffs, or, equivalently, the larger the fraction of potentially frivolous suits. In addition, it is more likely the smaller are C_p and C_d, and the larger is PJ. Since the fraction of legitimate suits among those actually filed is t in the free-entry equilibrium, the fraction of frivolous suits is $1 - t$. Thus, from (9.6), the fraction of frivolous suits is increasing in the costs of a trial for both parties and decreasing in the expected stakes of the case. Again, these are the same factors that increased the likelihood of settlement in previous models.

4.1.2. THE IMPACT OF FRIVOLOUS SUITS ON OVERALL LITIGATION COSTS

From a social perspective, an important concern regarding frivolous suits is their impact on overall litigation costs. These consist of the total filing costs plus trial costs for those cases not dropped or settled (recall that settlement costs are zero). The total number of cases filed is $\alpha + (1 - \alpha)\theta$, and the number of cases that go to trial is $\alpha(1 - \sigma)$. Thus, total litigation costs are

$$TC = [\alpha + (1 - \alpha)\theta]w + \alpha(1 - \sigma)(C_p + C_d). \tag{9.9}$$

Total costs in the equilibrium in which all frivolous suits are filed and all cases settle are found by substituting $\theta = 1$ and $\sigma = 1$ into (9.9). In that case, $TC = w$; that is, only filing costs are incurred.

Total costs in the free-entry equilibrium are found by substituting θ^* from (9.7) and σ^* from (9.8) into (9.9). The result, after simplification, is

$$TC = \alpha(w + C_p + C_d). \tag{9.10}$$

Thus, total costs equal the amount that would be spent if only legitimate suits were filed and all went to trial. Intuitively, free entry by frivolous suits in this equilibrium essentially eliminates all of the surplus from settling rather than going to trial. Figure 9.2 graphs total litigation costs under the two types of equilibria. The mixed-strategy equilibrium exists to the left of t, and the pure-strategy equilibrium exists to the right of t. The discontinuous drop in costs at t shows the savings that result from settlement compared to trial. An implication of (9.10) is that banning settlements in an effort to deter frivolous litigation would *not* succeed in lowering total litigation costs (Katz, 1990, p. 16). In the following sections, I therefore examine alternative methods for reducing the amount of frivolous litigation.

4.2. The English Rule and Frivolous Suits

Under the English rule for allocating legal costs,[19] recall that the plaintiff recovers her filing plus trial costs if she wins at trial, but she must pay the defendant's trial costs if she loses. Thus, the expected value of a legitimate suit at trial, once filing costs have been paid, is

$$P(\mathcal{J} + w) - (1 - P)(C_p + C_d) = P\mathcal{J} - C_p + P(w + C_p) - (1 - P)C_d. \tag{9.11}$$

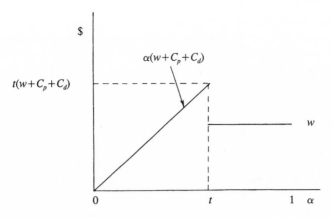

FIGURE 9.2 Total litigation costs as a function of the fraction of truly injured plaintiffs.

Compared to the value of a suit under the American rule, this expression differs by the terms $P(w + C_p) - (1 - P)C_d$, which may be positive or negative. Thus, once a case has been filed, it may be more or less valuable at trial under the English rule. The defendant's cost of taking a legitimate suit to trial under the English rule is

$$P(J + C_p + C_d + w) = PJ + C_d + P(w + C_p) - (1 - P)C_d. \qquad (9.12)$$

It thus differs from the cost under the American rule by the same extra terms. Let these extra terms be denoted by k—that is, $k = P(w + C_p) - (1 - P)C_d$.

Recall that in the free-entry equilibrium, the fraction of legitimate suits among those filed[20] equaled the threshold t in (9.6), which was the ratio of the plaintiff's expected value of a legitimate suit at trial to the defendant's expected cost of the suit at trial. Under the English rule, the corresponding threshold is given by the ratio of (9.11) to (9.12), or

$$t_E = [PJ - C_p + k]/[PJ + C_d + k]. \qquad (9.13)$$

Similarly, the equilibrium settlement rate under the English rule is given by

$$\sigma_E^* = w/(PJ - C_p + k). \qquad (9.14)$$

It is easy to show that t_E is increasing in k, and σ_E^* is decreasing in k. Thus, if $k > 0$—that is, if the English rule increases the value of legitimate suits at trial—then there are fewer frivolous suits filed and the settlement rate is lower. Intuitively, since legitimate suits are more valuable at trial, the defendant is less willing to settle because of the higher settlement demand plaintiffs will make ($k > 0$ is like an increase in the stakes of the case). And because of the lower settlement rate, fewer frivolous suits succeed (even though those that do succeed receive a higher settlement). Of course, the results are reversed if $k < 0$. It follows that in the current model, the English rule is not necessarily better at deterring frivolous litigation as compared to the American rule.

4.3. Sanctioning Frivolous Suits

Another possible way to discourage frivolous litigation is to give defendants legal recourse against frivolous claimants. An example is Rule 11 of the Federal Rules of Civil Procedure, which allows the court to impose financial sanctions on a plaintiff whose case is judged to have been frivolous. Polinsky and Rubinfeld (1993) examined the impact of a rule of this sort on the incidence of frivolous litigation and on litigation costs. They concluded that it can reduce the number of suits and overall litigation costs if the costs of imposing the sanctions are not too high and if the fraction of frivolous suits is not too large. They also noted the possibility, however, that mistaken imposition of sanctions might discourage some *legitimate* suits, though they showed that this effect can be offset by adjusting upward the award to winning plaintiffs in the original trial.

An important point regarding Rule 11-type sanctions is that the defendant can seek them only after winning at trial. In their model, Polinsky and Rubinfeld therefore assume that all suits go to trial (they ignore settlements), and they define frivolous suits to be those with a low (but still positive) probability of victory at trial. However, the fact that plaintiffs are willing to take low-probability suits to trial indicates that they nevertheless have a positive expected value.[21] Thus, these type of suits fail to meet our definition of frivolous suits, unless frivolous plaintiffs' chance of victory depends on legal error, as in section 2 above, or if some suits with $PJ - C_p > 0$ are defined to be frivolous—for example, those with low P.

In contrast to the model in Polinsky and Rubinfeld, frivolous suits never go to trial in the Katz (1990) model. Therefore, sanctions can have an impact only if (1) they reduce the defendant's inclination to settle, or (2) they make it less desirable for frivolous plaintiffs to file suit in the first place. Regarding the former, if we assume that the court correctly assesses the merits of plaintiffs' cases ex post (even when they lose), then defendants would never seek sanctions after the fact because they know that, in equilibrium, only legitimate suits ever go to trial. Thus, the sanctions would have no effect on the decisions of defendants. As for the latter, frivolous plaintiffs can be discouraged from filing only if they can be penalized for dropping their suits, given that they never go to trial. For example, Katz (1990, pp. 19–20) proposes that plaintiffs be required to post a bond when they file suit which they would forfeit if they end up dropping their suit. He shows that such a scheme can reduce the number of frivolous suits and lower litigation costs, again provided that the court correctly recognizes legitimate suits even when the plaintiff loses at trial.

In reality, of course, courts will sometimes make errors in imposing sanctions. I thus conclude this section by examining the impact of errors in imposing Rule 11-type sanctions in the context of the Katz model.[22] Note that an incorrectly imposed sanction is in effect a type II error (a false conviction) in that the court finds a legitimate suit frivolous. Thus, let q_2 be the probability that a winning defendant will prevail in an action for sanctions against a losing plaintiff. Also, let C_p' and C_d' be the litigation costs of an action for sanctions for the plaintiff and defendant, respectively, and let Υ be the sanction imposed on plaintiff, which I assume is paid to the defendant, if the defendant wins.[23] Given this setting, a winning defendant will bring an action for sanctions if $q_2\Upsilon - C_d' > 0$. I assume that this condition holds, for if it did not, then sanctions would have no impact.

The possibility of sanctions affects the expected value of the initial trial for legitimate plaintiffs, which, in this case becomes

$$PJ - C_p - (1 - P)(q_2\Upsilon + C_p'), \tag{9.15}$$

where $q_2\Upsilon + C_p'$ is the expected cost to a losing plaintiff of an action for sanctions. I assume that (9.15) is positive since, otherwise, the plaintiff would never go to trial. Note, however, that it is less than the value in the absence of sanctions, $PJ - C_p$. According to the derivation of equilibrium above, the defendant can either settle with all plaintiffs for an amount equal to (9.15), or refuse to settle, in which case his expected costs are

$$\alpha'[PJ + C_d - (1 - P)(q_2\Upsilon - C_d')], \tag{9.16}$$

where α' is defined as above to be the conditional probability that the suit is legitimate, given that it was filed. Note that the defendant's cost of a trial (the expression in brackets) is also less than the corresponding cost in the absence of sanctions, $PJ + C_d$.

As above, we can use (9.15) and (9.16) to define the threshold between the two types of equilibria:

$$t_s = \frac{PJ - C_p - (1 - P)(q_2\Upsilon + C_p')}{PJ + C_d - (1 - P)(q_2\Upsilon - C_d')} \tag{9.17}$$

Comparing this to (9.6), the threshold in the absence of sanctions, shows that $t > t_s$. Thus, the mixed-strategy (free-entry) equilibrium will hold for a smaller range of α when sanctions are available. Moreover, recall that when the free-entry equilibrium holds, t_s also represents the proportion of legitimate suits among those that file. Consequently, sanctions actually *increase* the proportion of frivolous suits that file (i.e., $1 - t_s > 1 - t$). This is because sanctions are imposed only on legitimate suits (mistakenly), given that true frivolous suits never go to trial. Thus, as was possible under the English rule, sanctions can have the effect of making legitimate suits less desirable.[24]

In addition, the equilibrium settlement rate increases to

$$\sigma_s^* = w/[PJ - C_p - (1 - P)(q_2\Upsilon + C_p')]. \tag{9.18}$$

This effect is also due to the lower value of legitimate suits, which makes the defendant more willing to settle. Sanctions therefore at least succeed in lowering the amount that frivolous claimants obtain in a settlement—from $P\mathcal{J} - C_p$ to the amount in (9.15)—though this happens at the expense of more frivolous suits succeeding. These results suggest that court-imposed sanctions on frivolous suits may not be an effective method for deterring such suits if most truly frivolous suits settle or are dropped before trial. Indeed, sanctions may have the opposite effect of deterring some legitimate suits.

4.4. Do Contingent Fees Promote Frivolous Litigation?

A common criticism of contingent legal fees is that they invite frivolous suits because the plaintiff is not responsible for her legal fees if she loses.[25] (In a sense, contingent fees therefore reverse the English rule, under which the plaintiff avoids paying legal fees if she *wins*.) What this criticism typically ignores is the role of the attorney in accepting or rejecting cases. Because the attorney assumes financial responsibility for a case, he or she will reject it if it promises an insufficient chance of recovery. This does not, however, rule out frivolous suits, since we have seen that they can result in recovery via settlement. Thus, the question to be answered in this section is, do contingent fees result in a higher fraction of frivolous suits being filed than do hourly fees?

I assume for purposes of the argument that attorneys earn zero profit, and that their effort does not affect the probability of success at trial.[26] This allows us to focus on their role in screening cases under a contingent fee. I also assume the plaintiff alone decides whether to settle or go to trial.[27] Finally, I assume that attorneys' costs are incurred by both parties during the pretrial bargaining period, whether or not a settlement is reached. Denote these costs R_p and R_d for the plaintiff and defendant, respectively.

4.4.1. HOURLY FEE

Under an hourly fee, the legal fees for both parties simply equal their attorneys' costs of litigation given zero attorney profit, and the plaintiff pays her own filing costs.[28] Thus, the plaintiff's total costs are $w + R_p$ if she settles and $w + R_p + C_p$ if she goes to trial. Similarly, the defendant's costs are R_d if the case settles and $R_d + C_d$ if it goes to trial.

The analysis of frivolous litigation under an hourly fee is thus identical to that in section 4.1, except for the addition of the settlement period costs. I thus begin with the defendant's decision to settle with all plaintiffs or go to trial with only legitimate plaintiffs. Under the former strategy, the defendant will offer at most the value of a legitimate suit at trial, or $S_h = P\mathcal{J} - C_p$, given that the plaintiff's filing and settlement costs are sunk. The cost of this strategy is $P\mathcal{J} - C_p + R_d$. If the defendant instead offers no settlement amount, his expected cost is $\alpha'(P\mathcal{J} + C_d) + R_d$, where α', the fraction of legitimate suits among those filed, is given by (9.5). Equating these costs yields the threshold separating the two strategies under the hourly fee:

$$t_h = (PJ - C_p)/(PJ + C_d), \tag{9.19}$$

which is identical to (9.6).

As above, when $\alpha > t_h$, all frivolous suits are filed and all cases settle. Total litigation costs in this case are thus $w + R_p + R_d$. When $\alpha < t_h$, the equilibrium again is a mixed strategy. As in section 4.1, $\alpha' = t_h$ in this equilibrium, which yields the fraction of uninjured plaintiffs who file suit:

$$\theta_h^* = [\alpha(C_p + C_d)]/[(1 - \alpha)(PJ - C_p). \tag{9.20}$$

This expression is identical to (9.7). Also, the settlement rate in the mixed-strategy equilibrium solves the equation $\sigma_h S_h - R_p - w = 0$, which, after substituting $S_h = PJ - C_p$, yields

$$\sigma_h^* = (w + R_p)/(PJ - C_p). \tag{9.21}$$

Note that this expression differs from (9.8) by the addition of R_p in the numerator.

Total costs in the mixed-strategy equilibrium under the hourly fee are

$$TC_h = [\alpha + (1 - \alpha)\theta_h^*](w + R_p + R_d) + \alpha(1 - \sigma_h^*)(C_p + C_d). \tag{9.22}$$

This expression differs from (9.9) by the addition of $R_p + R_d$ in the first term. Substituting (9.20) and (9.21) into (9.22) and simplifying yields expected costs in equilibrium:

$$TC_h = \frac{\alpha(PJ + C_d)}{(PJ - C_p)} \left[(w + R_p + R_d) + \left(\frac{C_p + C_d}{PJ + C_d} \right)(PJ - R_p - C_p - w) \right]. \tag{9.23}$$

4.4.2. CONTINGENT FEE

Under a contingent fee, the plaintiff's attorney receives a fraction of any proceeds from the suit, whether at trial or by settlement, and nothing if the plaintiff drops the suit or loses at trial. In most states, the plaintiff's attorney receives a third of any award, though in some states the percentage differs depending on whether the case settles or goes to trial. Here, I will allow the percentage to differ. Thus, let β_s be the fraction the attorney retains if the case settles and β_t the fraction if the case goes to trial.

Consider first the decision of an attorney whether or not to accept a frivolous suit. I assume that the attorney (unlike the defendant) can determine whether a suit is legitimate or frivolous before accepting it. Thus, since the latter can only yield a recovery by settling, the attorney's expected profit from accepting a frivolous suit is

$$\sigma_c \beta_s S_c - R_p \qquad (9.24)$$

where σ_c is the probability that the defendant will settle and S_c is the settlement amount under a contingent fee. Alternatively, since a legitimate suit can yield a recovery by settlement or trial, it yields an expected profit of

$$\sigma_c(\beta_s S_c - R_p) + (1 - \sigma_c)(\beta_t PJ - R_p - C_p) = \sigma_c \beta_s S_c - R_p$$
$$+ (1 - \sigma_c)(\beta_t PJ - C_p). \qquad (9.25)$$

Zero expected profits for attorneys implies that both (9.24) and (9.25) equal zero. This further implies that

$$\beta_s = R_p/\sigma_c S_c, \quad \text{and} \quad \beta_t = C_p/PJ, \qquad (9.26)$$

where σ_c and S_c are yet to be determined.

Now consider the defendant's decision to settle or go to trial. As above, the defendant either offers $S = 0$ or the lowest amount a legitimate plaintiff will accept. Under a contingent fee, the latter amount is the solution to $S_c(1 - \beta_s) = PJ(1 - \beta_t)$, where the left-hand side is the plaintiff's net return under a settlement and the right-hand side is the net expected return from trial. Substituting for β_t from (9.26) and solving yields

$$S_c = (PJ - C_p)/(1 - \beta_s). \qquad (9.27)$$

Note that, although we have yet to determine β_s, $S_c > S_h = PJ - C_p$ provided that $0 < \beta_s < 1$. That is, the settlement amount is *higher* under a contingent fee as compared to an hourly fee.

The threshold point under the contingent fee equates the defendant's cost of settling, $S_c + R_d$, and his cost of going to trial, $\alpha'(PJ + C_d) + R_d$. After substituting for S_c from (9.27), this yields

$$t_c = (PJ - C_p)/[(PJ + C_d)(1 - \beta_s)]. \qquad (9.28)$$

Comparing this to the threshold under the hourly fee in (9.19) shows that $t_c > t_h$, again given $0 < \beta_s < 1$.

In the free-entry (mixed-strategy) equilibrium, $\alpha' = t_c$ (the defendant is indifferent between his two strategies) and $\sigma_c S_c(1 - \beta_s) - w = 0$ (uninjured plaintiffs are indifferent between filing and not filing). These two equations can be solved simultaneously with (9.28), (9.27), and (9.26) to obtain the equilibrium probability of settlement

$$\sigma_c^* = w/(PJ - C_p) \qquad (9.29)$$

and the equilibrium probability that a frivolous plaintiff will file suit

$$\theta_c^* = \frac{\alpha(C_p + C_d)}{(1 - \alpha)(PJ - C_p)} - \frac{\alpha R_p(PJ + C_d)}{(1 - \alpha)(R_p + w)(PJ - C_p)}. \tag{9.30}$$

Comparing these to (9.20) and (9.21) shows that $\sigma_c^* < \sigma_h^*$ and $\theta_c^* < \theta_h^*$.[29] That is, the settlement rate is lower under the contingent fee, and a larger fraction of frivolous suits file under the *hourly* fee. The reason behind this counterintuitive result is that the higher settlement amount under the contingent fee makes the defendant less willing to settle, all else equal. This in turn reduces the expected value of a frivolous suit.

Although we have shown that the contingent fee actually leads to *fewer* frivolous suits in the free-entry equilibrium, we are also interested in how it affects total litigation costs. In the equilibrium where all frivolous suits file, total costs are again $w + R_p + R_d$. In the free-entry equilibrium, total costs are found by substituting (9.29) and (9.30) into (9.22) to get

$$TC_c = \frac{\alpha(PJ + C_d)w}{(PJ - C_p)(R_p + w)} \left[(w + R_p + R_d) + \frac{(C_p + C_d)(R_p + w)}{(PJ + C_d)w}(PJ - C_p - w) \right]. \tag{9.31}$$

A comparison of total costs under the two fee structures shows that

$$TC_c - TC_h = \frac{-\alpha R_p}{(PJ - C_p)(R_p + w)} [(PJ - C_p)(R_p + w) + R_d(PJ + C_d)] < 0. \tag{9.32}$$

Thus, total litigation costs under the contingent fee are lower in the free-entry equilibrium.

To this point, we have seen that, in the free-entry equilibrium, fewer frivolous suits are filed and litigation costs are lower under a contingent fee. It does not follow, however, that contingent fees *never* result in more suits or higher costs. To see why, recall that the threshold point separating the two types of equilibria was higher under the contingent fee (i.e., $t_c > t_h$). In addition, it can be shown that under both fee structures, as α approaches the threshold point from below, total litigation costs in the free-entry equilibrium rise above total costs when all cases settle. (The discontinuity, recall, is due to the savings in costs of settlements versus trials.)

The implications of this situation are shown in figure 9.3, where the solid line is total costs under the hourly fee and the dashed line is total costs under the contingent fee. Notice from the graph that, over the range between t_h and t_c, total costs are higher under the contingent fee. The higher costs are not due, however, to more frivolous suits. Rather, they are due to the higher number of trials under the contingent fee. Overall, figure 9.3 shows that costs are higher under the hourly fee between zero and t_h; higher under the contingent fee between t_h and t_c; and the same under the two fees between t_c and 1. The comparison of costs over the entire range is therefore ambiguous.

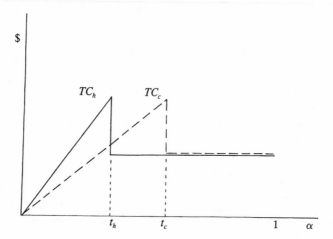

FIGURE 9.3 Total litigation costs under contingent fees (dashed line) and hourly fees (solid line).

A final point concerning contingent fees, not considered in the preceding model, is that they play an important role in providing access to the legal system for low-income plaintiffs who have a legitimate claim but otherwise could not afford the up-front cost of hiring an attorney. Thus, if contingent fees were not available, some legitimate suits would be deterred because, although $PJ > R_p + C_p + w$, the plaintiff's wealth is less than her filing plus litigation costs. In reality, this factor likely offsets those examined earlier, and may be the true basis for the claim that contingent fees promote more litigation than hourly fees. If so, then it might be more accurate to claim that hourly fees lead to *too little* litigation, and therefore possibly underdeterrence of defendants.[30]

4.5. Repeat Defendants and Frivolous Litigation

Many authors have argued that repeat defendants such as insurance companies and manufacturers of dangerous products might be able to deter frivolous suits by developing a reputation for not paying settlements.[31] The idea is that, by demonstrating a willingness to take all (or a substantial number of) cases to trial, the defendant can deter future frivolous plaintiffs from filing suit. In the case of one-time defendants, we have seen that, once a suit has been filed, defendants often prefer to settle rather than to incur trial or other defense costs, even though they know the suit may be frivolous. In this section, I derive the conditions under which repeat defendants can succeed in making a credible threat to go to trial often enough to deter frivolous suits from being filed.[32]

The model is identical to that in section 4.1, except that the defendant now faces a sequence of plaintiffs over an infinite number of discrete periods. Thus, the defendant's objective is to minimize the present value of his stream of expected litigation costs, rather than the costs of any given suit. The question is whether this difference in the objective function allows a repeat defendant to deter frivolous suits where one-time defendants cannot.

The key to achieving deterrence is for the defendant to commit to a strategy of going to trial frequently enough to make frivolous suits unprofitable. He does this by announcing to potential plaintiffs a policy of setting $\sigma < \sigma^*$ in each period, where, recall, σ^* is the lowest settlement rate that just allows a frivolous plaintiff to break even. If this policy is believable, then no frivolous plaintiffs will file suit (i.e., $\theta = 0$). (Note that such an announcement is not believable for a one-time defendant because in the above equilibria, $\sigma \geq \sigma^*$.)

Assume that potential plaintiffs adopt the following conditional or "trigger" strategy in response to the repeat defendant's threat: set $\theta = 0$ as long as the defendant continues to set $\sigma < \sigma^*$, but if he fails to do so in any period t (i.e., if he sets $\sigma \geq \sigma^*$), then revert to the equilibrium strategy for the one-shot game in all future periods.[33] Thus, if the defendant deviates from his threat, frivolous plaintiffs either set $\theta = 1$ or $\theta = \theta^*$, depending on the nature of the one-shot equilibrium (of course, all injured plaintiffs file suit regardless of the defendant's behavior).

In order to examine the conditions under which the defendant adheres to his threat, let us conjecture an equilibrium in which it is rational for him to do so (I will refer to this as a "deterrence equilibrium"). The per-period litigation costs of the defendant in this case are

$$\alpha[\sigma(P\mathcal{J} - C_p) + (1 - \sigma)(P\mathcal{J} + C_d)] \tag{9.33}$$

where $\sigma < \sigma^*$. The present value of this cost over an infinite number of periods is

$$[(1 + r)/r]\alpha[\sigma(P\mathcal{J} - C_p) + (1 - \sigma)(P\mathcal{J} + C_d)] \tag{9.34}$$

where r is the one period discount rate.

Equations (9.33) and (9.34) illustrate the problem a defendant has in sustaining his threat to set $\sigma < \sigma^*$. In particular, note that the derivative of (9.33) with respect to σ is $-\alpha(C_p + C_d) < 0$, which is the negative of the surplus from settling all legitimate suits rather than going to trial. Thus, in any period, the defendant ideally would like to set $\sigma = 1$ (i.e., settle all cases), given that only legitimate suits have been filed. If he does this, his cost in the *current period* falls from the amount in (9.33) to $\alpha(P\mathcal{J} - C_p)$. Subtracting this amount from (9.33) yields the resulting savings:

$$T(\sigma) = \alpha(1 - \sigma)(C_p + C_d). \tag{9.35}$$

Call this the defendant's "temptation" to settle once he has deterred all frivolous suits from filing.

The savings represented by $T(\sigma)$ is one time, however, given the conjectured response of frivolous plaintiffs to the observed deviation of the defendant from his threat to set $\sigma < \sigma^*$. In particular, they will disbelieve any future threat by the defendant to go to trial and behave according to their one-shot equilibrium strategy. To examine the potential impact of that response, consider the two possible one-shot equilibria.

First, when $\alpha > t$, all uninjured plaintiffs file suit in equilibrium ($\theta = 1$), and all cases settle ($\sigma = 1$). Thus, the defendant's per-period cost in all periods following deviation is $PJ - C_p$. The present value of this stream of costs, as of the period in which the defendant deviates, is

$$(PJ - C_p)/r. \tag{9.36}$$

Alternatively, the present value of costs over the same time frame if the defendant had not deviated from his threat is

$$\alpha[\sigma(PJ - C_p) + (1 - \sigma)(PJ + C_d)]/r. \tag{9.37}$$

The cost of deviating from his threat is thus the difference between (9.36) and (9.37), or

$$E(\sigma) = [(PJ - C_p) - \alpha(PJ + C_d) + \alpha\sigma(C_p + C_d)]/r. \tag{9.38}$$

Equation (9.38) is thus the "enforcement" of the defendant's threat because it represents the higher cost he faces in all periods following a deviation as a result of the entry of frivolous suits.

A necessary condition for existence of a deterrence equilibrium is that $E(\sigma) \geq T(\sigma)$, given the defendant's announced value of σ. Figure 9.4 shows that this condition holds for $\sigma \geq \sigma'$ where σ' solves the equation $T(\sigma) = E(\sigma)$. Figure 9.4 also shows that σ' is necessarily between zero and 1, given that $T(0) > E(0)$, $T(1) < E(1)$, $dT/d\sigma < 0$, and $dE/d\sigma > 0$. Explicitly solving this equation for σ yields

$$\sigma' = \frac{r}{1+r} + \frac{\alpha(PJ + C_d) - (PJ - C_p)}{\alpha(1+r)(C_p + C_d)}, \tag{9.39}$$

where the second term on the right-hand side is positive given $\alpha > t$.

Note that the condition $\sigma \geq \sigma'$ is only a necessary condition for existence of a deterrence equilibrium; it must also be true that $\sigma < \sigma^*$. In order to satisfy these conditions simultaneously, therefore, it must be true that $\sigma^* > \sigma'$, which may or may not hold. When it does, the defendant can simply announce a σ between σ' and σ^*, and he can credibly deter all frivolous suits. Further, because the present value of his costs in this equilibrium, given by (9.34), is decreasing in σ, his optimal strategy is to announce a σ as close as possible to σ^*—that is, he should settle as often as possible without making frivolous suits profitable. Finally, expressions (9.29) and (9.39) can be used to show that, for the case where $\alpha > t$, a deterrence equilibrium is more likely as w increases and as α, C_d, and r decrease. However, PJ and C_p have an ambiguous effect on existence.

The outcome in the other one-shot equilibrium when $\alpha < t$ is derived in a similar manner. Note that in this case, even one-shot defendants partially suc-

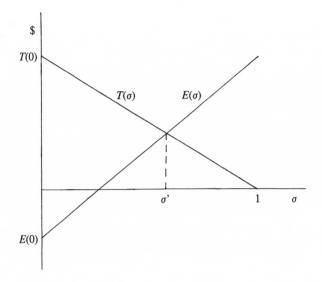

FIGURE 9.4 Necessary condition for a deterrence equilibrium.

ceed in deterring frivolous suits, since $\theta^* < 1$. However, a repeat defendant can again drive θ to zero if he can credibly set $\sigma < \sigma^*$. The temptation to deviate from this threat in this case continues to be given by (9.35), but the enforcement differs since it depends on the nature of the one-shot equilibrium. In particular, this procedure for deriving the enforcement yields[34]

$$E(\sigma) = \sigma\alpha(C_p + C_d)/r. \qquad (9.40)$$

Equating (9.40) and (9.35) yields the critical value of σ[35]

$$\sigma' = r/(1 + r). \qquad (9.41)$$

As above, existence of a deterrence equilibrium requires $\sigma' > \sigma^*$. Thus, such an equilibrium is more likely as w and C_p increase, and as r and PJ decrease. (In this case, existence is independent of α and C_d.) The shaded area in figure 9.5 shows where a deterrence equilibrium exists under the two types of equilibria.[36] Notice in general that an equilibrium does not exist as α becomes large. This is because, as the fraction of truly injured plaintiffs in the population increases, the benefits of deterring frivolous suits declines.

A final issue concerns the impact of a deterrence equilibrium (when one exists) on overall litigation costs. It turns out that when $\alpha < t$, a reputational equilibrium unambiguously lowers total litigation costs. Thus, when the free-entry equilibrium would prevail in the one-shot game, a deterrence equilibrium is socially beneficial. Conversely, when $\alpha > t$, a reputational equilibrium may or may not lower costs. In this case, because the fraction of legitimate suits is large, the social benefits of deterrence are smaller or nonexistent.[37]

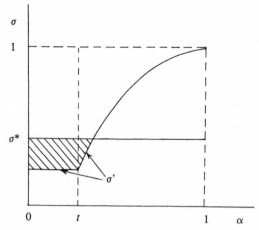

FIGURE 9.5 Area where a deterrence equilibrium exists.

5. Summary

This chapter continued the discussion of litigation costs by explicitly examining the problem of frivolous suits, or suits without merit that are filed solely in hopes of obtaining a settlement. In the same way that economic theory had a hard time explaining why rational litigants ever go to trial, it has a hard time explaining why defendants ever settle frivolous suits, given that a frivolous plaintiff would never take such a suit to trial. In this chapter I proposed several explanations for the success of frivolous suits, including higher costs of trial for the defendant than the plaintiff; court error in determining the merits of a case; the defendant's cost of mounting a defense against summary judgment; and private (asymmetric) information by plaintiffs about the merits of their case. I then used the asymmetric information model to examine several policies, including the English Rule and Rule 11 sanctions, aimed at curbing frivolous litigation. I concluded by asking whether contingent fees encourage more frivolous suits than do hourly fees, and whether repeat defendants can deter frivolous suits by developing a reputation for not settling.

NOTES

Chapter 1

1. See chapter 8 for a further discussion of the evolution of the law toward efficiency.

2. See Coase (1960).

3. This discussion is based on Coleman (1982), Murphy and Coleman (1990, chap. 5), and Miceli and Segerson (1995). Also see Atkinson and Stiglitz (1980).

4. Another way is to employ the political process to choose among noncomparable points.

5. See, for example, Posner (1980, 1992).

6. But see Murphy and Coleman (1990, pp. 224–227).

7. For example, Posner (1992, p. 523) states that "Although the correlation is far from perfect, judgemade rules tend to be efficiency-promoting, while those made by legislatures tend to be efficiency-reducing." Also see Kaplow and Shavell (1994).

8. The behavior of legislatures is generally studied under the heading of public choice theory.

9. That is, x^* is the herd size that a combined rancher-farmer would choose.

10. The second-order condition is satisfied given a decreasing marginal benefit ($\Pi'' < 0$) and an increasing marginal cost ($D'' > 0$).

11. See chapter 6 for a more detailed analysis of Pigouvian taxes (and subsidies) in comparison to other methods for controlling externalities.

12. See chapter 2, section 2.2.

13. For a more precise statement, including all of the underlying assumptions, see Coleman (1982) and Cooter (1982a).

14. But see Hovenkamp (1995, pp. 337–338).

15. Reassigning legal rights is like moving to a different starting point in the Edgeworth box. Although the market mechanism will still put the parties on the contract curve, their equilibrium wealth levels will be different.

16. The rancher's purchase price similarly will reflect the prevailing liability rule if the farmer was there first.

17. See the discussion of this issue in chapter 6 (section 2.5) and also in chapter 7 in the context of compensation for takings (section 2.4).

18. But see the case study by Ellickson (1991), which shows that parties involved in an externality situation often do cooperate to achieve a mutually beneficial outcome without

interference by the state. Also, see the experimental studies by Hoffman and Spitzer (1982, 1986).

19. See Coase (1988, chap. 6) and Hovenkamp (1995, p. 335). For an excellent introduction to law and economics based on the Coase theorem, see Polinsky (1983a).

20. See Calabresi (1970).

21. See the critiques in Coleman (1982), Dworkin (1980), Murphy and Coleman (1990, pp. 213–229), and Hovenkamp (1995).

22. See, e.g., Hart (1961, chap. VII), Ehrlich and Posner (1974), and Posner (1990, pp. 42–61).

23. This argument is perhaps best exemplified by the choice between property rules and liability rules as examined by Calabresi and Melamed (1972). See chapter 6.

24. This approach follows that of Cooter (1985a).

25. 159 F.2d 169 (1947).

26. 156 Eng. Rep. 145 (1854).

Chapter 2

1. Economists are also concerned with the distributional implications of tort rules, though less so.

2. An exception is when a product causes injuries to the consumer. See section 4.3 below.

3. See Cooter (1985a) for a unified approach to torts, contracts, and property from the perspective of the model of precaution.

4. For the most part, I will not consider the implications of risk aversion. See Shavell (1979, 1987), Landes and Posner (1987), and Miceli and Segerson (1995).

5. In the standard model only the victim suffers harm. For a model where both the injurer and the victim suffer harm, see Leong (1989) and Arlen (1990).

6. More generally, we could write expected damages as $p(x)L(x)$, where p is the probability of an accident and L is the victim's losses in the event of an accident. In this case both p and L are decreasing in x.

7. The second-order condition is satisfied given $D'' > 0$.

8. This assumes, of course, that the victim is able to prove that the injurer *caused* her injuries. See section 2 below.

9. See Brown (1973) for the first formal analysis of the various liability rules. Cooter (1982b) was the first to demonstrate the implications of the discontinuity in the injurer's costs (figure 2.1) implied by Brown's formalization of the negligence rule.

10. It turns out, however, that this conclusion regarding administrative costs is not necessarily true. See the discussion of litigation costs in section 1 of the next chapter.

11. In a Nash equilibrium, each player is maximizing his own objective function, taking as given the decisions of all the other players. See Shubik (1985, chap. 9).

12. See, for example, the discussion of sequential torts in section 3 of the next chapter.

13. See Keeton, et al. (1984, pp. 468–479) and Landes and Posner (1987, pp. 83–84).

14. For other analysis of comparative negligence, most of which argue for its efficiency, see Haddock and Curran (1985), Rea (1987), Cooter and Ulen (1988), Rubinfeld (1987), White (1989), and Curran (1992). Also see sections 2.2.1 and 3.2.4 in the next chapter.

15. 159 F.2d 169 (2d. Cir. 1947).

16. Although I refer to the injurer as the defendant, this rule can also be used to determine contributory negligent by the victim.

17. See, for example, Posner (1972, 1992), Brown (1973), Grady (1983), and Landes and Posner (1987). It is less clear, however, how much influence it has had on judges and

lawyers. For example, the Hand rule receives no special emphasis as a theory of negligence in Keeton, et al. (1984). Also see Landes and Posner (1987, p. 85).

18. The smaller is the untaken precaution proposed by the plaintiff, however, the more likely it is that the court will make an error and find the defendant nonnegligent.

19. 243 La. 829, 147 So.2d 646 (1962).

20. See Cooter (1987b), who therefore argues that a noneconomic theory is necessary to explain the importance of causation in tort law. Also see Epstein (1973) along these lines. In contrast, Shavell (1980c) has argued that causation can be incorporated into the positive economic theory of negligence. But see Burrows (1984) and Wright (1985) for critiques of Shavell's analysis.

21. This argument was first developed by Grady (1983), and later formalized and extended by Kahan (1989).

22. For a more detailed discussion of uncertainty over causation, see section 2.3 in the next chapter.

23. See, for example, *Haft v. Lone Palm Hotel*, 3 Cal.3d 756, 478 P.2d 465 (1970).

24. This doctrine arose from Judge Cardozo's majority opinion in the famous case *Palsgraff v. Long Island R.R.*, 248 N.Y. 339, 162 N.E. 99 (1928). See section 3.2.6 in the next chapter for discussion of the "direct consequences" doctrine of proximate case, which arose from Andrews's dissenting opinion in Palsgraff (Grady, 1984).

25. See Calabresi (1961), Cooter (1987b), Epstein (1973), and Coase (1960). Grady (1989, p. 156) has suggested that proximate cause is an "older" way of conducting negligence analysis. Also see Henderson and Pearson (1988, p. 524, esp. note 132).

26. Of course, this strategy is limited by reasonableness.

27. See Keeton, et al. (1984, section 39). The doctrine originated in the case of *Byrne v. Boadle*, 2 H.&C. 722, 159 Eng. Rep. 299 (1863), in which a pedestrian was injured by a barrel of flour that fell out of the window of a warehouse.

28. In section 5.1 I consider differences in victim susceptibility to injury and how this affects the calculation of damage awards.

29. See, for example, Png (1987).

30. In particular, $\partial x / \partial c_i = -1/p''(x)L < 0$.

31. See Murphy and Coleman (1990, p. 156) on objective versus subjective standards in the law. Cooter and Ulen (1988, pp. 11–12) provide a useful comparison of the reasonable person in law with the rational person in economics. Their distinction is essentially that rational individuals pursue their self-interest and therefore ignore external effects (in the absence of third-party sanctions), whereas reasonable individuals are expected to recognize and respond to external effects.

32. Keeton, et al. (1984, p. 175), quoting the Restatement (Second) of Torts, § 283.

33. This specification assumes that there are no "scale effects" in the activity level. That is, marginal and average damages per unit of activity are equal. In many cases, this will not be true, as when there are cumulative harmful effects from the ingestion of a drug. See Marino (1988) and Miceli, Pancak, and Sirmans (1996) for analyses of accident settings involving scale effects.

34. The second-order conditions are satisfied given our assumptions about w and D.

35. Landes and Posner (1987, pp. 66–67). However, see Gilles (1992), who argues that courts do actually condition negligence standards on activity levels when it is practicable to do so. Landes and Posner also make this point (1987, pp. 70–71).

36. The party bearing the damages in equilibrium is the victim under no liability, negligence, negligence with contributory negligence, and comparative negligence, and it is the injurer under strict liability and strict liability with contributory negligence.

37. Product-related accidents in which the victim is *not* the consumer but a third party are identical to accidents between strangers.

38. A similar analysis can be applied to accidents between employers and employees.

39. This section is based primarily on Shavell (1980b) and Landes and Posner (1985, 1987, chap. 10).

40. Both Landes and Posner (1985) and Shavell (1980b) assume that $c(q) = cq$; that is, there are constant returns to scale (marginal and average costs are equal). When this is the case, the optimal number of firms is indeterminate. In contrast, Polinsky (1980b) considers the case where average costs are U-shaped.

41. Together, of course, (2.26) and (2.27) imply that $c'(q) = c(q)/q$, or that marginal costs equal average costs.

42. Below I comment briefly on the impact of market power in this context.

43. Below I note the impact of consumer misperceptions about risk.

44. In particular, recall that the victim (consumer) bears the damages in equilibrium under negligence, negligence with contributory negligence, and comparative negligence, whereas the injurer (producer) bears it under strict liability with contributory negligence.

45. Both of these bargains are examples of the Coase theorem (Coase, 1960).

46. Others have argued that products liability law is not generally efficient. See, for example, Epstein (1980, 1995), Huber (1990), and Viscusi (1991).

47. See Spence (1977), Shavell (1980b), and Polinsky and Rogerson (1983).

48. See *Vosburg v. Putney*, 80 Wis. 523, 50 N.W. 403 (1891).

49. This is true assuming that the due standard is set at the efficient level of care x^*. See the discussion of errors in setting the due standard in section 2 of the next chapter.

50. Specifically, the derivative of the right-hand side with respect to α is $(1 + p'(x)\alpha L)(\partial x/\partial \alpha) + p(x)L$, which is positive since the first term equals zero at the optimal value of x.

51. Cooter and Ulen (1988, p. 352) provide a graphical demonstration of this result.

52. To see this, note from (2.15) that if the injurer is negligent in this case, his costs are $x_\alpha + \alpha[p(x_\alpha)L - p(x^*)L]$ (where $px)L = D(x)$), which is less than x^* for $\alpha < 1$. (Note that x_α here is identical to the value that minimizes the right-hand side of (2.37).)

53. This explanation is based on Cooter and Ulen (1988, pp. 388–397). Also see Cooter (1982b).

54. Kahan and Tuckman (1995) examine statutes enacted in some states that require successful plaintiffs to hand over a portion of their punitive damages to the state. These statutes represent a form of "decoupling" whereby the amount that the plaintiff receives is different than the amount the defendant pays. Section 2.2 of the next chapter examines the economics of decoupled liability.

55. The following argument is based on Shavell (1986). Also see Shavell (1987, pp. 179–182).

56. I assume that there is no uncertainty about causation in the sense that it is known that each of the n injurers contributed to the risk. See the discussion of uncertainty over causation in section 2.3 of the next chapter.

57. For a more detailed analysis of the problem of multiple injurers, see Shavell (1987, chap. 7), Landes and Posner (1987, chap. 7), Tietenberg (1989), and Miceli and Segerson (1991b).

58. For a more detailed analysis of the effects of joint and several liability, see Kornhauser and Revesz (1991).

59. See Shavell (1987, pp. 178–179) for the formal proof.

Chapter 3

1. This section is based on Shavell (1987, chap. 11) and Hylton (1990b). Also see Miceli and Segerson (1991a).

2. It is not necessary for the parties to go to trial for there to be litigation costs. For example, the costs could be pretrial bargaining costs. See Polinksy and Rubinfeld (1988b) for a model that compares the deterrence effects of trials and settlements. Also see Png (1987).

3. But see Polinsky and Rubinfeld (1988a), who show that the optimal zero-litigation cost outcome can be achieved under strict liability with a suitable adjustment in compensatory damages.

4. See Shavell (1982b), Menell (1983), Kaplow (1986a), and Rose-Ackerman and Geistfeld (1987).

5. See, in particular, Polinsky and Che (1991), on which the following analysis is based, and Kahan and Tuckman (1995). Also see the related analysis of Kaplow (1993).

6. See the discussion of legal errors in implementing a negligence rule in the next section.

7. This assumes that victims observe the injurer's care level with certainty.

8. On this point, see Ordover (1978) and Hylton (1990b).

9. Shavell (1987, pp. 274–275). Miceli and Segerson (1991a) show that contingent fees for plaintiffs' attorneys may lower overall costs under both strict liability and negligence if their effect is to make it easier for plaintiffs to bring suit.

10. See the discussion of this in the context of the standard of proof for determining negligence in section 2.2.4. Also see Goldberg (1994), who argues that it is not necessarily true that a strict liability case involves lower litigation costs than a negligence case.

11. But see Goldberg (1994).

12. See Rizzo (1987) for an argument along these lines.

13. The model is based on Craswell and Calfee (1986).

14. Of course, if the support of F has a finite upper limit, the injurer can avoid liability with certainty by choosing that limit. I will assume, however, that this level of care is too costly.

15. Recall that other reasons for noncompliance with the negligence standard (too little care) are, differences in the cost of care across injurers (section 3 of chap. 2) and litigation costs (section 1 this chapter). Cooter (1991) has identified "lapses" by injurers as another reason.

16. I thus follow the terminology of Polinsky and Shavell (1989) and Hylton (1990a). Png (1986) reverses the numbers of the errors. From statistics, a type I error is when the null hypothesis is falsely rejected, and a type II error is when the null hypothesis is falsely accepted. Thus, the terminology I will employ is based on the null hypothesis that the defendant failed to comply with the due standard.

17. In   particular, $[p_n(1 - q_1) - p_c q_2]D - (p_n - p_c)D = [p_n q_1 - p_c(1 - q_2)]D > < 0$ given $q_1 < 1 - q_2$. In a more general model in which care is continuous and courts observe the injurer's care with error, Shavell (1987, pp. 93–95) and Cooter and Ulen (1986) show that legal error tends to make injurers take too much care (i.e., it results in overdeterrence).

18. The assumption that $p_{cn} = p_{nc}$ is not crucial for the results provided that the two inequalities hold.

19. The intuition is identical to that in the continuous care case. See section 1.2 in the previous chapter.

20. However, I assume that the errors are independent.

21. Recall that the zero-litigation cost condition includes only the first term on the right-hand side, which corresponds to the Hand rule for discrete choices of care in the previous chapter (see equation (2.13)).

22. Rubinfeld and Sappington (1987) employ a similar specification, though they assume that the defendant can shift the distribution of e to the left (i.e., increase the probability that $e < e_s$) by defense expenditures. Also see Miceli (1990).

23. The figure is drawn as if the right-hand side of (3.27), $G(e_s)$, is strictly decreasing in e_s, though a positively sloped segment cannot be ruled out.

24. More generally, injurers will vary in their cost of care, x, so that for any $e_s < 1$, some injurers will take care and some will not. However, we expect that more will take care the lower is e_s (Hylton, 1990a).

25. See Hylton (1990a, p. 441) for a similar result. Also see chapter 9 for further discussion of frivolous suits (especially section 2).

26. I am assuming no uncertainty regarding the relevant law, though this of course is also a possibility.

27. See, for example, *Summer v. Tice*, 33 Cal.2d 80, 199 P.2d 1 (1948).

28. The analysis is based largely on Shavell (1985, 1987, chap. 5). Also see Miceli and Segerson (1991b) and Landes and Posner (1987, p. 212).

29. This would not be true if q affected $p(x)$ multiplicatively.

30. Shavell (1985, 1987) also shows that the injurer chooses efficient care if he is held liable for a portion of all accidents that occur, where that portion is $p(x)/[p(x) + q]$. To see why, note that the injurer's expected costs in this case are given by

$$x + [p(x) + q]\{p(x)/[p(x) + q]\}D = x + p(x)D$$

which is minimized at $x*$. The court actually employed a version of this sharing rule in *Sindell v. Abbott Laboratories*, 163 Cal. Rptr. 132, 607 P.2d 924 (1980). The case concerned a drug that produced harmful side effects, but where the victim did not recall which of several manufacturers she purchased the drug from. The court therefore assigned liability to each company in proportion to its market share. See Shavell (1985, p. 607), Marino (1991), and Rose-Ackerman (1990).

31. The analysis of these questions is based on Shavell (1992).

32. See in general Hirshleifer and Riley (1992).

33. See Endres (1992).

34. 10 M.&W. 546, 152 Eng. Rep. 588 (1842).

35. Kornhauser and Revesz (1991) consider a model in which a *single* tortfeasor makes sequential choices of care.

36. Grady (1988) refers to situations in which the victim consciously chooses too little care in hopes of inducing compensating precaution by the injurer as an "injurer's trap".

37. I consider comparative negligence below.

38. Since the proofs are virtually identical to those for the simultaneous care case, I omit them.

39. This is the standard Shavell (1983) considers, though his model is slightly different.

40. Note that in cases where the *injurer* moves first and victims face a standard of $y^*(x)$, we would have to consider the contributory negligence rules and omit simple negligence, which imposes no standard on victims.

41. See section 3.2.4 for a discussion of comparative negligence in sequential tort cases.

42. Grady (1988, p. 21) refers to a victim's obligation to take compensating precaution as the *doctrine of avoidance*. Most cases, however, involve an injurer confronting a negligent victim, the scenario I am considering.

43. See Bradford and Carlson (1962).

44. Recall the analysis of negligence with contributory negligence above allowed the injurer to escape liability if $y < y^*$, in which case he chose $x = 0$.

45. See the Restatement (Second) of Torts, §479 (helpless plaintiff) and §480 (inattentive plaintiff).

46. 21 N.E.2d 625 (1939).

47. 89 S.E.2d 49 (1955).

48. *Anderson v. Payne*, 54 S.E.2d 82, 86 (1949).

49. See Keeton, et al. (1984, pp. 468–470).

50. In an empirical study, White (1989) showed, first, that contributory negligence created stronger incentives for care than did comparative negligence, and second, that incentives for care under comparative negligence were weaker than was efficient. Not surprisingly, therefore, Low and Smith (1995) found that comparative negligence creates stronger incentives to hire a lawyer and file a suit compared to contributory negligence.

51. See Rea (1987) for the more general proof.

52. Strictly speaking, $D(x,y)$ is not actual damages in the model we are employing, but expected damages. That is, $D(x,y) = p(x,y)L(x,y)$, where $p(x,y)$ is the probability of an accident, and $L(x,y)$ is actual damages in the event of an accident. This distinction is not important for the current discussion or any of the analysis in this section.

53. This includes the defense of contributory negligence.

54. See Rose-Ackerman (1989) for discussion of a similar rule.

55. Since it applies to the victim in the current model, it is a contributory negligence rule.

56. Also see Grady (1988, p. 17).

57. Actual decisions in sequential tort cases are sometimes based on proximate-cause principles, sometimes on last clear chance principles, and sometimes both. For example, in *Greear v. Noland*, the court held that "The last clear chance doctrine . . . allows a negligent plaintiff to recover only if his negligence was not proximate cause, but only a remote cause or condition, of the accident, and the negligent defendant was the sole proximate cause" 89 S.E.2d 49, 53 (1955).

Chapter 4

1. The analysis in this section is based largely on Shavell (1980a). Also see Rogerson (1984), Shavell (1984); and Cooter and Ulen (1988, chap. 7).

2. The timing of payment is inessential to the model. Its only effect, we shall see, is on the amount of the various damage payments.

3. I thus treat the buyer's valuation of performance as nonstochastic (given r). Alternatively, one could treat V as a random variable, reflecting uncertainty by the buyer about the value of the good at the time of delivery. See Shavell (1980a) for a discussion of this and other possible sources of contract uncertainty.

4. For example, Shavell (1980a) considers the more general case where r has some value in the event of nonperformance.

5. Note that if the price were not prepaid, $D_e = V(r)$. Also, if there were a salvage value of r, this amount would be subtracted from D_e.

6. If the buyer prepaid the price, $D_r = r + P$—i.e., the seller would have to refund the price as well.

7. If competition drives sellers to zero profit, however, reliance damages will lead to efficient breach since $V(r) - P - r = 0$.

8. If the buyer prepaid, the seller will perform if $P - C \geq P - D_s = 0$, which yields the same result.

9. See Cooter (1985a) for a general discussion of the similarity between the economic model of torts and contracts.

10. In general, any lump-sum damage amount (including zero) induces efficient reliance. However, only $V(r^*) - P$ also induces efficient breach by the seller.

11. 9 Exch. 341 (1854).

12. For similar arguments, see Cooter (1985a), Cooter and Ulen (1988, p. 309–316), Craswell (1989), Sykes (1990, p. 61), and Chung (1992). Also see Rose-Ackerman (1989) for a related discussion in the context of tort law (in particular, she discusses the efficiency of a type of limited strict liability rule).

13. See generally Wittman (1981), Goetz and Scott (1983), Cooter (1985a, pp. 15–16) and Craswell and Schwartz (1994, p. 66).

14. See the Restatement (Second) of Torts, §918 (Avoidable Consequences). Also, see Shavell (1987, pp. 158–159).

15. This section is based on Polinsky (1983b).

16. Polinsky (1983b) also examines a model in which the risk is due to uncertain offers from third parties for the seller's good.

17. See section 3.1 of chapter 5 for a generalization of this model that endogenizes the breach decision.

18. In this section I assume the price is prepaid so that the restitution damage measure does not coincide with no damages. I will note the impact of assuming that the price is payable on performance in footnotes.

19. If the price were payable on performance, the denominator of the left-hand side would be $U_b'(D - r)$, and the denominator on the right-hand side would be $U_s'(-D)$.

20. This verifies that optimal risk sharing entails $C_l \leq D < C_h$ (given $V < C_h$), as asserted above.

21. If the price is payable on performance, optimal risk sharing implies that $C_l - P \leq D^* \leq V - P$. Note that, since $P > C_l$, the first inequality implies that $D^* < 0$ may be optimal if the seller is very risk averse. This will be important for the discussion of impossibility in section 3.2 of the next chapter.

22. The analysis of this function of the *Hadley* v. *Baxendale* rule is based on Bebchuk and Shavell (1991).

23. Although the model here is based on Bebchuk and Shavell (1991), the approach is somewhat different.

24. I assume that there is no reliance decision by promisees, or that it is fixed.

25. Rather than choosing when to breach, promisors in Bebchuk and Shavell (1991) choose a level of precaution against breach. Thus, the value of information in their model is that promisors can tailor their level of precaution to the promisee's actual type. Their results, however, are identical to those obtained here. For other models of precaution in contract settings, see Cooter (1985a), Craswell (1988), and Cremer and Khalil (1992). Also see the general discussion in Posner (1992: pp. 126-127).

26. I assume that promisees do not make false statements. Bebchuk and Shavell (1991) demonstrate that they do not have an incentive to do so in equilibrium.

27. This result is in part a consequence of the fact that the promisee obtains all of the surplus from the contract. The basic result would not be changed if the promisor expected to receive a share as well. The only difference would be that the magnitude of the gain of revelation to the promisee would fall.

28. In particular, if we subtract I/α from the left-hand side of (4.23) we obtain

$$\frac{1}{\alpha} \int_{V_1}^{V^c} (V^c - C) dF(C) > 0.$$

29. See, for example, Hirshleifer and Riley (1992).

30. In the context of moral hazard and insurance, see Shavell (1979). In the context of adverse selection and insurance, see Rothschild and Stiglitz (1976).

31. Alternatively, the seller could choose P and D to maximize V_s subject to $V_b \geq V_b^0$, or the parties could choose P and D jointly to maximize the sum of their expected values subject to $r = r(P, D)$. The results under this specification are identical to those obtained below.

32. The constraint $r = r(P, D)$ is included by substitution. The terms associated with $\partial r/\partial P$ and $\partial r/\partial D$ drop out of (4.28) and (4.29) by the Envelope theorem given (4.26).

33. Chung (1992) examines a more general version in which the incumbent buyer chooses reliance.

34. I assume that the seller and incumbent buyer are not able to renegotiate the original price after the entrant makes his offer. For a model that allows this, see Spier and Whinston (1995). On the enforceability of renegotiation in general, see section 4 in the next chapter.

35. In this case, P and D are not necessarily Pareto-optimal owing to the presence of a third party.

36. Other analyses that show inefficiencies arising from unlimited stipulated damages are Diamond and Maskin (1979) and Aghion and Bolton (1987). Spier and Whinston (1995) show that liquidated damages are set efficiently when there are no reliance expenditures and the seller and incumbent buyer can renegotiate the contract after the entrant makes his offer. However, when reliance and renegotiation both occur, liquidated damages are again set inefficiently high.

37. See the discussion of formation defenses in section 2 of the next chapter.

38. See Cooter and Ulen (1988, pp. 293–296), Goldberg (1989, part VI), and Rea (1984).

39. I discuss subjective values further in the next section in the context of specific performance. Also see the discussion in chapters 6 and 7 in the context of private property.

40. This can be seen by noting in (4.27) that $\partial V_s/\partial D < 0$ and $\partial V_s/\partial P > 0$.

41. See, for example, Cooter and Ulen (1988, pp. 320–324), Ulen (1984), and Friedmann (1989), from which much of the current argument is drawn.

42. The difference is identical to that between a property rule and a liability rule. See Calabresi and Melamed (1972) and the discussion in chapter 6.

43. 382 P.2d 109, cert. denied, 375 U.S. 906 (1962).

44. Friedmann (1989) notes that money damages are analogous to the government's right of eminent domain in that, in eminent domain takings, the landowner does not have the right to refuse the sale. In contrast, private parties do not have such a right and can acquire property only by bargaining with the owner, as under specific performance. Thus, as we shall see in chapter 7, the economic analyses of takings law and contract law have much in common.

45. The analysis is based on Rogerson (1984, pp. 50–51). Also, see Lewis, Perry, and Sappington (1989).

46. The situation thus resembles the analysis of contract modification in section 4 of the next chapter.

47. I am assuming the original price P is payable on performance.

48. Specifically, $D \leq V$ when the price is prepaid, and $D \leq V - P$ when it is payable on performance. In contrast, (4.35) shows that $S \geq V(r) - P$.

Chapter 5

1. This discussion is based on Cooter and Ulen (1988, pp. 214–217).

2. 124 N.Y. 538, 27 N.E. 256 (Court of Appeals of New York 1891).

3. Posner (1992, §4.2) suggests several economic functions that the doctrine of consideration may serve.

4. This type of argument is the basis for the analysis of formation defenses in Cooter and Ulen (1988, pp. 249–277). Also see Posner (1992, §§4.6, 4.7).

5. I examine this form of duress in more detail in section 4 below in the context of rules governing contract modification.

6. A well-known example of contract provisions overturned on the grounds of unconscionability are "add-on" clauses. See, for example, *Williams* v. *Walker-Thomas Furniture Co.*, 350 F.2d 445 (D.C. Cir. 1965). For a humorous case involving the unconscionability defense, see *Vokes* v. *Arthur Murray, Inc.*, 212 S.2d 906 (Fla. 1968).

7. Note the analogy to the tort doctrine of *res ipsa loquitur*, which, recall, allows a defendant to be judged negligent based on the circumstance of the accident without the need for the plaintiff to prove negligence. (See section 2.4 in chapter 2.)

8. 66 Mich. 568, 33 N.W. 919 (1887).

9. Restatement (Second) of Contracts, §§152, 154. One piece of evidence of risk assignment is a price different than is justified by the presumed nature of the object. For example, Posner (1992, p. 102) suggested that the cow in *Sherwood* v. *Walker* sold for a price higher than its value for slaughter. This implies that the buyer is paying for the *expected* value of the cow given a slight chance that it is fertile, and is therefore assuming the risk of the cow's value.

10. Restatement, §§153, 154.

11. The analysis in this section is based on Smith and Smith (1990).

12. This assumption does not affect the analysis because its only effect is distributional.

13. Smith and Smith (1990) show more generally that, in order to minimize the probability of resale, the seller will sell initially to a butcher if $q > 1/2$ and initially to a breeder if $q < 1/2$. The expected number of transactions in the first case is $(2 - q)$ and in the second it is $(1 + q)$. When $q = 1/2$, the seller is indifferent about whom to sell to and the expected number of transactions is 1.5 in both cases.

14. Note that this reverses the facts of the baseball card case where the buyer apparently had superior information.

15. I assume that the seller can verify the cow's type to a buyer at no cost.

16. Note in particular that αq is the fraction of barren cows owned by informed sellers, $(1 - \alpha)q$ is the fraction of barren cows owned by uninformed sellers, and $(1 - \alpha)(1 - q)$ is the fraction of fertile cows owned by uninformed sellers. q^* is found by taking the ratio of barren cows to total cows in this remaining population.

17. That is, it results in a *separating equilibrium*, as opposed to a pooling equilibrium which occurs under no excuse.

18. This assumes that the seller pays t for the initial sale to the butcher, and promises to pay t for a resale to the breeder if the cow turns out to be fertile (which the seller knows will never happen in this case).

19. Obviously, she will reveal a fertile cow. She will also reveal a barren cow because if she tried to sell it at V^c, it would be returned with certainty yielding a return of $V^B - L < V^B$.

20. Also see Posner (1992, §4.5); and Cooter and Ulen (1988, pp. 277–284).

21. The idea of preventing a contingency from occurring in a contract setting is similar to the notion of precaution against an accident in a tort setting. I will make this similarity clearer in section 3.4 below. Also, see Cooter (1985a).

22. White's model is an extension of Polinsky's (1983b) model to include consideration of the breach decision. White does not, however, consider the choice of reliance.

23. The analysis is based on Sykes (1990).

24. More specifically, the Uniform Commercial Code allows discharge if performance is "made impracticable by the occurrence of a contingency the non-occurrence of which was a basic assumption on which the contract was made . . . " (UCC, article 2, §615). In addition, the promisor must not have foreseen or caused the contingency, and must not have assumed (directly or indirectly) the risk of its occurrence. See Cooter and Ulen (1988, pp. 284–288).

25. See section 1.1 in the previous chapter.

26. Note that if $T < P$, the seller will breach for $C \geq P$ and will perform for $C < P$. Thus, the particular value of T in this case would have no effect.

27. There is an analog in property law, however. Specifically, a developer who over-relies in anticipation of a regulation is not entitled to claim a vested right—either to compensation or exemption from the regulation—because he did not act in good faith. See the discussion in section 2.5 of chapter 7.

28. This is similar to the result from the economics of negligence law that, in an efficient equilibrium, no injurers are actually negligent.

29. For similar interpretations, see Cooter (1985a) and Rasmusen and Ayres (1993, p. 327).

30. See Posner (1977, 1992, §4.2). Also see Dnes (1995).

31. 11 N.W. 284 (1882).

32. 117 F. 99 (1902).

33. Section 2-209, Comment 2 (1977).

34. Section 89 (1981).

35. The model is based on Miceli (1995). Also see Graham and Peirce (1989); Lewis, Perry, and Sappington (1989); Aivazian, Trebilcock, and Penny (1984); Cooter (1982a); and Leff (1970).

36. I ignore risk-sharing considerations in the discussion. On this point, see Aivazian, Trebilcock, and Penny (1984).

37. See Shavell (1984) and Schwartz (1992).

38. I assume that the cost of renegotiating the price is zero, though it is only necessary that renegotiation be less costly than breach.

39. See, for example, Shavell (1984) and Aivazian, Trebilcock, and Penny (1984) for arguments along these lines.

40. The case of *Recker* v. *Gustafson*, 279 N.W.2d 744 (1979), depicts the importance of litigation costs in inducing promisees to accept modification. Specifically, the evidence presented in court indicated that, "Prior to agreeing to . . . less favorable terms, Reckers [plaintiffs] were told by [defendant Gustafsons's attorney] that the Gustafsons were willing to go to court to get out of the [original] agreement and that litigation was expensive" (747).

41. I assume the same m for both types, though this is not essential.

Chapter 6

1. I do not consider a third rule, inalienability, which prevents transfer of entitlements under any circumstances (Calabresi and Melamed, 1972).

2. Also see Polinsky (1980a) and Coleman (1988, chap. 2).

3. 257 N.E.2d 870 (1970).

4. There are exceptions. Private ownership of land is protected by a liability rule vis-à-vis the government in the case of eminent domain acquisitions (see the discussion in the next chapter), and private individuals can acquire land without the owner's consent under the doctrine of adverse possession (see section 3.2).

5. For convenience I ignore theft of property in violation of property rule protection. Klevorick (1985) provides an ingenious economic theory of criminal sanctions based on the need to deter such violations. Also see Coleman (1988, chaps. 2 and 6) on this point.

6. This same entry problem potentially arises in the externality context. See section 2.5.

7. Kaplow and Shavell (1996) similarly distinguish between protection of interests in objects and protection of the entitlement to be free of externalities.

8. See, for example, Keeton, et al. (1984, §§87, 88A). Also see Merrill (1985).

9. Also see Landes and Posner (1987, pp. 42–53) for a similar argument.

10. Merrill (1985) thus emphasizes the dichotomy between high and low court intervention (rules versus discretion), as opposed to the choice between property rules and liability rules.

11. See, for example, Polinsky (1979), White and Wittman (1979), and Cornes and Sandler (1986).

12. See Polinsky (1979) for a discussion of alternative assignments of entitlement in externality contexts.

13. 494 P.2d 701 (1972).

14. Compare this example to the farmer-rancher example in chapter 1.

15. The other forms of the negligence rule also induce optimal abatement by both parties; see chapter 2.

16. The preceding conclusions are also demonstrated in Kaplow and Shavell (1996).

17. See Starrett (1972) and Cornes and Sandler (1986) for a general discussion of a nonconvexity problem associated with the possibility of exit (shutdown) by the victim of an externality. Cooter (1980) discusses how the law resolves this nonconvexity problem.

18. The model is based on Frech (1979) and Polinsky (1980b).

19. Note that this differs from the welfare function in the analysis of product liability (chapter 2, section 4.3) in that here, the victim is not a customer of the injurer.

20. For a formal demonstration, see Frech (1979).

21. However, this essentially transforms liability rules into property rules (Frech (1979, p. 266)).

22. This is essentially the point made by Coleman (1982) regarding the distributional effects of different assignments of rights according to the Coase theorem. See section 2 in chapter 1.

23. An exception is Houston, which relies primarily on private covenants (Siegan, 1972).

24. The practice of zoning as a legitimate exercise of the government's police power was upheld in *Village of Euclid* v. *Ambler Realty*, 272 U.S. 365 (1926).

25. In addition to controlling externalities, economists have also examined of the role of zoning in preventing free-riding in the consumption of local public goods (Fischel, 1985).

26. Hirsch (1988, chap. 4) also raises questions about the efficiency of zoning in controlling externalities.

27. Adelstein and Edelson (1976) consider an intermediate case in which a new development is planned within an existing community. In this case, the developer will internalize the costs and benefits of new entrants into the development, but he will ignore any external effects on existing residents of the community. The authors examine subdivision exactions (i.e., Pigouvian taxes) imposed on the developer by a local government as a solution to this problem.

28. See, for example, Posner (1992, chap. 3).

29. Of course, this is not universally true—automobiles represent an example of personal property protected by a filing system.

30. Although this characterization is something of a simplification, it is a useful way to frame the general question of how best to deal with the inevitable problem of title flaws. Note that this problem is similar to that addressed by the doctrine of mutual mistake in contract law, where the general concern is how to allocate unavoidable risks optimally between two innocent parties.

31. The analysis is based on Miceli and Sirmans (1995b).

32. Specifically, $p = BW_0/OL_0$.

33. Note that $pL_0 = BW_0$ given the definition of p in the previous note.

34. Quoted in Merrill (1985, p. 1131). Also see Holmes (1897, p. 477), "A thing which you have enjoyed and used as your own for a long time, whether property or opinion, takes root in your being and cannot be torn away without your resenting the act and trying to defend yourself, however you came by it."

35. Compare the discussion of the *Peevyhouse* case in chapter 4, and the relationship between market value versus willingness to accept as measures of compensation for government takings in chapter 7.

36. This conclusion, of course, is based on the assumption that all other aspects of the two systems are held constant. In reality they are not. See Miceli and Sirmans (1995b) for a discussion of qualifications of this conclusion based on various features of the recording and registration systems.

37. Note that there is no moral hazard associated with title insurance since the probability of a claim is beyond the control of the insured. Thus, deductibles are not necessary for incentive purposes.

38. This will be true if, as seems likely, the landowner purchases the insurance prior to investing. In order to break even, the insurance company will therefore have to set $p = \theta V(x^*)$.

39. However, the two systems may have different distributional effects. Under system B the landowner pays p, and under system A he may have to pay a registration fee to fund indemnification of claimants (as under the Torrens system).

40. All fifty states have enacted a variation of this doctrine, with the statutory period ranging from five to thirty years across the states. See Netter, Hersch, and Manson (1986) for an empirical analysis of the factors that determine this variation in the statutory period.

41. See, for example, Seidel (1979) and Mascolo (1992).

42. The argument is based on Miceli and Sirmans (1995a). Similar analyses are found in Merrill (1986); (1985, pp. 37–38). Also see Ellickson (1986) and Netter, Hersch, and Manson (1986).

43. See Mascolo (1992) and Helmholz (1983). Also see *Predham* v. *Holfester*, 108 A.2d 458 (1954).

44. See, for example, *Brand* v. *Prince*, 324 N.E.2d 314 (1974).

Chapter 7

1. Specifically, the relevant clause reads, "nor shall private property be taken for public use, without just compensation."

2. The argument in this section is based on Posner (1992, §3.7) and Munch (1976).

3. See L. Cohen (1991) for a general discussion of the holdout problem.

4. However, Ulen (1992) describes cases in which the government has used its taking power to convey property to private interests.

5. As figure 6.2 in the previous chapter showed, fair market value is equal to BW_o, whereas the amount necessary to leave the owner indifferent between the land and wealth is DW_o, where the latter exceeds the former by BD. Moreover, this difference increases as the convexity of indifference curve increases—that is, as land and wealth become less substitutable.

6. See the discussion of this issue in Knetsch and Borcherding 1979).

7. BRS use a general equilibrium model to derive their result. Here, I use a simple partial equilibrium model based on Miceli (1991) and Fischel and Shapiro (1989).

8. The total tax revenue is therefore $(n - m)T$, and a balanced budget implies that $mC(x) = (n - m)T$, or $T = mC(x)/(n - m)$. Thus, for small m and large n, T is small relative to $C(x)$.

9. Note the similarity of this problem and the problem of choosing efficient reliance and breach in a contract setting. In particular, the taking decision corresponds to the breach decision and the investment decision corresponds to the reliance decision. See section 1.1 of chapter 4. Cooter (1985a) draws a similar parallel.

10. Note that this is consistent with the result that expectation damages lead to efficient breach. See chapter 4.

11. These rules both assume that the social value of the taking is public knowledge. Hermalin also considers the case where the social value is privately known by the government.

12. See, for example, Rose-Ackerman (1992, p. 34).

13. The following argument is based on Miceli (1991).

14. In particular, differentiating (7.6) shows that $\partial m/\partial x = v'/nB'' < 0$ given $B'' < 0$.

15. See section 2.5 below and Miceli and Segerson (1996, chaps. 7, 8).

16. See *Mugler* v. *Kansas*, 123 U.S. 393 (1887).

17. 260 U.S. 623 (1922).

18. 438 U.S. 104 (1978).

19. 112 S.Ct. 2886 (1992).

20. The analysis is based on Miceli and Segerson (1994, 1996).

21. Note that E is never actually realized given efficient regulation since development is only permitted when $E = 0$ is realized.

22. I treat C as lump-sum compensation.

23. Note that setting C between zero and full compensation cannot resolve this conflict because any $C < \Delta V$ will result in overregulation.

24. See Miceli and Segerson (1994, 1996) for a more formal proof.

25. For a formal proof of these results, see Miceli and Segerson (1994, 1996).

26. Holmes's opinion in *Penn Coal* is consistent with the ex post rule.

27. See the discussion of the efficiency of nuisance law in chapter 6.

28. See, for example, Friedman (1986).

29. 480 U.S. 470 (1987).

30. 494 P.2d 701 (Ariz. 1972).

31. But see *Hadacheck* v. *Sebastian*, 239 U.S. 394 (1915), in which compensation was not paid to a preexisting brick factory that was shut down as a nuisance. The ruling in this case therefore resembles the ex post rule in that no compensation was dictated by the ex post efficiency of the regulation as opposed to the ex ante efficiency of the land use.

32. The following is based on Miceli and Segerson (1996, chap. 7).

33. See Miceli and Segerson (1996, chap. 7) for an analysis of the case where the probability of a regulation depends on whether or not the landowner invested r.

34. *Callender* v. *Marsh*, 1 Pick. 417, 430 (1823). For a more recent case that employed this reasoning, see *HFH Ltd.* v. *Superior Court*, 542 P.2d 237 (1975).

35. See, for example, Fischel (1985), Epstein (1985), Fischel and Shapiro (1988), and Miceli and Segerson (1996, chap. 6).

36. The following illustration is based on Miceli and Segerson (1996, chap. 6).

37. See, generally, Mandelker (1993, pp. 234–244). Note that grandfather clauses provide similar protection (Kaplow, 1986b).

38. See Miceli and Segerson (1996, chap. 8) for details.

Chapter 8

1. See Shavell (1993) for an analysis of the settlement-litigation decision for the case of disputes not involving monetary compensation. With some exceptions, the basic principles are the same.

2. The higher trial rate in state courts may partially reflect the fact that the denominator is cases disposed of rather than commenced. There is considerable variability in trial rates across state courts that report disposition, ranging from 0.4 percent in Hawaii to 38.8 percent in Missouri. *State Court Caseload Statistics: Annual Report* (1988, text table 8, p. 60).

3. This model was originally developed by Gould (1973) and Landes (1971). Also, see Shavell (1982a), Posner (1992, chap. 21), and Cooter and Rubinfeld (1989).

4. The model closely resembles the one in Shavell (1982a) and Posner (1992).

5. In this chapter and the next, I will adopt the convention of using the feminine pronoun for the plaintiff and the masculine pronoun for the defendant.

6. See, for example, Cooter, Marks, and Mnookin (1982).

7. Also see Wittman (1985) and Priest (1985).

8. See, for example, Rubin (1977), Priest (1977), Cooter and Kornhauser (1980), and Terrebone (1981).

9. The analysis in this section is based on Hylton (1993b).

10. Hylton (1993b) provides evidence in favor of this prediction.

11. However, a mixed strategy equilibrium might exist in which trials occur. For example, see section 4 of the next chapter for such an equilibrium in the context of frivolous suits.

12. For economic analyses of decision by precedent, see Cooter, Kornhauser, and Lane (1979); Blume and Rubinfeld (1982); Heiner (1986); Macey (1989); and Kornhauser (1989). Also see Landes and Posner (1976) for an empirical analysis of precedent that views it as a stock of legal capital that depreciates over time as conditions change.

13. See, for example, Rizzo (1987).

14. See, for example, Posner (1995, chap. 3).

15. See, for example, Higgins and Rubin (1980), M. Cohen (1991), Posner (1990b), and Miceli and Cosgel (1994).

16. But see Posner (1995, pp. 131–132).

17. See Galantner (1974) on the different interests of one-time versus repeat players, and Miller (1987) on agency problems in the attorney-client relationship.

18. They illustrate their theory in the context of products liability law, but suggest that it is more pervasive.

19. See, for example, Posner (1992, pp. 523–524).

20. Also see Rosen (1992).

21. This model is overly simple in assuming that all disputes are identical and therefore that all either settle or go to trial. White shows that the conclusions are not altered when disputes are heterogeneous.

22. See, for example, Bebchuk (1984) and Nalebuff (1987).

23. The model I will use is closest to the one in Bebchuk (1988).

24. Other possibilities are that the defendant has private information about his guilt (Bebchuk, 1984; Nalebuff (1987), or one of the parties has private information about the cost of a trial. See Schweizer (1989) for a model in which both parties have private information.

25. Recall that the relevant factor was the difference between trial and settlement costs.

26. Adding a positive filing cost to this model has no effect on the results. I introduce filing costs in section 3.

27. For a model that examines the dynamics of pretrial bargaining under one-sided asymmetric information, see Spier (1992).

28. The latter type of plaintiffs are frivolous in the sense that the expected return from the case at trial, PJ, is less than the trial cost even though $P > 0$ and $J > 0$. An alternative definition of a frivolous suit would be that the case has no merit, that is, either $P = 0$ or $J = 0$. See the next chapter.

29. Note that an offer of $S^* = 0$ may be optimal if the defendant believes that the fraction of plaintiffs with $P_p J - C_p < 0$ is high, since the latter would simply drop their suits. I will focus generally on the case where $S^* > 0$. See Nalebuff (1987) for the implications of having some plaintiffs with $P_p J - C_p < 0$ in a model where the *plaintiff* makes the take-it-or-leave-it settlement demand.

30. The second-order condition for a minimum, $f - f'[(C_p + C_d)/J] > 0$, is assumed to hold.

31. See generally Posner (1992, pp. 570–572) and Donohue (1991a).

32. These simplifications do not affect the results.

33. See section 4.2 of chapter 9 for a discussion of the English rule in a model of frivolous suits.

34. See Katz (1987) and Hause (1989) for formal analyses. Based on simulations, Katz estimates that a switch from the American to the English rule could cause per trial expenditures to increase by more than 100 percent in a typical case. Hause obtains qualitatively similar results.

35. This assumes that the increases in C_p and C_d have exactly offsetting effects on $P_p - P_d$.

36. A risk-averse plaintiff or defendant may still prefer the English rule, however, if it significantly increases the expected value of a trial compared to the American rule.

37. The foregoing comparison of the American and English rules has ignored their possible impact on the incentives of parties to take precaution to avoid disputes in the first place. On this point, see Rose-Ackerman and Geistfeld (1987), Hylton (1993a), and Buckner and Katz (1995).

38. They were able to do this because Florida mandated fee shifting in such cases during the period 1980–1985.

39. The higher drop rate, however, created a bias in claims not dropped that favored settlement. Thus, the settlement rate *conditional* on the case not being dropped was higher under the English rule.

40. These results cannot be said to support the conclusion of Hause (1989) that settlements are more likely under the English rule due to higher per trial expenditures because expenditures were held fixed in the experiments.

41. The results of Coursey and Stanley (1988) have to be qualified, however, by the fact that their analysis was based on a model of symmetric beliefs about the outcome of a trial (i.e., $P_p = P_d$).

42. Hensler et al. (1991, p. 136) found that in a sample of 387 tort suits, 87 per cent were filed under a contingent fee, 4 per cent under a flat rate, less than one percent under an hourly fee, and 8 per cent under some other arrangement.

43. In section 4.4.2 in the next chapter, I develop a more sophisticated model of the impact of contingent fees. In that model, I allow the rate to differ depending on whether the plaintiff receives a judgment at trial or accepts a settlement offer.

44. This condition is based on the assumption that the plaintiff alone makes the settlement decision. It therefore ignores agency problems between the plaintiff and her lawyer (Miller, 1987).

45. This sanction does not generally include attorney's fees, a fact that I do not explicitly incorporate.

46. See, in particular, Miller (1986), Spier (1994), and Anderson (1994).

47. Spier (1994) undertakes a more sophisticated analysis in the context of the asymmetric information model.

48. Miller (1986, p. 108) reaches similar conclusions.

49. In Spier's (1994) model, the defendant chooses the settlement amount to minimize his expected costs.

50. The work-product doctrine sets a limit on discoverable information. See Allen et al. (1990) for an economic theory of limits on discovery. Their basic argument is that protecting some information from discovery gives clients a greater incentive to reveal it to their attorney.

51. The analysis in this section is based on Cooter and Rubinfeld (1994).

52. Cooter and Rubinfeld also show that discovery increases the settlement rate when it reduces the variance of the distributions from which $P_p J_p$ and $P_d J_d$ are drawn. This is true because a distribution with a lower variance will produce fewer extreme (i.e., excessively optimistic) realizations of these variables.

53. Note that the settlement amount in (8.12) is a special case of this expression when $P_p = P_d$, $J_p = J_d$, and $R_p = R_d = 0$.

54. Hay (1994) argues, however, that silence by an informed party signals unfavorable information. Under ideal circumstances, this prevents concealment of information and makes mandatory disclosure unnecessary. See Shavell (1989) for a formal analysis of voluntary disclosure of information prior to trial in the context of the asymmetric information model.

55. I therefore ignore the possibility of a breakdown in bargaining for reasons other than differing perceptions or expectations.

56. The results are qualitatively the same under different assumptions about the distribution of the surplus from settling.

57. Given positive filing costs, I assume that without discovery, $S^* > w$ so that it always pays for plaintiffs to file and settle for S^* regardless of their P.

58. This section is based on Miceli (1992).

59. On this point, see Miller (1987).

Chapter 9

1. One apparent consequence of this growth in litigation has been an increasing demand for lawyers, which has "sustained the price of lawyers' services in the face of huge entry during the 1970s" (Rosen, 1992, p. 235). Also see Epstein (1995), especially the Introduction.

2. Though there certainly is a popular view that this is the case. See, for example, Huber (1990), Olson (1991), and Howard (1994).

3. And, as we shall see in this chapter, frivolous suits are more likely to settle or be dropped before trial as compared to meritorious suits.

4. Such a suit may be better referred to as a *negative expected value* suit.

5. This section is based on Cooter and Rubinfeld (1989, pp. 1083–1084).

6. See equation (8.12) in chapter 8.

7. See Cooter and Ulen (1988, p. 486).

8. See equation (8.13) in chapter 8.

9. ·See Png (1983) for a model in which frivolous suits succeed despite the absence of a credible threat by the plaintiff to go to trial.

10. Hylton (1990a, p. 441) notes, however, that such suits are not frivolous in the sense that plaintiffs do expect to recover at trial (also see Katz (1990, p.3)). Note that the plaintiff's threat to go to trial is therefore credible in this model.

11. This, of course, is not essential. If they assess different probabilities, the analysis would proceed exactly as in the previous chapter for the case where $P_p \neq P_d$.

12. As shown in the previous chapter, discovery will reduce the likelihood of frivolous suits. However, defendants may elect to settle rather than engage in costly discovery. Thus, frivolous suits may still succeed.

13. The equilibrium concept is a sequential equilibrium. See Katz (1990) for details.

14. I interpret a defendant's refusal to make a settlement offer as an offer of $S = 0$.

15. Note that the filing cost has no effect on the decision of either type of plaintiff because it is sunk at the time the settlement decision is made.

16. Thus, $PJ - C_p$ is a pooling offer, and zero is a separating offer.

17. This follows from Bayes' rule. Implicit in this formula is the fact that legitimate plaintiffs file suit with probability one.

18. Results (2) and (3) are found by differentiating t in (9.6) with respect to the relevant variables, given that α is more likely to exceed t the smaller is t.

19. This section is based on Katz (1990, pp. 17–19).

20. I assume, following Katz (1990), that the English rule does not affect the desirability of filing a legitimate suit in the first place.

21. See, in particular, Polinsky and Rubinfeld (1993, p. 427).

22. Also see Polinsky and Rubinfeld (1993, pp. 419–421) for an analysis of errors in the imposition of sanctions.

23. Polinsky and Rubinfeld (1993) note that Rule 11 sanctions are usually paid to the defendant, though they discuss the possible desirability of "decoupling" awards (pp. 417–419).

24. Compare this to the case where $k < 0$ under the English rule.

25. This section is based on Miceli (1994).

26. There is an extensive literature on the role of contingent fees in providing attorneys an incentive to work hard for their clients. See, for example, Danzon (1983) and Rubinfeld and Scotchmer (1993).

27. See Miller (1987) and Thomason (1991) for discussions of the conflicts of interest between attorneys and clients in this context.

28. I assume the parties incur no additional time costs besides their legal fees.

29. It can also be shown that, in the free-entry equilibrium, $\beta_s = R_p/(R_p + w)$, which is between zero and one as required.

30. In general, there seems no reason to believe that low-income plaintiffs are more likely to file frivolous claims.

31. See, for example, Ross (1970), Galanter (1974), Png (1983), and Rowe (1984).

32. The analysis is based on Miceli (1993).

33. This is only one type of conditional strategy that the plaintiff could adopt. For example, she could revert to her one-shot strategy for a finite number of periods. See, for example, Taylor (1976). The strategy examined in the text, however, is the simplest analytically. Friedman (1971) was the first to examine conditional strategies of this sort in repeated games (or "supergames').

34. Note the E in this case is therefore greater than the value in (9.38) given $\alpha < t$.

35. This expression for σ' is therefore less than σ' in (9.39) when $\alpha < t$.

36. The graph assumes that $\sigma^* > r/(1 + r)$.

37. See Miceli (1993, p. 142) for details.

REFERENCES

Adelstein, R., and N. Edelson. 1976. "Subdivision Exactions and Congestion Externalities." *J. Legal Stud.* 5(1): 147–163.

Aghion, P., and P. Bolton. 1987. "Contracts as a Barrier to Entry." *American Econ. Rev.* 77: 388–401.

Aivazian, V., M. Trebilcock, and M. Penny. 1984. "The Law of Contract Modifications: The Uncertain Quest for a Bench–mark of Enforceability." *Osgoode Hall L. J.* 22(2): 173–212.

Akerlof, G. 1970. "The Market for Lemons: Qualitative Uncertainty and the Market Mechanism." *Quarterly J. Econ.* 84: 488–500.

Allen, R., M. Grady, D. Polsby, and M. Yashko. 1990. "A Positive Theory of the Attorney–Client Privilege and the Work Product Doctrine." *J. Legal Stud.* 19(2): 359–397.

Anderson, D. 1994. "Improving Settlement Devices: Rule 68 and Beyond." *J. Legal Stud.* 23(1): 225–246.

Arlen, J. 1990. "Re–examining Liability Rules When Injurers as well as Victims Suffer Losses." *Int'l Rev. Law and Econ.* 10(3): 233–239.

Atkinson, A., and J. Stiglitz. 1980. *Lectures on Public Economics.* New York: McGraw-Hill.

Baird, D., and T. Jackson. 1984. "Information, Uncertainty, and the Transfer of Property." *J. Legal Stud.* 13(2): 299–320.

Bebchuk, L. 1988. "Suing Solely to Extract a Settlement Offer." *J. Legal Stud.* 17: 437–450.

Bebchuk, L. 1984. "Litigation and Settlement Under Imperfect Information." *Rand J. Econ.* 15 (3): 404–415.

Bebchuk, L., and S. Shavell. 1991. "Information and the Scope of Liability for Breach of Contract: The Rule of *Hadley v. Baxendale.*" *J. Law, Econ., & Org.* 7(2): 284–312.

Blume, L., and D. Rubinfeld. 1987. "Compensation for Takings: An Economic Analysis." *Research in Law and Econ.* 10: 53–104.

Blume, L., and D. Rubinfeld. 1982. "The Dynamics of the Legal Process." *J. Legal Stud.* 11 (2): 405–419.

Blume, L., D. Rubinfeld, and P. Shapiro. 1984. "The Taking of Land: When Should Compensation Be Paid?" *Quarterly J. Econ.* 99(1): 71–92.

Bradford, A., and P. Carlson. 1962. "Last Clear Chance in Automobile Negligence Cases." *Defense Law J.* 11: 61–77.

Brown, J. P. 1973. "Toward an Economic Theory of Liability." *J. Legal Stud.* 2(2): 323–349.

Buckner, C., and A. Katz. 1995. "The Incentive Effects of Litigation Fee Shifting When Legal Standards are Uncertain." *Int'l Rev. Law and Econ.* 15(2): 205–224.

Burrows, P. 1984. "Tort and Tautology: The Logic of Restricting the Scope of Liability." *J. Legal Stud.* 13: 399–414.

Calabresi, G. 1970. *The Cost of Accidents*. New Haven, CT: Yale University Press.

Calabresi, G. 1961. "Some Thoughts on Risk Distribution and the Law of Torts." *Yale L. J.* 70: 499–553.

Calabresi, G., and A.D. Melamed. 1972. "Property Rules, Liability Rules, and Inalienability: One View of the Cathedral." *Harvard L. R.* 85: 1089–1128.

Chung, T. 1992. "On the Social Optimality of Liquidated Damage Clauses: An Economic Analysis." *J. Law, Econ., & Org.* 8(2): 280–305.

Coase, R. 1988. *The Firm, The Market, and the Law*. Chicago: University of Chicago Press.

Coase, R. 1960. "The Problem of Social Cost." *J. Law and Econ.* 3: 1–44.

Cohen, L. 1991. "Holdouts and Free Riders." *J. Legal Stud.* 22 (2): 351–362.

Cohen, M. 1991. "Explaining Judicial Behavior, or What's Constitutional About the Sentencing Commission?" *J. Law, Econ., & Org.* 7: 183–199.

Coleman, J. 1988. *Markets, Morals and the Law*. New York: Cambridge University Press.

Coleman, J. 1982. "The Economic Analysis of Law." in *Ethics, Economics, and the Law: NOMOS XXIV*. J. Pennock and J. Chapman, eds. New York: NYU Press.

Cooter, R. 1991. "Lapses, Conflicts, and Akrasia in Torts and Crimes: Towards an Economic Theory of the Will." *Int'l Rev. Law and Econ.* 11(2): 149–164.

Cooter, R. 1989. "Punitive Damages for Deterrence: When and How Much?" *Alabama L. R.* 40: 1143–1196.

Cooter, R. 1987a. "Why Litigants Disagree: A Comment on George Priest's 'Measuring Legal Change'. *J. Law, Econ., & Org.* 3(2): 227–234.

Cooter, R. 1987b. "Torts as the Union of Liberty and Efficiency: An Essay on Causation." *Chicago–Kent L. R.* 63: 523–551.

Cooter, R. 1985a. "Unity in Tort, Contract, and Property: The Model of Precaution." *Cal. L. R.* 73(1): 1–51.

Cooter, R. 1985b. "Defective Warnings, Remote Causes, and Bankruptcy: A Comment on Schwartz." *J. Legal Stud.* 14(3): 737–750.

Cooter, R. 1982a. "The Cost of Coase." *J. Legal Stud.* 11(1): 1–33.

Cooter, R. 1982b. "Economic Analysis of Punitive Damages." *Southern Cal. L. R.* 56: 79–101.

Cooter, R. 1980. "How the Law Circumvents Starrett's Non–Convexity." *J. Econ. Theory* 22: 499–504.

Cooter, R., and L. Kornhauser. 1980. "Can Litigation Improve the Law Without the Help of Judges?" *J. Legal Stud.* 9(1): 139–163.

Cooter, R., L. Kornhauser, and D. Lane. 1979. "Liability Rules, Limited Information, and the Role of Precedent." *Bell J. Econ.* 10: 366–373.

Cooter, R., S. Marks, and R. Mnookin. 1982. "Bargaining in the Shadow of the Law: A Testable Model of Strategic Behavior." *J. Legal Stud.* 11(2): 225–251.

Cooter, R., and D. Rubinfeld. 1994. "An Economic Model of Legal Discovery." *J. Legal Stud.* 23(1): 435–463.

Cooter, R., and D. Rubinfeld. 1989. "Economic Analysis of Legal Disputes and Their Resolution." *J. Econ. Lit.* 27 (3): 1067–1097.

Cooter, R., and T. Ulen. 1988. *Law and Economics*. New York: HarperCollins.

Cooter, R., and T. Ulen. 1986. "An Economic Case for Comparative Negligence." *N. Y. U. L. R.* 61: 1067–1110.

Cornes, R., and T. Sandler. 1986. *The Theory of Externalities, Public Goods, and Club Goods.* Cambridge: Cambridge University Press.

Coursey, D., and L. Stanley. 1988. "Pretrial Bargaining Behavior within the Shadow of the Law: Theory and Experimental Evidence." *Int'l Rev. Law and Econ.* 8: 161–179.

Craswell, R. 1989. "Performance, Reliance, and One–sided Information." *J. Legal Stud.* 18(2): 365–401.

Craswell, R. 1988. "Precontractual Investigation as an Optimal Precaution Problem." *J. Legal Stud.* 17(2): 401–436.

Craswell, R., and J. Calfee. 1986. "Deterrence and Uncertain Legal Standards." *J. Law, Econ., & Org.* 2(2): 279–303.

Craswell, R., and A. Schwartz. 1994. *Foundations of Contract Law.* New York: Oxford University Press.

Cremer, J., and F. Khalil. 1992. "Gathering Information Before Signing a Contract." *Amer. Econ. Rev.* 82(3): 566–578.

Curran, C. 1992. "The Spread of the Comparative Negligence Rule." *Int'l Rev. Law and Econ.* 12(3): 317–332.

Danzon, P. 1983. "Contingent Fees for Personal Injury Litigation." *Bell J. Econ.* 14: 213–224.

Diamond, P., and E. Maskin. 1979. "An Equilibrium Analysis of Search and Breach of Contract, I: Steady States." *Bell J. Econ.* 10: 282–316.

Dnes, A. 1995. "The Law and Economics of Contract Modification: The Case of *Williams v. Roffey*." *Int'l Rev. Law and Econ.* 15(2): 225–240.

Donohue, J. 1991a. "The Effects of Fee Shifting on the Settlement Rate: Theoretical Observations on Costs, Conflicts, and Contingency Fees." *Law and Contemp. Probs.* 54(3): 195–222.

Donohue, J. 1991b. "Opting for the British Rule, or If Posner and Shavell Can't Remember the Coase Theorem, Who Will?" *Harvard L. R.* 104: 1093–1119.

Dworkin, R. 1980. "Why Efficiency: A Response to Professors Calabresi and Posner." *Hofstra L. R.* 8: 563–590.

Ehrlich, I., and R. Posner. 1974. "An Economic Analysis of Legal Rulemaking." *J. Legal Stud.* 3(1): 257–286.

Eisenberg, T. 1990. "Testing the Selection Effect: A New Theoretical Framework with Empirical Tests." *J. Legal Stud.* 19(2): 337–358.

Ellickson, R. 1991. *Order Without Law.* Cambridge, MA: Harvard University Press.

Ellickson, R. 1986. "Adverse Possession and Perpetuities Law: Two Dents in the Libertarian Model of Property Rights." *Wash. Univ. L. Quarterly* 64: 723–737.

Ellickson, R. 1973. "Alternatives to Zoning: Covenants, Nuisance Rules, and Fines as Land Use Controls." *U Chi. L. R.* 40: 681–782.

Endres, A. 1992. "Strategic Behavior under Tort Law." *Int'l Rev. of Law and Econ.* 12(3): 377–380.

Epstein, R. 1995. *Simple Rules for a Complex World.* Cambridge, MA: Harvard University Press.

Epstein, R. 1985. *Takings: Private Property and the Power of Eminent Domain.* Cambridge, MA: Harvard University Press.

Epstein, R. 1980. *Modern Product Liability Law.* Westport, CT: Quorum Books.

Epstein, R. 1985. "Unconscionability: A Critical Reappraisal." *J. Law and Econ.* 28: 293–315.

Epstein, R. 1973. "A Theory of Strict Liability." *J. Legal Stud.* 2: 151–204.

Fischel, W. 1985. *The Economics of Zoning Laws*. Baltimore: Johns Hopkins University Press.

Fischel, W., and P. Shapiro. 1989. "A Constitutional Choice Model of Compensation for Takings." *Int'l Rev. Law and Econ.* 9: 115–128.

Fischel, W., and P. Shapiro. 1988. "Takings, Insurance, and Michelman: Comments on Economic Interpretations of 'Just Compensation" Law." *J. Legal Stud.* 17: 269–293.

Frech, H. 1979. "The Extended Coase Theorem and Long Run Equilibrium: The Nonequivalence of Liability Rules and Property Rights." *Economic Inquiry* 17: 254–268.

Friedman, J. 1971. "A Non–cooperative Equilibrium for Supergames." *Rev. Econ. Stud.* 38: 1–12.

Friedman, L. 1986. "A Search for Seizure: *Pennsylvania Coal v. Mahon* in Context." *Law and History Rev.* 4(1): 1–22.

Friedmann, D. 1989. "The Efficient Breach Fallacy." *J. Legal Stud.* 18(1): 1–24.

Galanter, M. 1974. "Why the 'Haves' Come Out Ahead: Speculations on the Limits of Legal Change." *Law and Society Rev.* 9: 95–160.

Gilles, S. 1992. "Rule–based Negligence and the Regulation of Activity Levels." *J. Legal Stud.* 21(2): 319–363.

Goetz, C., and R. Scott. 1983. "The Mitigation Principle: Toward a General Theory of Contractual Obligation." *Virginia L. R.* 69: 967–1025.

Goldberg, V. 1994. "Litigation Costs Under Strict Liability and Negligence." *Research in Law and Economics* 16: 1–15.

Goldberg, V., ed. 1989. *Readings in the Economics of Contract Law*. New York: Cambridge University Press.

Goldberg, V. 1988. "Impossibility and Related Excuses." *J. Institutional and Theoretical Econ.* 144: 100–116.

Goodman, J. 1978. "An Economic Analysis of the Evolution of the Common Law." *J. Legal Stud.* 7(2): 393–406.

Gould, J. 1973. "The Economics of Legal Conflicts." *J. Legal Stud.* 2(2): 279–300.

Grady, M. 1989. "Untaken Precautions." *J. Legal Stud.* 18(1): 139–156.

Grady, M. 1988. "Common Law Control of Strategic Behavior: Railroad Sparks and the Farmer." *J. Legal Stud.* 17(1): 15–42.

Grady, M. 1984. "Proximate Cause and the Law of Negligence." *Iowa L. R.* 69: 363–449.

Grady, M. 1983. "A New Positive Economic Theory of Negligence." *Yale L. J.* 92: 799–829.

Graham, D., and E. Peirce. 1989. "Contract Modification: An Economic Analysis of the Hold–up Game." *Law and Contemp. Probs.* 52: 9–32.

Greenberg, P., and J. Haley. 1986. "The Role of the Compensation Structure in Enhancing Judicial Quality." *J. Legal Stud.* 15(2): 417–426.

Haddock, D., and C. Curran. 1985. "An Economic Theory of Comparative Negligence." *J. Legal Stud.* 14: 49–72.

Hart, H. L. A. 1961. *The Concept of Law*. London: Oxford University Press.

Hause, J. 1989. "Indemnity, Settlement, and Litigation, or I'll Be Suing You." *J. Legal Stud.* 18(1): 157–179.

Hay, B. 1994. "Civil Discovery: Its Effects and Optimal Scope." *J. Legal Stud.* 23(1): 481–515.

Heiner, R. 1986. "Imperfect Decisions and the Law: On the Evolution of Legal Precedent and Rules." *J. Legal Stud.* 15(2): 227–261.

Helmholz, R. 1983. "Adverse Possession and Subjective Intent." *Wash. University L. Quarterly* 61: 331–358.

Henderson, J., and R. Pearson. 1988. *The Tort Process*, 3rd. ed. Boston: Little, Brown.

Hensler, D., et al. 1991. *Compensation for Accidental Injuries in the United States*. Rand: Institute for Civil Justice.

Hermalin, B. 1995. "An Economic Analysis of Takings." *J. Law, Econ. and Org.* 11(1): 64–86.

Higgins, R., and P. Rubin. 1980. "Judicial Discretion." *J. Legal Stud.* 9: 129–138.

Hirsch, W. 1988. *Law and Economics*, 2nd. ed. Boston: Academic Press.

Hirshleifer, J. 1971. "The Private and Social Value of Information and the Reward to Inventive Activity." *American Econ. Rev.* 61: 561–574.

Hirshleifer, J., and J. Riley. 1992. *The Analytics of Uncertainty and Information*. New York, Cambridge University Press.

Historical Statistics of the U.S. From Colonial Times to 1970 (Part 1), U.S. Department of Commerce, Bureau of the Census, Washington, D.C.

Hoffman, E., and M. Spitzer. 1986. "Experimental Tests of the Coase Theorem with Large Bargaining Groups." *J. Legal Stud.* 15(1): 149–171.

Hoffman, E., and M. Spitzer. 1982. "The Coase Theorem: Some Experimental Results." *J. Law and Econ.* 25: 73–98.

Holderness, C. 1989. "The Assignment of Rights, Entry Effects, and the Allocation of Resources." *J. Legal Stud.* 18(1): 181–189.

Holmes, O. W. 1897. "The Path of the Law." *Harvard L. R.* 10: 457–478.

Hovenkamp, H. 1995. "Law and Economics in the United States: A Brief Historical Survey." *Cambridge J. Econ.* 19: 331–352.

Howard, P. 1994. *The Death of Common Sense*. New York: Random House.

Huber, P. 1990. *Liability: The Legal Revolution and its Consequences*. New York: Basic Books.

Hughes, J., and E. Snyder. 1995. "Litigation and Settlement Under the English and American Rules: Theory and Evidence." *J. Law and Econ.* 38(1): 225–250.

Hughes, W., and G. Turnbull. 1996. "Restrictive Land Covenants." *J. Real Estate Finance and Econ.* 12(1): 9–21.

Hylton, K. 1993a. "Litigation Cost Allocation Rules and Compliance with the Negligence Standard." *J. Legal Stud.* 22(2): 457–476.

Hylton, K. 1993b. "Asymmetric Information and the Selection of Disputes for Litigation." *J. Legal Stud.* 22(1): 187–210.

Hylton, K. 1990a. "Costly Litigation and Legal Error Under Negligence." *J. Law, Econ., & Org.* 6(2): 433–452.

Hylton, K. 1990b. "The Influence of Litigation Costs on Deterrence under Strict Liability and under Negligence." *Int'l Rev. Law and Econ.* 10(2): 161–171.

Johnson, M. 1977. "Takings and the Private Market." In *Planning without Prices*, B. Siegan, ed. Lexington, MA: D. C. Heath.

Kahan, M. 1989. "Causation and Incentives to Take Care under the Negligence Rule." *J. Legal Stud.* 18(2): 427–447.

Kahan, M., and B. Tuckman. 1995. "Special Levies and Punitive Damages: Decoupling, Agency Problems, and Litigation Expenditures." *Int'l Rev. Law and Econ.* 15(2): 175–185.

Kaplow, L. 1993. "Shifting Plaintiffs' Fees versus Increasing Damage Awards." *Rand J. Econ.* 24(4): 625–630.

Kaplow, L. 1986a. "Private versus Social Costs in Bringing Suit." *J. Legal Stud.* 15(2): 371–385.

Kaplow, L. 1986b. "An Economic Analysis of Legal Transitions." *Harvard L. R.* 99: 509–617.

Kaplow, L., and S. Shavell. 1996. "Property Rules versus Liability Rules." *Harvard L. R.*, 109(4): 713–790.

Katz, A. 1990. "The Effect of Frivolous Litigation on the Settlement of Legal Disputes." *Int'l Rev. of Law and Econ.* 10(1): 3–27.

Katz, A. 1988. "Judicial Decisionmaking and Litigation Expenditure." *Int'l Rev. of Law and Econ.* 8: 127–143.

Katz, A. 1987. "Measuring the Demand for Litigation: Is the English Rule Really Cheaper?" *J. Law, Econ., & Org.* 3(2): 143–176.

Keeton, W.P, D. Dobbs, R. Keeton, and D. Owen. 1984. *Prosser and Keeton on Torts.* St. Paul, MN.: West.

Klein, B., R. Crawford, and A. Alchian. 1978. "Vertical Integration, Appropriable Rents, and the Competitive Contracting Process." *J. Law and Econ.* 21: 297–326.

Klevorick, A. 1985. "On the Economic Theory of Crime." In *Criminal Justice: NOMOS XXVII,* J. Pennock and J. Chapman, eds. New York: NYU Press.

Knetsch, J., and T. Borcherding. 1979. "Expropriation of Private Property and the Basis for Compensation." *University of Toronto L. J.* 29: 237–252.

Kornhauser, L. 1989. "An Economic Perspective on Stare Decisis." *Chicago–Kent L. R.* 65: 63–113.

Kornhauser, L., and R. Revesz. 1991. "Sequential Decisions by a Single Tortfeasor." *J. Legal Stud.* 20(2): 363–380.

Kronman, A. 1978. "Mistake, Disclosure, Information, and the Law of Contracts." *J. Legal Stud.* 7(1): 1–34.

Kull, A. 1992. "Unilateral Mistake: The Baseball Card Case." *Wash. University Law Quarterly* 70: 57–84.

Landes, W. 1971. "An Economic Analysis of the Courts." *J. Law and Econ.* 14(1): 61–107.

Landes, W., and R. Posner. 1987. *The Economic Structure of Tort Law.* Cambridge, MA: Harvard University Press.

Landes, W., and R. Posner. 1985. "A Positive Economic Theory of Products Liability." *J. Legal Stud.* 14(3): 535–567.

Landes, W., and R. Posner. 1979. "Adjudication as a Private Good." *J. Legal Stud.* 8(2): 235–284.

Landes, W., and R. Posner. 1976. "Legal Precedent: A Theoretical and Empirical Analysis." *J. Law and Econ.* 19(2): 249–307.

Leff, A. 1970. "Injury, Ignorance and Spite—The Dynamics of Coercive Collection." *Yale L. J.* 80(10): 1–46.

Leong, A. 1989. "Liability Rules When Injurers As Well as Victims Suffer Losses." *Int'l Rev. Law and Econ.* 9: 105–111.

Lewis, T., M. Perry, and D. Sappington. 1989. "Renegotiation and Specific Performance." *Law and Contemp. Probs.* 52: 33–48.

Low, S., and J. Smith. 1995. "Decisions to Retain Attorneys and File Lawsuits: An Examination of the Comparative Negligence Rule in Accident Law." *J. Legal Stud.* 24(2): 535–557.

Macey, J. 1989. "Internal and External Costs and Benefits of Stare Decisis." *Chi–Kent L. R.* 65: 93–113.

Mandelker, D. 1993. *Land Use Law,* 3rd. ed. Charlottesville, VA: Michie Co.

Marino, A. 1991. "Market Share Liability and Economic Efficiency." *Southern Econ. J.* 57(3): 667–675.

Marino, A. 1988. "Products Liability and Scale Effects in a Long–Run Competitive Equilibrium." *Int'l Rev. Law and Econ.* 8: 97–107.

Mascolo, E. 1992. "A Primer on Adverse Possession." *Conn. Bar J.* 66: 303–320.

Menell, P. 1983. "A Note on Private versus Social Incentives to Sue in a Costly Legal System." *J. Legal Stud.* 12(1): 41–52.

Merrill, T. 1986. "Property Rules, Liability Rules, and Adverse Possession." *Northwestern University L. R.* 79: 1122–1154.

Merrill, T. 1985. "Trespass, Nuisance, and the Cost of Determining Property Rights." *J. Legal Stud.* 14(1): 13–48.

Miceli, T. 1995. "Contract Modification when Litigating for Damages Is Costly." *Int'l Rev. Law and Econ.* 15: 87–99.

Miceli, T. 1994. "Do Contingent Fees Promote Excessive Litigation?" *J. Legal Stud.* 23: 211–224.

Miceli, T. 1993. "Optimal Deterrence of Nuisance Suits by Repeat Defendants." *Int'l Rev. Law and Econ.* 13: 135–144.

Miceli, T. 1992. "The Strategic Benefit of In–House Counsel for Products Liability Defendants." *J. Products Liability.* 14: 113–119.

Miceli, T. 1991. "Compensation for the Taking of Land Under Eminent Domain." *J. Institutional and Theoretical Econ.* 147(2): 354–363.

Miceli, T. 1990. "Optimal Prosecution of Defendants Whose Guilt Is Uncertain." *J. Law, Econ., and Org.* 6(1): 189–201.

Miceli, T., and M. Cosgel. 1994. "Reputation and Judicial Decisionmaking." *J. Econ. Behavior and Org.* 23: 31–51.

Miceli, T., K. Pancak, and C. F. Sirmans. 1996. "An Economic Analysis of Lead Paint Laws." *J. Real Estate Finance and Econ.* 12(1): 59–75.

Miceli, T., and K. Segerson. 1996. *Compensation for Regulatory Takings: An Economic Analysis with Applications.* Greenwich, CT: JAI Press.

Miceli, T., and K. Segerson. 1995. "Defining Efficient Care: The Role of Income Distribution." *J. Legal Stud.* 24(1): 189–208.

Miceli, T., and K. Segerson. 1994. "Regulatory Takings: When Should Compensation Be Paid?" *J. Legal Stud.* 23(2): 749–776.

Miceli, T., and K. Segerson. 1991a. "Contingent Fees for Lawyers: The Impact on Litigation and Accident Prevention." *J. Legal Stud.* 20(2): 381–399.

Miceli, T., and K. Segerson. 1991b. "Joint Liability in Torts: Marginal and Infra–marginal Efficiency." *Int'l Rev. Law and Econ.* 11: 235–249.

Miceli, T., and C. F. Sirmans. 1995a. "An Economic Theory of Adverse Possession." *Int'l Rev. Law and Econ.* 15(2): 161–173.

Miceli, T., and C. F. Sirmans. 1995b. "The Economics of Land Transfer and Title Insurance." *J. Real Estate Finance and Econ.* 10: 81–88.

Michelman, F. 1967. "Property, Utility, and Fairness: Comments on Ethical Foundations of 'Just Compensation' Law." *Harvard L. R.* 80: 1165–1258.

Miller, G. 1987. "Some Agency Problems in Settlement." *J. Legal Stud.* 16(1): 189–215.

Miller, G. 1986. "An Economic Analysis of Rule 68." *J. Legal Stud.* 15(1): 93–125.

Munch, P. 1976. "An Economic Analysis of Eminent Domain." *J. Pol. Econ.* 84: 473–497.

Murphy, J., and J. Coleman. 1990. *The Philosophy of Law*, 2nd ed. Boulder: Westview Press.

Nalebuff, B. 1987. "Credible Pretrial Negotiation." *Rand J. Econ.* 18(2): 198–210.

Netter, J., P. Hersch, and W. Manson. 1986. "An Economic Analysis of Adverse Possession Statutes." *Int'l Rev. Law and Econ.* 6: 217–227.

Olson, W. 1991. *The Litigation Explosion.* New York: Dutton.

Ordover, J. 1978. "Costly Litigation in the Model of Single Activity Accidents." *J. Legal Stud.* 7(2): 243–261.

Png, I. 1987. "Litigation, Liability, and Incentives for Care." *J. Public Econ.* 34: 61–85.

Png, I. 1986. "Optimal Subsidies and Damages in the Presence of Legal Error." *Int'l Rev. Law and Econ.* 6(1): 101–105.

Png, I. 1983. "Strategic Behavior in Suit, Settlement, and Trial." *Bell J. Econ.* 14: 539–550.

Polinsky, A. M. 1983a. *An Introduction to Law and Economics.* Boston: Little, Brown.

Polinsky, A. M. 1983b. "Risk Sharing Through Breach of Contract Remedies." *J. Legal Stud.* 12(2): 427–444.

Polinsky, A. M. 1980a. "On the Choice Between Property Rules and Liability Rules." *Economic Inquiry* 18(2): 233–246.

Polinsky, A. M. 1980b. "Strict Liability vs. Negligence in a Market Setting." *American Econ. Rev.* 70(2): 363–367.

Polinsky, A. M. 1979. "Controlling Externalities and Protecting Entitlements: Property Right, Liability Rule, and Tax–Subsidy Approaches." *J. Legal Stud.* 8(1): 1–48.

Polinsky, A. M., and Y. Che. 1991. "Decoupling Liability: Optimal Incentives for Care and Litigation." *Rand J. Econ.* 22(4): 562–570.

Polinsky, A. M., and W. Rogerson. 1983. "Products Liability, Consumer Misperceptions, and Market Power." *Bell J. Econ.* 14: 581–589.

Polinsky, A. M., and D. Rubinfeld. 1993. "Sanctioning Frivolous Suits: An Economic Analysis." *Georgetown L. R.* 82(2): 397–435.

Polinsky, A. M., and D. Rubinfeld. 1988a. "The Welfare Implications of Costly Litigation for the Level of Liability." *J. Legal Stud.* 17(1): 151–164.

Polinsky, A. M., and D. Rubinfeld. 1988b. "The Deterrent Effects of Settlements and Trials." *Int'l Rev. Law and Econ.* 8: 109–116.

Polinsky, A. M., and S. Shavell. 1989. "Legal Error, Litigation, and the Incentive to Obey the Law." *J. Law, Econ. and Org.* 5(1): 99–108.

Posner, R. 1995. *Overcoming Law.* Cambridge, MA: Harvard University Press.

Posner, R. 1992. *Economic Analysis of Law.* 4th ed. Boston: Little, Brown.

Posner, R. 1990a. *The Problems of Jurisprudence.* Cambridge, MA: Harvard University Press.

Posner, R. 1990b. *Cardozo: A Study in Reputation.* Chicago: University of Chicago Press.

Posner, R. 1980. "The Ethical and Political Basis of the Efficiency Norm in Common Law Adjudication." *Hofstra L. R.* 8: 487–507.

Posner, R. 1977. "Gratuitous Promises in Economics and Law." *J. Legal Stud.* 6: 411–426.

Posner, R. 1972. "A Theory of Negligence." *J. Legal Stud.* 1(1): 29–96.

Posner, R., and A. Rosenfield. 1977. "Impossibility and Related Doctrines in Contract Law: An Economic Analysis." *J. Legal Stud.* 6: 83–118.

Priest, G. 1987. "Measuring Legal Change." *J. Law, Econ., & Org.* 3(2): 193–225.

Priest, G. 1985. "Reexamining the Selection Hypothesis: Learning from Wittman's Mistakes." *J. Legal Stud.* 14(1): 215–243.

Priest, G. 1977. "The Common Law Process and the Selection of Efficient Rules." *J. Legal Stud.* 6(1): 65–82.

Priest, G., and B. Klein. 1984. "The Selection of Disputes for Litigation." *J. Legal Stud.* 13(1): 1–55.

Rasmusen, E., and I. Ayres. 1993. "Mutual and Unilateral Mistake in Contract Law." *J. Legal Stud.* 22(2): 309–343.

Rawls, J. 1971. *A Theory of Justice.* Cambridge, MA: Harvard University Press.

Rea, S. 1987. "The Economics of Comparative Negligence." *Int'l Rev. of Law and Econ.* 7: 149–162.

Rea, S. 1984. "Efficiency Implications of Penalties and Liquidated Damages." *J. Legal Stud.* 13(3): 147–167.

Rizzo, M. 1987. "Rules versus Cost–Benefit Analysis in the Common Law." In *Economic Liberties and the Judiciary*, J. Dorn and H. Manne, eds. Fairfax, VA: George Mason University Press.

Rogerson, W. 1984. "Efficient Reliance and Damage Measures for Breach of Contract." *Rand J. Econ.* 15(1): 39–53.

Rose-Ackerman, S. 1992. "Regulatory Takings: Policy Analysis and Democratic Principles." In *Taking Property and Just Compensation*, N. Mercuro, ed. Boston, Kluwer Academic Publishers.

Rose–Ackerman, S. 1990. "Market–Share Allocations in Tort Law: Strengths and Weaknesses." *J. Legal Stud.* 19(2): 739–746.

Rose–Ackerman, S. 1989. "Dikes, Dams, and Vicious Hogs: Entitlement and Efficiency in Tort Law." *J. Legal Stud.* 18(1): 25–50.

Rose–Ackerman, S., and M. Geistfeld. 1987. "The Divergence Between Social and Private Incentives to Sue: A Comment on Shavell, Menell, and Kaplow." *J. Legal Stud.* 16(2): 483–491.

Rosen, S. 1992. "The Market for Lawyers." *J. Law and Econ.* 35(2): 215–246.

Rosenberg, D., and S. Shavell. 1985. "A Model in Which Suits are Brought for Their Nuisance Value." *Int'l Rev. of Law and Econ.* 5: 3–13.

Ross, H. L. 1970. *Settled Out of Court*. Chicago: Aldine.

Rothschild, M., and J. Stiglitz. 1976. "Equilibrium in Competitive Insurance Markets: An Essay in the Economics of Imperfect Information." *Quarterly J. Econ.* 90: 629–650.

Rowe, T. 1984. "Predicting the Effects of Attorney Fee Shifting." *Law and Contemp. Problems* 47: 139–171.

Rubin, P. 1977. "Why is the Common Law Efficient?" *J. Legal Stud.* 6(1): 51–63.

Rubin, P., and M. Bailey. 1994. "The Role of Lawyers in Changing the Law." *J. Legal Stud.* 23(2): 807–831.

Rubinfeld, D. 1987. "The Efficiency of Comparative Negligence." *J. Legal Stud.* 16(2): 375–394.

Rubinfeld, D., and D. Sappington. 1987. "Efficient Awards and Standards of Proof in Judicial Proceedings." *Rand J. Econ.* 18(2): 308–315.

Rubinfeld, D., and S. Scotchmer. 1993. "Contingent Fees for Attorneys: an Economic Analysis." *Rand J. Econ.* 24(3): 343–356.

Sax, J. 1971. "Takings, Private Property, and Public Rights." *Yale L. J.* 81: 149–186.

Sax, J. 1964. "Takings and the Police Power." *Yale L. J.* 74: 36–76.

Scheppele, K. 1988. *Legal Secrets*. Chicago: University of Chicago Press.

Schwartz, A. 1992. "Relational Contracts in the Courts: An Analysis of Incomplete Agreements and Judicial Strategies." *J. Legal Stud.* 21(2): 271–318.

Schwartz, A. 1977. "A Reexamination of Nonsubstantive Unconscionability." *Virginia L. R.* 63: 1053–1083.

Schweizer, U. 1989. "Litigation and Settlement Under Two–Sided Incomplete Information." *Rev. Econ. Stud.* 56: 163–178.

Seidel, G. 1979. *Real Estate Law*. St. Paul, MN.: West.

Shanley, M. 1991. "The Distribution of Posttrial Jury Awards." *J. Legal Stud.* 20(2): 463–481.

Shavell, S. 1994. "Acquisition and Disclosure of Information Prior to Sale." *Rand J. Econ.* 25(1): 20–36.

Shavell, S. 1993. "Suit versus Settlement When Parties Seek Nonmonetary Judgments." *J. Legal Stud.* 22(1): 1–13.

Shavell, S. 1992. "Liability and the Incentive to Obtain Information About Risk." *J. Legal Stud.* 21(2): 259–270.

Shavell, S. 1989. "Sharing of Information Prior to Settlement or Litigation." *Rand J. Econ.* 20(2): 183–195.

Shavell, S. 1987. *Economic Analysis of Accident Law.* Cambridge, MA: Harvard University Press.

Shavell, S. 1986. "The Judgment Proof Problem." *Int'l Rev. Law and Econ.* 6: 45–58.

Shavell, S. 1985. "Uncertainty Over Causation and the Determination of Civil Liability." *J. Law and Econ.* 28(3): 587–609.

Shavell, S. 1984. "The Design of Contracts and Remedies for Breach." *Quarterly J. Econ.* 99(1): 121–148.

Shavell, S. 1983. "Torts in Which Victim and Injurer Act Sequentially." *J. Law and Econ.* 26: 589–612.

Shavell, S. 1982a. "Suit, Settlement, and Trial: A Theoretical Analysis Under Alternative Methods for the Allocation of Legal Costs." *J. Legal Stud.* 11(1): 55–81.

Shavell, S. 1982b. "The Social versus the Private Incentive to Bring Suit in a Costly Legal System." *J. Legal Stud.* 11(2): 333–339.

Shavell, S. 1980a. "Damage Measures for Breach of Contract." *Bell J. Econ.* 11(2): 466–490.

Shavell, S. 1980b. "Strict Liability versus Negligence." *J. Legal Stud.* 9(1): 1–25.

Shavell, S. 1980c. "An Analysis of Causation and the Scope of Liability in the Law of Torts." *J. Legal Stud.* 9: 463–516.

Shavell, S. 1979. "On Moral Hazard and Insurance." *Quarterly J. Econ.* 93: 541–562.

Shubik, M. 1985. *Game Theory in the Social Sciences: Concepts and Solutions.* Cambridge, MA: MIT Press.

Siegan, B. 1972. *Land Use Without Zoning.* Lexington, MA: Lexington Books.

Smith, J., and R. Smith. 1990. "Contract Law, Mutual Mistake, and Incentives to Produce and Disclose Information." *J. Legal Stud.* 19(2): 467–488.

Snyder, E., and J. Hughes. 1990. "The English Rule for Allocating Legal Costs: Evidence Confronts Theory." *J. Law, Econ., & Org.* 6(2): 345–380.

Spence, M. 1977. "Consumer Misperceptions, Product Failure and Producer Liability." *Rev. Econ. Stud.* 44: 561–572.

Spier, K. 1994. "Pretrial Bargaining and the Design of Fee–Shifting Rules." *Rand J. Econ.* 25(2): 197–214.

Spier, K. 1992. "The Dynamics of Pretrial Negotiation." *Rev. Econ. Stud.* 59: 93–108.

Spier, K., and M. Whinston. 1995. "On the Efficiency of Privately Stipulated Damages for Breach of Contract: Entry Barriers, Reliance, and Renegotiation." *Rand J. Econ.* 26(2): 180–202.

Stanley, L., and D. Coursey. 1990. "Empirical Evidence on the Selection Hypothesis and the Decision to Litigate or Settle." *J. Legal Stud.* 19(1): 145–172.

Starrett, D. 1972. "Fundamental Non–convexities in the Theory of Externalities." *J. Econ. Theory* 4: 180–199.

Statistical Abstract of the United States, years 1971–1994, U.S. Department of Commerce, Bureau of the Census, Washington, D.C.

Sykes, A. 1990. "The Doctrine of Commercial Impracticability in a Second–Best World." *J. Legal Stud.* 19(1): 43–94.

Taylor, M. 1976. *Anarchy and Cooperation.* New York: Wiley.

Terrebonne, R. 1981. "A Strictly Evolutionary Model of Common Law." *J. Legal Stud.* 10(2): 397–407.

Thomas, R. 1995. "The Trial Selection Hypothesis without the 50 Percent Rule: Some Experimental Evidence." *J. Legal Stud.* 24(1): 209–228.

Thomason, T. 1991. "Are Attorneys Paid What They're Worth? Contingent Fees and the Settlement Process." *J. Legal Stud.* 20(1): 187–223.

Tietenberg, T. 1989. "Indivisible Toxic Torts: The Economics of Joint and Several Liability." *Land Econ.* 65(4): 305–319.

Ulen, T. 1992. "The Public Use of Private Property: A Dual–Constraint Theory of Efficient Government Takings." In *Taking Property and Just Compensation*, N. Mercuro, ed. Boston: Kluwer Academic Publishers.

Ulen, T. 1984. "The Efficiency of Specific Performance: Toward a Unified Theory of Contract Remedies." *Mich. L. R.* 83: 341–403.

Viscusi, W. K. 1991. *Reforming Products Liability*. Cambridge, MA: Harvard University Press.

Waldfogel, J. 1995. "The Selection Hypothesis and the Relationship Between Trial and Plaintiff Victory." *J. Political Econ.* 103(2): 229–260.

White, M. 1992. "Legal Complexity and Lawyers' Benefit From Litigation." *Int'l Rev. of Law and Econ.* 12(3): 381–395.

White, M. 1989. "An Empirical Test of the Comparative and Contributory Negligence Rules in Accident Law." *Rand J. Econ.* 20(3): 308–330.

White, M. 1988. "Contract Breach and Contract Discharge Due to Impossibility: A Unified Theory." *J. Legal Stud.* 17(2): 353–376.

White, M. 1975. "Fiscal Zoning in Fragmented Metropolitan Areas." In *Fiscal Zoning and Land Use Controls*, E. Mills and W. Oates, eds. Lexington, MA: Lexington Books.

White, M., and D. Wittman. 1979. "Long Run versus Short Run Remedies for Spatial Externalities: Liability Rules, Pollution Taxes, and Zoning." In *Essays on the Law and Economics of Local Governments*, D. Rubinfeld, ed., Washington, DC: Urban Institute.

Wittman, D. 1985. "Is the Selection of Cases for Trial Biased?" *J. Legal Stud.* 14(1): 185–214.

Wittman, D. 1984. "Liability for Harm or Restitution for Benefit." *J. Legal Stud.* 13: 57–80.

Wittman, D. 1981. "Optimal Pricing of Sequential Inputs: Last Clear Chance, Mitigation of Damages, and Related Doctrines in the Law." *J. Legal Stud.* 10: 65–91.

Wittman, D. 1980. "First Come, First Served: An Economic Analysis of 'Coming to the Nuisance'." *J. Legal Stud.* 9(3): 557–568.

Wright, R. 1985. "Actual Causation vs. Probabilistic Linkage: the Bane of Economic Analysis." *J. Legal Stud.* 14: 435–456.

INDEX